The Fight Against Cancer

How did cancer, a pathology identified for over 2,000 years, turn suddenly at the beginning of the twentieth century into the scourge of our modern times?

Why and how did an illness that is not an epidemic, and is not contagious, end up being considered a threat to the very balance of society?

Between the two World Wars an illness that mainly affects adults over fifty years old became so prominent that it superseded both tuberculosis and syphilis in importance.

As Patrice Pinell shows, the effect of cancer in France before the Second World War reached far beyond the question of its mortality rates. Pinell's socio-historical approach to the early developments in the fight against cancer describes how scientific, therapeutic, philanthropic, ethical, social, economic and political interest combined to transform medicine.

Patrice Pinell is Directeur de recherche at the Institut National de la Recherche Médical (INSERM). He is an historian and sociologist of medicine, and has worked on topics such as the medicalisation of school failures (*Un siécle d'éches scolaires*), the anti-cancer war (*Naissance d'un Fléau*), the AIDS movement in France (*Un épidémie politique*), and the history of muscular dystophy.

Routledge Studies in the History of Science, Technology and Medicine

Edited by John Krige, CRHST, Paris, France

Routledge Studies in the History of Science, Technology and Medicine aims to stimulate research in the field, concentrating on the twentieth century. It seeks to contribute to our understanding of science, technology and medicine as they are embedded in society, exploring the links between the subjects on the one hand and the cultural, economic, political and institutional contexts of their genesis and development on the other. Within this framework, and while not favouring any particular methodological approach, the series welcomes studies which examine relations between science, technology, medicine and society in new ways, e.g. the social construction of technologies, large technical systems, etc.

Also published by Routledge in hardback and paperback:

Science and Ideology
A comparative history
Mark Walker

The Fight Against Cancer
France 1890–1940

Patrice⌐Pinell

*Translated from the French
(excluding the notes) by*
David Madell

London and New York

First published 2002 by Routledge
11 New Fetter Lane, London EC4P 4EE

Simultaneously published in the USA and Canada
by Routledge
29 West 35th Street, New York, NY 10001

Routledge is an imprint of the Taylor & Francis Group

Typeset in Baskerville by Exe Valley Dataset Ltd, Exeter
Printed and bound in Great Britain by
MPG Books Ltd, Bodmin, Cornwall

British Library Cataloguing in Publication Data
A catalogue record for this book is available from the British Library

Library of Congress Cataloging in Publication Data

Pinnel, Patrice
    [Naissance d'un fléau English]
    The fight against cancer: France 1890–1940/Patrice Pinell; translated from the French
by David Madell.
    p. cm.
Includes bibliographical references and index.
1. Cancer–France–History–20th century. I. Title

RC279.F8 P5613 2002
616.99'4'0944–dc21   2002069902

ISBN 0–415–27923–2

Contents

Acknowledgements

The teaching of Pierre Bourdieu, which deeply affected my sociological training, has always been a source of intellectual stimulation for me.

My friends Hervé Friedman and Jean-Claude Salomon introduced me to the world of cancerology and have proved themselves to be worthy guides.

I have found François Delaporte, Sylvia Klingberg, Ilana Löwy and Jacques Maître to be patient listeners and invariable pertinent critics.

I know that I am indebted to the competence, efficiency and kindness of Marie Bézard.

My thanks to all.

Publisher's note

Tables referred to in the text are to be found in the Appendices at the end of the book.

Introduction

Alban Berg finished composing his first opera, *Woyzeck*, in 1917. Apart from making a few cuts to compress the action, the libretto closely followed a piece written eighty years earlier by Georg Büchner. There was a single addition to the original text, four short lines at the beginning of scene 2 of act II:

THE DOCTOR: A woman dead, in four weeks. (Discreetly). Cancer of the
     womb. I've already had twenty patients in that state. In four weeks . . .
THE CAPTAIN: Doctor, don't frighten me. People die of fright, just fright!
THE DOCTOR: In four weeks! This will make for an interesting autopsy.
THE CAPTAIN: Oh dear, oh dear![1]

With these few words the doctor gained ascendancy over the captain, who found the very mention of cancer enough to terrify him. The orchestra emphasised the meaning of these words by playing a short musical sequence constructed around the note *B*, a note which comes to symbolise death, throughout the opera.

Although minor compared with Büchner's work, the change introduced by Alban Berg was nevertheless significant of a trend in cultural development; it expressed a change underway in the perception of cancer, the emergence of a new look at a disease known and dreaded since Antiquity.

A turning point in the history of cancer

Contrary to accepted belief, cancer is not a new disease, that has appeared with modern civilisation. It even seems, following palaeopathological discoveries, that it has been experienced by animals and the human race since remote times.[2] Its history, as a category of medical knowledge, has its roots in classical Greece and the Hippocratic School. The generic term of Karkinos (cancer in its Latin translation) was created at the time to designate a particular type of tumour which could cause death.[3] During the course of this story, which is over 2,000 years old, the definition of cancer has been subject to considerable revisions, and the theoretical frameworks from which doctors analyse its aetiology and its pathogenicity are changing. Long perceived as a general disease connected with melancholia, because it appeared to be caused by black bile (or melancholic blood), cancer was given a new kind of interpretation at the end of the eighteenth century, which considered it a pathology whose origin was local. The progress in clinical anatomy which then took place regarded it as a specific lesion affecting various tissues. Dominant during the first half of the nineteenth century, this tissular theory, elaborated by Bichat, was later gradually abandoned in favour of a new concept which situated the original distur-bance typifying cancer in the cell.[4] If, between the fifth century BC and the end of the nineteenth century AD, scientific ideas had considerably pro-gressed and no longer had very much in common apart from certain descriptive elements of clinical signs (which led to the discovery of 'cancers' in the current sense of the term, hidden behind the word *Karkinos*), the social perception of the disease remained more or less the same in the long term. The disease was terrifying, and all the medical treatises, such as the so-called 'lay' ones, agreed on this point. It was terrifying because the very appearance of the tumour was that of the claws of a crab (Galien), and also because of that other similarity with the animal in that it was impossible to make it let go (Paul d'Egine).[5] It was terrifying because it ate away at every-thing it grabbed hold of: 'It is a disease which gets into the flesh and gnaws away at it little by little like a type of gangrene', wrote Antoine Furetière in his *Dictionnaire Universel* in 1684.[6] It was terrifying because of its stealth, its apparent lack of malignancy and the abrupt reversal which occurred when the tumour, insensitive up to now caused 'terrible pains'.[7] Finally, it was terrifying because of the abjectness which was caused by the wounds it made. It is not surprising that this disease found a place in the records of the religious orders. Saint Francis of Assisi kissed lepers; at the end of the fourteenth century, Catherine of Sienna herself tested her charitable heroism by collecting in a bowl the pus from the breast of a cancerous woman to drink it like Christ's blood.[8] She began a new series of images in religious hagiography. In the seventeenth century, in edifying narratives, 'the kiss on the open wounds of a cancerous woman' replaced the common-place act of kissing lepers.[9] After a gap, the theme reappeared in the nineteenth century with the renewal of the mystical movements, to inspire the practices of an institution dedicated exclusively to the care of incurable cancers, the 'Oeuvre du Calvaire'. Fear and horror of cancer were now feelings attached to the history of this medical category and indeed are as ancient as this. But – and it is here that there was a turning point which began at the beginning of the nineteenth century – those feelings which, until then, had been experienced as a response to an 'exceptional' disease – both because of its characteristics and because of its nature – began to be expressed in public conversation, as the disease took on a 'social' dimension . . . a dimension which Alban Berg introduced specifically in his

Woyzeck. The opera was not 'modern' because it associated cancer with death, but because of its choice of cancer to evoke mass death: the doctor terrifies his listener, by emphasising the number, by making cancer of the womb a scourge, a disease which kills his women patients like an epidemic.

The dramatist captured something of the atmosphere of the times and, in fact, his opera was contemporary with events which revealed signs of a turning point in the history of cancer. For several years, cancer had been the subject of epidemiological research in Germany and in the English-speaking countries.[10] The initiative came from hospital doctors supported by the authorities or, as in the United States, by certain large insurance companies.[11] The idea that this disease represented, because of its incidence, a threat to society took on more and more substance; at the same time, learned societies and specialised treatment centres appeared in Europe, Germany, North America and Japan.[12] The change was observed after the armistice which ended the First World War. Many voices were raised to demand that measures be taken to stop the progress of this new social scourge.

The era of policies to combat cancer then began. The governments of an increasing number of countries came on the scene, the League of Nations was involved and set up a Cancer Commission in 1925, to co-ordinate efforts. Cancer leagues, which grew throughout nearly all the world, decided to join in an International Union. This was inaugurated in 1934, and brought together associations from thirty-four countries.[13] On the eve of the Second World War, in the 'developed' countries, cancer was – or was beginning to be – recognised as the most worrying disease socially, whilst, in contrast, obsession with the up to now great dominating scourges of tuberculosis and syphilis was receding in a marked fashion. During these years between the wars, a transition was taking place: the popularisation of the danger of cancer accompanied a new process of transformation which deeply affected the medical field, and, more completely, the place of medicine in the functioning of Western societies, because the fight against cancer created a situation without any historical equivalent. For the first time, social organisations had termed as a scourge a disease which escaped 'classical' methods of action through social hygiene. Contrary to the infectious diseases, such as rickets and alcoholism, which were partly controllable by preventative measures, cancer, according to the medical knowledge of the period, had only one treatment. The old saying 'prevention is better than cure' had no relevance here; since there was a lack of adequate prevention, the reduction of mortality depended only on the successes of surgery and radiotherapy. Hence cancer policies whose objective was to assist in the development of specialised treatment centres. The requirements of cancer treatment were very out of tune with the traditions of individualism within the medical profession. The eradication of malignant tumours was taking over from teamwork based on collaboration by specialists in supplementary professions. It also involved recourse to ever more costly 'heavy' technologies, which put 'the art of healing' in the category of the application of the rising science of radiation physics.

Cancerology, between the wars, showed signs of developments to come, making way for a change in hospitals and for a redefinition of the relationships between 'specialists' and 'generalists'. It sharply posed the question of methods of financing health policies, and, as a repercussion, that of the relationship between the public sector and private medicine. In other words, the construction of a 'leading' sector within health systems which were still largely dependent on the heritage of the nineteenth century highlighted the need for reforms and adaptation to the emergence of new conditions for the practising of medicine.

But treatment alone – however 'progressive' it might be – could not resolve the problem of the control of the disease. For it was only potentially effective on one condition: that cancer must be diagnosed sufficiently early, while still localised. Hence a second strategy was put forward by all parties concerned in the fight against cancer: the 'premature diagnosis'. Diagnosis, not screening, since no test was able to reveal the existence of a cancer. And this difficult diagnosis required experienced practitioners who needed to be trained. Moreover, even the best clinician could do nothing if his patient consulted him too late. Potential patients – that is, the whole population – had therefore to be educated, educated to be concerned about bodily symptoms which up to then had been considered 'normal'. In fact, acute suffering, which doctors had known to be characteristic of cancer, for centuries, only took place at an advanced stage of the disease when treatment was ineffective. Changing the way in which each person perceived his body became a necessity since the effectiveness of the whole policy depended on the development of habits which aimed to make a detective of the potential patient, discovering in himself the signs of 'disease'. The control of the 'modern-day scourge' passed through the internalisation stage of new standards of self-supervision. At this point, the history of cancer met the history of the process of civilisation as analysed by Norbert Elias.[14] During the years between the wars, the question of cancer therefore assumed an importance which was well beyond its incidence and its effect on mortality.

This disease itself crystallised the social preoccupations relating to the 'modernisation' of Western societies, of which one of the major challenges was the redefining of the role of medicine within the realms of possibility.

Ambitions and limits of a problem

This preamble describes the general aim of this book. The socio-historical analysis of the first developments called by its instigators the 'fight against cancer' is a central theme. It allows us to start the process of social development during which transformations appear that give rise to contemporary medicine. In this way, we demonstrate the importance, within the history of the medical field, of these years of transition between the wars. Many questions considered characteristic of our age originated then in their first form. It is, moreover, one of them which initiated my research.

As a sociologist, my interest in cancer began with my participation in the National Congress on Cancer, which the French Ministry of Health organised in 1982–3. Following this, I began a first draft on the social representations of this disease. It was time to take the drama out of it. Political chiefs, associations of sufferers, journalists and, of course, doctors all agreed that cancer was one of the great 'myths' of our age and that the consequences of this were harmful.[15] Their message began with one observation: an excessive and uncontrollable fear is attached to the image of cancer, which hinders the effectiveness of medical treatment, since it produces irrational behaviour in the population as a whole, as well as in sufferers: either a cancer phobia which sends individuals constantly scurrying to the their doctor's waiting rooms, or a flight from reality which makes them postpone the time for diagnosis. Cancerologists, in particular, were surprised at the lack of impact which progress made within the realms of treatment had on the mind.

Here, before their very eyes, was a true paradox, since cancer was generally one of the serious diseases for which medicine was getting the best therapeutic results. Hence the idea that, because of a lack of information, mistaken beliefs had been allowed to develop and that, with the help of a human tendency towards irrationality, cancer had ended up polarising on itself all the obsessions of the modern world. It is the structure of this 'myth' which analysis of its representations has allowed us to perceive.[16] Cancer is one part of the vision of a threatening and threatened social world, strongly carcinogenic – because of pollution, stress, working conditions, tobacco, alcohol, manufactured food, sexuality, etc. – but also cancerous, scourged by unemployment, inflation, communism, the unknown. It is therefore disease which turns social disorder into a public event, so as to make it part of the body, where it becomes organic disorder. And this evil incarnate finally invokes the image of the 'bad death', the expected death whose outcome cannot be denied.[17] But a sociological approach is not satisfied with being merely descriptive. In a certain sense, my first work followed the nature of the myth and contributed to writing it in a learned form. To abandon this nature would mean a break with beliefs. It was necessary for these beliefs to be made historical and to understand why and how they grew up.

The existence of very strong cancer associations was a start, and little courage was necessary to suggest the hypothesis of their involvement in this construction. Hence a return to the beginning of our century, at the historical point where the emergence of the 'scourge of cancer', the institutionalisation of cancerology as a specialised sector and the beginning of movements in the fight against cancer converged. The emphasising of such a convergence made my question problematic: the transformation into a 'modern scourge' of this 2,000-year-old disease is an international phenomenon, related to transformations which seem to affect, wherever they appear, the medical field and, more globally, social organisations. At least this is what came to light from a first analysis of the talks held by representatives and the institutions engaged in the fight against cancer. For I could hardly rely only on these 'topical' works and on any historical notices relating to the main institutions set up at the time. In fact, this 'turnabout' in the history of cancer and anti-cancer institutions hardly seemed to have originated any research in social science. It was not particularly astonishing that the abundant sociological literature dealing with cancer did not even appear aware of it. Those who produced it shared, for the most part, theoretical opinions which led them to approach social facts in a sort of timeless present, where history had no place.

The absence of historians was more surprising, even more so since there is no lack of research on medical knowledge regarding cancer 'down the ages'. But those who complain about a 'history of ideas' seem to incline towards the peremptory opinion of L.J. Rather, who, in a book describing the development of theories on the origin of cancer since Ancient Greece,[18] does not find it necessary to extend his analysis beyond the end of the nineteenth century, because, he notes, the period starts at that time which one can, according to the theories advanced, call 'the ice age', a period which he presumes is perhaps being completed with the revolution in molecular biology.[19] As regards sociologists and the social historians of medicine, they are very interested in cancerology, but only after the 1950s.[20] We note elsewhere that, on a more general level, medicine between the wars has not been very well studied up to now, as if this period was only a minor interval, a sort of void linking the great periods of the nineteenth and the second half of the twentieth centuries. Could it be that medical sociologists and historians are inclined to share the prejudices of professionals, for whom the essential lies in what their generations have achieved (or are in the process of achieving), and who are naturally inclined to only value what, 'from other times', offers them the excitement of the exotic? In fact, the start of the fight against cancer was only tackled in a single work, *The Dread Disease* by James T. Patterson,[21] a 'cultural history' of cancer in the United States from 1880 to the present. The author's ambition was mainly to prove the fact that this disease 'can originate from the thought processes and behaviour of North American society', and his approach to the development of knowledge and medical practices remains superficially descriptive and, unfortunately, throws hardly any light on the scientific, professional, and social interests and challenges of which cancer and its control could have been the subject.[22]

Since the process of social transformation which I wanted to analyse has not provided material from any other study, I was faced with a problem concerning research strategy. In fact, this process is carried out on an international scale. Wherever cancer is considered as a scourge, a consensus of opinion is formed on the main outlines of action concerning the 'fight against cancer': building treatment centres, developing research on causes, educating the 'public', organising early diagnosis and fighting all forms of 'charlatanism'. But the determining factors at the origin of this process and the dynamics of its development mainly vary according to nation-states for obvious reasons. If practices relating to cancer are modified, by and large, according to the same general objectives, they are included and develop in historically differentiated and relatively independent national areas. This means that the challenges presented by cancer, the interests of the various representatives, groups and institutions invested in these practices, their alliances and oppositions, their strategies and, consequently, the interpenetration of their strategies, in short everything which contributes to the dynamics of cancer policies is neither similar, nor in principle transferable, from one country to another. It is because it is not possible to economise on specific analyses at a national level that a study of the 'French case' is justified and is relevant. It would be no less true that since interdependence between states and, particularly, between national medical fields is an undeniable reality, we could not act as if the fight against cancer was a French peculiarity.

Production of information on cancer, and also on the biological activity of radiation, codification of know-how, and technological progress evolve at a supranational level, so it is necessary to understand their effects on a given country. This is especially so as reference to foreign countries, the 'importation' of practices or the international position occupied are an integral part of the 'internal' challenges. In addition, elements of comparison must be introduced as soon as one wishes to discover the particularities of the national case studied.

The absence of works studying the beginnings of the fight against cancer in other countries limited the analysis. The comparative approach could only concern the most easily identified objective facts (such as the creation of specialised institutions, their composition, their explicit aims, etc.). However, although rough, the available data gave evidence of certain singularities of the 'French case', the importance of which would be decisive for the exposition of my problem. Also, in France more than anywhere else, the First World War played a major role in the birth of a specialised cancerologist sector. The upheavals which it caused allowed obstacles to be removed, which, until then, had opposed its adoption. At the beginning of the 1920s, the political authorities recognised that in this field the country had fallen behind. The questions posed by the existence of this delay were to direct the analysis of the whole process as it developed in France between the end of the nineteenth century and the beginning of the 1940s.

Understanding the causes of this in fact involved, in the period before the war, studying the impact on the medical field of the renewal of the challenges regarding cancer, linked to the first therapeutic successes obtained by surgery and radiotherapy – a discipline then in the process of being set up. It was necessary to identify the groups involved in the study and treatment of cancer, and the questions which they were asking themselves. It was necessary to define their interests and ambitions, the relationships which they had with each other, and their areas of agreement and conflict. But it would not be possible to assess the condition of pre-war 'cancerology' institutions without placing them in the more general context of the hospital-university medicine of the age, its organisation, its hierarchies and its method of reproduction.

It is under these conditions, and only under these conditions, that the 'historical-structural nature' of the deciding factors which, on the one hand, were delaying the perception of cancer as a social disease and, on the other hand, were an obstacle to the creation of specialised treatment centres, could be established. Hence the first chapters of this book, the outline of which is given by this thesis.

To attribute the delay in France to the structural determining factors of the medical field would logically lead us to reflect on the conditions which prevented them from being obstacles: What did the war change? What made it possible for a fight against cancer to emerge and a specific policy in this field to be adopted? These are questions which could only be answered by analysing the influence of all the changes in the health system initiated by the war. This force was motivated by the opposition which, dealing with the field of power, turned the definition of the role of the state in public health and the boundaries of its intervention into a political issue. The war revealed the extent of the shortcomings in the nation's health organisation and the authorities laid the foundations for a policy of fight against the great scourges. The new aims intended to compensate for the shortcomings without transforming either the hospital-university structures or the relationships between public medicine and the private sector, in order not to alienate the majority of the medical body. The result of a compromise, this will to reform without affecting the existing situation could only cause contradictions, the extent of which would later be revealed in all their extent in the fight against cancer. This was because the deciding structural factors which were the obstacle before 1914 to the creation of cancer institutions were only temporarily 'neutralised' by the war. They would then progressively influence and burden the sector development: hence the contradictory opinions confronting them from the start of the programme in the fight against cancer. Conflicts regarding political orientation become linked to medical–scientific advances regarding treatment techniques. These different perceptions of what 'cancer treatment' should be became in reality a great disparity of practices and an explosion of institutional structures. The phenomenon was accentuated even more by the combined effect of successive rearrangements carried out by ministerial policy and the introduction of 'heavy' treatment technologies. On the eve of the Second World War, cancerology, because of its very heterogeneous nature, produced the most arresting image of the transition which was taking place in the medical field.

If the analysis of this dynamism in the development of the cancerology sector is at the centre of this work, the last chapters propose to deal with the social transformations which this process involved. If public hospitals became the only possible place to practice 'state-of-the-art medicine' in France, the whole regulation of the health system would have to be changed if we wished to adapt to the changes in the social world. Because if hospitals were becoming places where the cost of treatment was the first priority concerning therapeutic effectiveness, a complete series of new problems was emerging. The conditions for effectiveness were not only technical, they were also social, they required an increased division of medical work, in a spirit contrary to the ideology which dominated the profession. In addition, the effectiveness obtained was only relative. Cures did increase, but rather less than cases of temporary remission: and what should therefore be done with this type of sufferer?

We shall see that all these problems give us the opportunity to ask, in terms whose topicality is always our own, questions about relationships between doctors, between doctors and 'the public', between doctors and patients.

Finally, whether they have already been put into practice or are still to come, the transformations which the fight against cancer is bringing about are speculated upon by the institution itself, which by providing cancer publicity elaborates on the official public line. Hence a mirror image which links the face of the modern-day scourge to that of the medicine of the future, and which, at the end of a long but necessary detour, provides a reply to the question which caused me to undertake this research.

1 A fatal and incurable disease

Rheims owes the distinction of being the first town in the world with a 'cancer hospital' to the compassion of a Jansenist Canon. But, little realising the future historical interest of the project, the majority of the inhabitants tried to oppose it. They even went so far as to send a petition to the king for the institution to be set up elsewhere. The *intendant* of Champagne responsible for sorting out the matter dismissed the complainants and the hospital was able to open its doors in 1742: it was to operate in this way for a century, and then lose its specific nature and become a hospice annex for incurable patients of all types.

Having fallen completely into oblivion, the Rheims experience was resurrected at the beginning of the twentieth century when a thesis was written. The candidate, Ledoux-Lebard, dealt with a previously unpublicised theme (as the subject of his thesis), that of the 'Fight against cancer'. The approach was critical and emphasised the shortcomings of French medicine regarding cancer organisation.[1] In this subtle but still dangerous exercise, which consisted of emphasising the superiority of work done abroad – principally in Germany, the United Kingdom and the United States – the hospital founded by Canon Godinot allowed Ledoux-Lebard to preserve national pride. Even in this area, where delay nonetheless occurred, the French were forerunners. This 'completely new initiative', presented as the first tangible sign of a will to fight cancer, became a compulsory reference in the cancerology promoters' argument. In 1926, Doctor Pol Gosset, delving into the Rheims hospital archives, wrote its history, and called this 'cancer hospital' the forerunner of the cancer centres.[2] In addition, when retracing the controversy which took place over its creation, he opposed the open-mindedness of the instigators to the false beliefs of the inhabitants, who, persuaded that cancer was a contagious disease, were hostile to it being established in the town. But this flattering vision, inspired by the wish to establish a bridge between the past and the present does not hold up to the analysis of the documents which he himself mentioned in his text.

Charitable spirit and sense of opportunity

In 1738, Jean Godinot, Canon, doctor of theology, Vicar General of the
Sainte-Chapelle in Paris and Vicar General of the Abbaye Saint-Nicaise in
Rheims, made a donation of 14,000 *livres* to the administrators of the Saint-
Marcoul hospital to ensure its support in perpetuity of two poor cancer
sufferers, on condition that they were Christians and natives of Rheims. The
man was moved because 'the poor of this town who have been affected by
the disease that is vulgarly known as cancer are not sufficiently cared for'.[3]
The Rheims General Hospital, although charged by two royal decrees (the
first by François II, the second by Charles IX) with the care of cancer
sufferers, did not rest until it had succeeded in abandoning this duty, going
so far as to give small amounts of money to patients to get them to go home.

Its administrators explained: 'After several visits to all the sites of this
General Hospital, [they] recognised that it was overcrowded everywhere
and that cancer patients could not be sheltered in it without harming other
patients and even the public, as the General Hospital is in the heart of the
town.'[4] The cause of its potential harmfulness was the stench which their
badly bandaged wounds produced. The 'stench' was not just bad odours in
the sense in which we understand them. According to the medical opinion
of those days, marked by the renewal of 'Hippocratic airism', stench,
pestilence or anything which contributes to the production of polluted air
is a source of infection and a menace to those exposed to it. A cancer
patient whose bandages are suppurating is a nuisance and a danger if he is
enclosed in a limited space with others, since there is overcrowding. Hence
the argument which puts forward the topography – of the hospital firstly (it
was crowded everywhere) – and of the place it occupied in the city area (in
the town centre).

Mindful of these arguments, the Canon considered another hospital,
Saint-Marcoul, because it was situated in a large green area in the 'fresh
air'. But there he met with a rejection. Saint-Marcoul was a special hospital
reserved for patients with 'scrofula'. The medical arguments advanced by
its administrators returned to the risk of infection:

> Scrofula is a scirrhous tumour which you recover from, but cancer is a
> hard tumour, full of melancholic and silted blood, which is so incurable
> that, according to doctors, it is the worst disease that affects man.
> These two types of disease are infectious, therefore they infect each
> other. The individual affected by scrofula, in this weak state is very
> susceptible to poor air, and far from getting better, runs the inevitable
> risk of being at any moment infected by an incurable disease.[5]

Once more, the arguments seemed irrefutable to the Canon, who did not
persist and decided to look for other solutions. His obstinacy was finally
rewarded.

The administrators of the General Hospital, who should not have been completely unaware of the amount of the donation (which in the meantime had risen to 25,000 *livres*), decided to turn a house that belonged to them in the Bourg Denis into a hospital exclusively reserved for cancer patients. They argued that the house was surrounded by gardens and built on a plot with only a very narrow strip opening on to the road, thus ensuring favourable conditions for isolation. The donation was made, the site was ready to be arranged, when the inhabitants of the Bourg Denis using the same arguments protested and presented a petition to the king for the hospital to be built elsewhere.

The *intendant* of Champagne, after hearing the different parties, took the side of those responsible for the General Hospital who, even if they acknowledged the 'bad odour of cancer suppurations', denied 'formally, with all the doctors and pharmacists and from the most extensive experience, that the air was infectious and contagious'[6]; the proof of this was that the servants of a rich middle-class person did not get cancer, nor did the charitable ladies who took care of cancer victims. The ease with which these same persons were capable of developing opposing arguments, according to whether they wanted to refuse to accommodate the cancer patients in the General Hospital or to explain that grouping them together in a special hospital did not pose any risk to neighbouring citizens, at least showed the vagueness which existed regarding the possibility of trans-mitting cancer. The weight of the argument concerning the 'most famous experiment' did not overcome the doubts, since a site guaranteeing isolation was chosen. In this type of uncertain situation where, at the end of the day, all arguments were valid, decisions were taken according to pure social influence. If the hospital was finally built in spite of the protests of the neighbouring population, it was because they were confronted with a more powerful coalition of interests centred around the donation. The General Hospital became more prosperous (under acceptable conditions for its efficient operation, cancer patients would be kept apart) and the *intendant* of Champagne was certainly mindful that a large part of the money would fill the kingdom's coffers. In other words, it could be said that it was a long way from a victory of medical enlightenment over working-class obscurantism.

It is very difficult to see an outline of future cancer treatment centres in the cancer hospital. The staff who looked after the few patients (the number of beds was to increase progressively from two to twelve) would decrease to one nurse carrying out the job of manager and to one, then two maids. Even if the establishment received a weekly visit from two nuns, the doctor himself visited it only occasionally, whenever the need to treat an acute case was felt to be necessary. This same doctor (practising in the General Hospital) confined himself to the annual examination (in March) of the patients 'well enough to be sent home to their families'.[7] Under no cicumstances was there a question of his undertaking the slightest cancer treatment, an abstentionist line which was perfectly in tune with the institution's mission. Canon Godinot had wanted to remedy the unjust situation of certain cancer patients only. The criteria for admission specified that patients to be received were the poor with ulcerated cancers. If doctors sometimes tried to treat cancers by various methods, including cauterisation or surgical removal, while having few illusions on the effectiveness of their method, they did not risk attacking ulcerated cancers. A person seen at this stage was considered an incurable patient, someone whose disease would never improve because it thwarted the *vis medicatrix naturae*, the 'healing force of nature'. Medical orthodoxy adopted a relatively fixed position of non-treatment on this point, as remedies, whatever they were, were only complementary to the action of nature and could only, since the latter was impotent, be harmful.

The cancer hospital was from the beginning an 'asylum for incurables'. It was established in the eighteenth century, when the king gave his approval to the Cardinal of La Rochefoucauld to establish an institution 'conceived for the well-being and the relief of our poor subjects afflicted with incurable diseases and to remove a hideous and pitiable spectacle from the eyes of the people'.[8] It was, as with all asylums, a question of offering a refuge to unfortunates 'whose condition renders them incapable of earning their living by working or begging',[9] and to alleviate in some way a social disability which became evident when the tumour opened to the exterior and ulcerated. The need felt to open a special establishment for incurable cancer sufferers did not come from any concern for treatment. It arose from the refusal of other hospitals to accept the patients, a refusal which, we have seen, originated from the uncertainty of medical knowledge on the question of the 'contagiousness' of cancer. Is this refusal peculiar to Rheims? Historical information is not sufficient to provide us with an answer. One thing at least seems certain, the hospital, after a century of operation, was transformed into a hospice annex for incurables and was to disappear without there being any emulators, even in Paris, which was, after all, the city where institutional specialisation appeared the most advanced.

Cancer was, therefore, one of those diseases where it was thought that treatment and care were not matters for any particular institutional measure, even though, as we shall see later, the admission of patients into general hospitals could be problematic. In order not to stop at this simple declaration and to understand the reasons for a situation which would last for the whole of the nineteenth century and until the First World War, it is necessary to make a detour and replace the question within the context of the changes in the medical field brought about by the French Revolution and their conceptual, institutional and political incidence.

The modern hospital and clinical medicine: origin of new knowledge about cancer

On the eve of the Revolution, there was no real institution devoted exclusively to the 'art of healing'. General hospitals fulfilled the functions of care, asylum and police at the same time. They received poor patients, but were also used to confine vagrants of all types, and many had a custodial section.

The opening of special establishments sometimes originated from a decision to isolate patients affected by an epidemic (thus the Saint-Louis hospital was built in Paris in 1607 in order to be used as an isolation hospital for the 'pestiferous'). More often, it was in response to initiatives from Church officials (Canon Godinot for cancer patients, the Cardinal of La Rochefoucauld for incurables, Abbot de l'Epée for the deaf-and-dumb). Their purpose was not to respond to a specific medical problem, but to supply a refuge for those categories of people unable to make a living.

The revolutionary crisis and its developments were to profoundly affect this situation by changing, chiefly, the nature of the hospital in order to transform it into a more 'specialist' institution in the study and treatment of diseases. After having advocated closing hospitals for a time, the Republic began to favour reforming the institution by removing its police role. The hospital's provision of health care created a new structure able to generate new attitudes in doctors. The charitable aspect became secondary, or, more specifically, was viewed in a different light, a tacit agreement between the rich and the poor whereby, in return for the care taken of him, a poor man offered his body for medical research, so contributing to the gathering of knowledge about the disease. This is the origin of the clinic examined by Michel Foucault,[10] a new step emphasising observation at the expense of theory. From this there progressively emerges a rearrangement of the classification of diseases based on a concept of disease inspired by sensualist philosophy, which broke with centuries of 'humoralism'. The classification of symptoms (fevers, coughs, pains, etc.) into pathological entities was based on the idea of lesion – the disease is in a local area, indicated by the seat of the lesion which is revealed by pathological anatomical examination. Using the *post mortem* to cast light on the *in vivo*, the 'clinic' invents a whole arsenal of observation techniques (percussion, palpation, auscultation) using the senses, as well as instruments in order to amplify acuity (the stethoscope), or facilitate examination (the speculum), which revolutionised diagnosis.[11]

Cancer occupied an important place within the intense output of which the Ecole de Paris was the epicentre. With the decline of the humoral theory and the growth of localist ideas, it changed 'nature' to become, according to Bichat, a disease of the tissues, affecting the intimate structure of the organs.[12] At the same time, as descriptions were refined and typologies were elaborated, distinguishing between different forms of cancer according to the nature of the tissues affected, more and more internal organs were discovered which were likely to provide a seat for cancer, and the differentiation between malignant and benign tumours became established pathological anatomical foundations. Until then, because of a lack of pertinent criteria, differential diagnosis of benign tumours and malignant tumours was carried out according to the progress of the disease; Laënnec differentiated from cancers serous cysts of the kidneys and ovaries as well as uterine fibromas. Bayle identified benign breast tumours. The concept of cancer as a local disease also led to a different thinking about the way it developed and its dissemination. C.A. Récamier established the first meticulous descriptions of the metastatic phenomenon. In fifty years, the vision of cancer profoundly changed, even if, at one time, new knowledge considered today as 'an important advance' was waiting in the wings of a medical scene occupied by the theories of Broussais (who saw the origin of all diseases, including cancer, as a local inflammation of the intestine). It had to wait until his doctrine was discredited in order to come into its own.[13] However, this major turn-around in knowledge had no direct impact on the treatment field. This contradiction was not peculiar to cancer. The Ecole de Paris had made few innovations in the area of treatment and professed a scepticism bordering on abstention. If we set aside the fashionable treatment of 'fasting and leeches' (the famous antiphlogistic method invented by Broussais, which he advised for cancer), healing methods had hardly changed and pessimism was in order. The gloomy reflections in Geoffroy's *Manuel de médecine pratique* published in 1800 were topical until the last years of the century.

> Internal cancer is always incurable and fatal, the doctor can only try to alleviate and calm the acute pains which the patients suffer. When external cancer is confirmed, there is no recourse but removal. This is often impracticable if the cancer is adherent, useless if other glands are already engorged and if the mass of blood is infected with the cancerous evil; and however beneficial such an operation might seem, when circumstances become more favourable, very often the cancer affects another gland and at the end of a certain time, the same illness appears in another part of the body.[14]

Certainly, Claude Anthelme Récamier may well have dared and succeeded in carrying out, in 1829, the first total hysterectomy on a cancer of the womb, but this feat was too closely associated with the amazing skill of the surgeon to be repeated. Of the twenty-one patients who had a hysterectomy in 1832, none survived the operation: so it was quickly decided not to repeat the experience.[15] Similarly, if Lisfranc removed certain cancers of the rectum (the first in 1826) and could boast about an 'acceptable' post-operative result (five patients out of nine), his relative success remained 'technical', as the patients still died of recurrences.[16] At best, some progress was made in accomplishing palliative operations, such as the diversion of the intestine to the surface with the insertion of an artificial anus, conceived by Amussat and attempted for the first time in 1839.

The invention of anaesthetics (chloroform and ether) made these various attempts possible. It also, and above all, encouraged surgeons to operate more on breast cancers, long considered as the most favourable site for removal. The poor rate of success obtained, however, hindered this trend and certain surgeons openly questioned the relevance of their intervention. An enquiry by Leroy d'Etiolles, dating from 1844, showed that survival at thirty months was less frequent in women who were operated on than those treated by drugs or who remained untreated. Having said this, in each case, survival was an exception (18 out of 1,192 for those not operated on, and 4 out of 804 for those operated on).[17] We understand that in this context where any method could be attempted, eclecticism reigned supreme. Broussais's leeches, the grey lizard treatment once advocated by Bayle,[18] treatments with zinc or cod liver oil favoured by Velpeau[19] were not, from experience, more or less effective than surgical removal. If the latter seemed more legitimate, it owed this particularly to the prestige attached to the profession. In other words, in practice, the contribution of 'clinical knowledge' to cancer did not fundamentally change the status of the patients who all remained incurable. The twofold task of a place of study and care in a hospital was hardly exercised, as the condition of the cancerous patient was recognised as being beyond the reach of treatment. Hence there was a confirmed tendency to discharge him, so that he did not take up the bed of another patient for whom hospital care might be beneficial. Moreover, he was not the only one in this position. By becoming a medical institution, the modern hospital tends to be differentiated from a hospice, by keeping for itself only 'patients for whom the aid of the curing arts is presently necessary', and by relegating to hospice-type institutions 'those whose illnesses are chronic and those for whom attempts at treatment would be useless and possibly dangerous',[20] as well as all of those – orphans, foundlings, old people without resources – who result from charitable action. This practical differentiation between hospital and hospice, which was in evidence under the First Empire, is included in a movement towards institutional specialisation – particularly pronounced in Paris – the argument of which should be grasped, if only to understand the reasons why it would not concern cancer, or at least not before the beginning of the twentieth century.

The determining factors in the process of hospital specialisation

The provision of health care within a hospital was not the outcome of the progressive development of medical practice, but the product of a political and ideological break with the past. Within this revolution, which was total and which even affected the age-old arrangement of time by imposing a new calendar, hospital reform was only one item in a project which aimed at redefining the place of medicine in a society which was to be rebuilt on different foundations. The idea that medicine had a social role to play was not foreign to the Ancien Régime, the doctors of the Royal Society of Medicine did not neglect to draw attention to the miserable living conditions in the countryside,[21] but with the advent of the Republic, this idea completely influenced the nation's principles on government.[22] By becoming social, medicine saw its vocation extend well beyond that of 'the art of healing'. It had to contribute to the establishment of a new order founded on reason and adjust to its requirements. It had to react each time that problems needing its intervention were identified. Its range was extensive, from prevention of 'mass diseases' to various matters required by the law, including collection of information regarding the people's state of health.[23] Hence the flourishing of institutions adapted to 'treatments' required by different 'social demands' which, when the problem concerned a particular category of people, took the form of a specialised hospital. The new medical order partly grew up in opposition to what was considered the former disorder, and was dedicated to ending the 'insupportable over-crowding' in hospital institutions. Also the specialist hospital as a medical institution went hand in hand with the establishment of methods of action which were required to suit different groups who did not have a common status. The reasons which led to discrimination between certain categories so that they could be treated separately can be systematically linked to two main types of problem. In the first case, the aim was to adjust to the requirements of particular methods of socialisation. The most well-known example is that of the insane. As R. Castel states, behind the separation of the insane from the criminals, the establishment of contractual order fixed by republican law is at stake.[24] Although he is neither a whole person, because he has no sanity, nor, because of this fact, punishable, the insane person must nonetheless be controlled. The law abolishing '*Lettres de cachets*' [official orders for imprisonment] gave him the status of a sick person and allocated him a place of treatment enshrined in law. Called to overcome the shortcomings in the law, medicine invented a new form of supervision, the end result of which was to define the status of an insane person as that of a completely supervised minor, registered under the 1838 law. At the same time, it marked the field of intervention which was entrusted to it with the introduction of an institutional *ad hoc* arrangement, responsible for treating this 'minor': the mental asylum.

Another 'minor' for which a particular medico-social treatment was considered was the child. Philippe Ariès's analysis[25] is a clue to those who wish to understand and interpret the creation of the first children's hospitals. The importance, for the middle classes, of an educational example which made school an area of socialisation where the child was kept apart from the ordinary world of the adult, largely explains this institutional innovation. The mingling of all sorts of ages in a single room could only shock those who ceaselessly tried to preserve childish innocence from the pernicious influences of maturity. Hospital segregation, by removing the child from a sight which is only too often an introduction to vice, fulfils under this heading the function of a moral prevention.

In the case of the deaf-and-dumb and the blind, specialisation went another way. Institutions intended as educational asylums had been created under the Ancien Régime. When they passed under the supervision of the state during the Revolution, they became medical institutions, and carried out for a while an intermediary role where educational and clinical practices co-existed and supported each other in the acquirement of knowledge regarding the sense organs and their relationship to the higher functions.

Finally, preoccupations concerning moral and physical prevention were combined to contribute to the development of the first maternity hospitals, which acted as refuges for women in labour.

The second type of problem which the creation of specialised hospitals attempted to resolve was that posed by the care of contagious diseases. It was a question of isolating those diseases which were capable of transmitting themselves through contact. The pathologies, and therefore the patients involved, were the subject of a great debate which pervaded the medical world and concerned the definition of criteria for differentiating between 'contagious' diseases and 'infectious' diseases. Medical theories offering to explain the appearance of diseases affecting the community were mainly focused on the question of dealing with the method of transmission. The existence of 'invisible' causal agents, indifferently called miasmas, viruses, and particles was put forward as a definitive explanation. Gradually, two possible methods of penetration by these agents became evident, the result being a division of these diseases into two groups: infectious diseases, in which active germs present in the air introduced themselves into the body by penetrating the natural orifices, and contagious diseases, which were transmitted through the intermediary of personal contacts, the skin being in this case the obligatory point of passage of the 'contagion'.[26] The violent controversy which exploded at the start of the nineteenth century, at first regarding the particular case of yellow fever, then cholera, polarised the two camps of the 'contagionists' and the 'infectionists'.

The controversy had direct socio-political implications on the preventive measures to be taken. The fight against 'infections' was through control of the environment, whilst the control of 'contagion' depended on the application of isolation techniques. In the one case, it was a question of purifying the air and water, disinfecting both the rural and urban environments (cemeteries were placed outside the towns, sewers were installed, etc.), and also improving the food supply and housing conditions of the people. In the other case, it was a question of installing *cordons sanitaires*, imposing quarantine on ships and building asylums and isolation hospitals. But, as F. Delaporte showed, the confrontation of the two doctrines did not necessitate the global rejection of one or the other theory: it was focused on the definition of relevant criteria allowing the classification of a disease as infectious or contagious.[27]

Even the most convinced 'infectionist' will recognise the contagious nature of diseases whose manifestations limit themselves to attacking the skin, and those, such as smallpox, which are transmissible by inoculation, that is – and the list is very limited – venereal diseases, syphilis and gonorrhoea (which, moreover, inoculation experiments have enabled us to differentiate). This consensus could be found in the range of hospitals for the contagious which were constructed. Syphilitics were taken to and isolated at the Hôpital du Midi, rue Saint-Jacques. The 'scabby', the 'mangy' and the 'wormy' were assembled in the Saint-Louis hospital, which became the clinic for skin diseases. The contagionists, who then occupied a position of strength in 1820, at the time of the threat of the yellow fever epidemic, obtained the construction of quarantine hospitals, such as that on the island of Frioul, facing Marseilles.[28] But when, a few years later, it was cholera's turn to manifest itself, the 'infectionist' theses dominated. The failure of attempts to inoculate against diseases is an argument which proves their infectious nature, no isolation measures having been taken, with the disastrous consequences of which we are aware. In addition, the contagiousness of tuberculosis was unquestionably denied by the majority of the medical profession, who were convinced of the hereditary nature of the disease and also the absence of proof 'through inoculation' appeared prohibitive. It was necessary to wait for the Pasteur revolution to lead to a total theoretical reformulation of the problem of mass diseases, so that isolation measures could begin to be taken, both for cholera sufferers (the opening of a special hospital in 1883, the Broussais hospital) and for tuberculosis sufferers.

If a belief in segregation is fundamental to the great majority of specialised establishments, the whole phenomenon cannot be ascribed to it. The invention of certain techniques requiring the use of complicated instruments was also a decisive factor in the setting up of facilities exclusively for their use. Therefore, it was on the initiative of the manufacturers of corsets and equipment whose purpose was the amelioration of bodily deformities that the first private orthopaedic clinics managed by doctors were opened.[29] The other technique whose perfection had institutional effects was lithotripsy. Its purpose was to allow a destruction of vesical stones without recourse to a bloody operation, since even if the surgery of the 'vesical cut' had attained a high degree of technical perfection, the results were often catastrophic for sufferers who died of infection. The inventor of the first French lithotripter, Civiale, obtained in 1829 a small department of 'urinaries' at the Necker hospital where he could develop his technique, which he did successfully.[30] It was with his successor, Félix Guyon, that what were merely methods centred on a technique developed into a new discipline, urology. Guyon, a 'general' surgeon, would extend the range of his operations beyond the treatment of vesical stones to the whole of the pathologies of the 'urinary apparatus'.[31]

This diagrammatic view of the logic which lay behind the creation of specialised institutions allows us to better understand why cancer sufferers are not concerned in this process. The treatment of cancer does not challenge techniques needing the use of complicated apparatus. The invention of radiotherapy, which was to change the perception of the problem, was not effective until the beginning of the twentieth century. In addition, there was no reason for the isolation of cancer sufferers because of a risk of contagion. Not that the hypothesis of transmission by contact with cancer had not been raised, but it had not been possible to prove it. I do not allude to the dispute in Rheims mentioned above. At the time when Canon Godinot made his contribution, the 'infectionist' and 'contagionist' theories were not yet in existence: if the reference corpus was 'airist', the infection/contagion distinction was not current and was never mentioned. The hypothesis of 'contagiousness' (in the sense of transmission by contact) came much later and arose because of the experiments carried out on smallpox. In 1773, Bernard Peyrilhe, a member of the Royal Academy of Surgery, delivered a memorandum to the Lyons Academy of Science, Literature and Arts, in which he defended the idea that cancer should be attributed to the action of a particular toxic virus. But his attempt at inoculating a dog with an extract of human cancer failed.[32] At the beginning of the nineteenth century, Alibert, a doctor at the Saint-Louis hospital (in Paris), tried without success to inoculate himself with cancer, and the (more prudent) experiments of Dupuytren on animals were a resounding flop. The contagionist analysis therefore lost, for some time, all credit.[33]

Finally, the care of cancer sufferers did not appear to relieve specific medico-social problems other than those relating to 'chronic incurables'. In other words, as soon as their incurability was established (relapse after treatment or 'ulcerated cancer'), these patients, more or less theoretically, came under the hospice.

When charity supplements public medicine: the growth of the 'Oeuvre du Calvaire'

The overcrowding of hospitals and hospices, due to the influx of poor patients, became a permanent condition from the 1830s, particularly in the large cities. The lack of space favoured discrimination, and patients were rejected who were not from the same district as the establishment, as well as those whose presence was the cause of trouble or inconvenience. The insistence with which ministerial circulars affirmed the need to grant a place to certain incurables demonstrated the hospital administration's unwillingness in this regard.[34] The names of three categories appear regularly amongst those rejected: venereal disease sufferers who had not been admitted to the specialist hospitals and who were considered a danger, and tuberculosis and cancer sufferers, because they aroused horror and disgust. The poor cancer sufferer, abandoned by all, condemned to wandering whilst waiting for death to carry him off, nevertheless generated charitable efforts of a particular type.

In the year 1834, which marked a tragic turning point in her life, Jeanne Françoise Garnier-Chabot had just had her twenty-third birthday. This young girl, daughter and wife of Lyons shopkeepers, lost her two children and her husband in rapid succession. A fervent Catholic, of a passionate nature which attracted her towards active mysticism, she overcame the trial and again brought meaning to her existence by throwing herself 'body and soul' into the creation of a charitable enterprise which was to survive her and make her influence felt after her death: the *Association des dames du Calvaire* [the Association of the Ladies of Calvary].[35]

A short time after the death of her husband, Jeanne Garnier-Chabot by chance met an 'unfortunate woman afflicted by a horrible disease which had covered her body with wounds', living alone in a slum. She took responsibility for her, treated her, and mainly tried 'to cure her tortured mind'.[36] This experience decided her vocation, and she then dedicated herself to relieving the physical and mental suffering of women affected by cancer whom the hospitals and hospices had abandoned. The extent of her task led her to persuade other widows to join her. The support of Cardinal Bonald, archbishop of Lyons, allowed her to obtain the necessary funds to buy a house which would be used for accommodation. The initiative was institutionalised in 1842, with the creation of the *Association des dames du Calvaire*. The enthusiasm of its founder attracted a larger and larger number of widows. Thanks to the gifts made by new members and money from collections, the association was able to establish itself in a large property in the district of Fourvière and welcome several dozen sufferers. The idea of the foundation of the association was original:

> It is of course a Catholic work, composed of lay widows, who are not attached to any religious order, who pay their pension to have the honour of caring for cancer sufferers and have no other attachment to the Calvaire than their love of God and the sick.[37]

Widowhood was a compulsory condition in order to be able to participate in the active life of the institution:

> Only a woman who has suffered is prepared for such a task. Only those for whom the love of material things is no longer important will be given the task.[38]

The rules drawn up by Mme Garnier-Chabot distinguished, in the association's organisation, between resident ladies managing the house and 'associated widows' who lived in the outside world and came to put on dressings on set days, 'devotees' who begged for charity and organised collections, and 'associates' who were responsible for helping with the upkeep of the house. Admission as a *'dame du Calvaire'* was subject to a 'training' of one year, during which the recipient had to give proof of her ability to overcome her repulsion when faced with the sight of the illnesses before her eyes. Once accepted, she received a silver cross on which the following four words were engraved: *Prayer, Humility, Charity, Sacrifice*.

Every morning, before attending their patient, the ladies would recite to themselves a prayer written by Mme Garnier, which ended with these words: 'Lord, grant your sufferers patience and resignation, and give us the spirit of faith and charity'.[39] A sort of unveiling ritual then began in which each lady undid the previous day's bandages and uncovered the wounds before cleaning them and starting to re-bandage them. The 'Oeuvre du Calvaire', a charity which Félix Rocquain called 'heroic',[40] operated on the basis of the daily performance of these extreme forms of behaviour.

The relationship which these widows had with the sufferers appeared much closer to J. Le Brun's descriptions of the *exempla* which cancer produced in convents in the seventeenth century than that which existed between carers and patients in the Rheims cancer hospital. The expression of this type of vocation, connected to the renewal of the wider mystical currents of the Roman Catholic Church, found its roots in the development of a 'mentality' within the ruling classes. It demonstrated the significance of a model of femininity inculcated in the religious schools which, more often than not, were responsible for the education of girls. This model, where the body was deeply distrusted and its subjection was made an obsession, found its ideal form in the creation of convent life.[41] The 'holy and implacable hate' which it was necessary to cultivate for one's own body by imposing on it a shackle of various restrictions, that is mortifying it, was opposed and mirrored by the love for a suffering body of another, and it is this duality which lies behind the nuns' deeds towards sufferers. We can see everything that, in the system of religious referents proper to Roman Catholicism, brings the condition of a widow 'who has regained her virginity through misfortune'[42] closer to that of a nun, which in its turn makes work like that at Calvaire attactive. All the more so since the latter offers several possibilities for putting into practice this ideal of behaviour. The 'resident mistress' may, without giving up her possessions and freedom, experience the life of a religious community more closely, while the status of 'associated widow' remains compatible with life in the world outside, even more so, that of an 'enthusiast', which does not entail contact with sufferers. Hence the reaction which met Jeanne Garnier-Chabot's initiative amongst the women of the middle classes and the aristocracy. Several hundred widows joined the association, which, after the death of its founder in 1853, set up 'daughter houses' in several towns in France (Paris and Saint-Etienne in 1874, Marseilles in 1881, Rouen in 1891, Bordeaux in 1909) and also abroad (Brussels in 1886, New York in 1899, Bethlehem in 1920).

However, membership of the Calvaire was not just a simple secular imitation of entry into the convent; it involved being able to bear the daily sight of the 'horror', the expression of suffering and the all-pervading presence of death, 'since only being able to relieve the patients' suffering and not cure them. On being received at the Calvaire, they were received for death'.[43] Only those could enter whom the Calvaire had helped to overcome an irreparable change in their life (the rules also stated that only 'young widows' of forty-five and under could be accepted). But this opportunity for watching over the dying also created a symbolic situation in the reversal of social relationships:

> This work, finer than all others in that its charity does more than mingle and equalise rank, makes of the woman who has birth and wealth and for whom the world seems to have reserved enjoyment, not only the companion but also the servant of the most wretched.[44]

'A sad wreck cast up by the tide of society'[45] the poor woman who was admitted to the Calvaire underwent a transformation; she became extremely devoted and practised humility and self-denial, as cancer changed her into a being whose open wounds and tribulations were likened to those of Christ on the cross ('Calvary'). If, here too, we find an association – between the woman suffering from cancer and Christ – which J. Le Brun tells us is at the heart of the representations of cancer in the convents of the classical period,[46] the difference because of the institutional atmosphere and the fact that the widow kept her rank lent a new character to this representation: that of raising the poor sufferer above the society woman. It is also appropriate to note that by defining the limits where, very temporarily, social positions were reversed, the houses of the Calvaire assured the 'elite' of its 'clear conscience' and served as an excuse for an edifying story, such as that which should charm the audience at the Academy of Moral and Political Sciences.

> One of these women, whose extreme misery sometimes makes rebellious, had entered the Calvaire, angry, defiant, hardly believing in the pity which she had received and hating those who are fortunate in this world. Finally, moved, in spite of everything, by the care taken of her, she asked for the name of the lady who administered it. They told her it was one of the famous names of France. After a moment of astonishment: 'So here are,' she replied, 'the rich people I thought so hard-hearted and they come to bandage the wounds of poor women like me.' . . . Her heart, which rage and hate had closed, opened and she wept.[47]

The model of 'heroic charity' which appeared in the Calvaire had no equivalent anywhere else, since even religious orders who could put it into practice did so only occasionally and not on a daily basis. Even more so, Mme Garnier-Chabot's institution was clearly very different from 'lay' works of charity which thrived with the inauguration of the Third Republic. Coming after the Paris Commune, these philanthropic activities had in common, to different degrees, the wish to contribute to a better organisation of society, a condition of the restoration of order.[48] Those who came forward involved themselves with certain types of illness and did so in a medico-social environment in which the aims were preventative. The first 'clinics' appeared. Mainly targeted at the prevention of childhood illnesses, protection of children in danger, screening for tuberculosis and the fight against alcoholism, none of these new institutions was interested in any way in the suffering of the poor from cancer. The latter could, once treated, be sent from hospitals to hospices who, using as an excuse the considerable complications of the care needed, often refused to take them, and nothing, except in part the work of the Calvaire, made up for this lack of public provision. In fact, the conditions had not yet been met for patients to be perceived as a group unit. Public institutions treated them as so many 'hopeless' and/or 'difficult' cases and contributed to their dispersal, by refusing to take responsibility for them in a lasting fashion. In the only place which accepted them (and only if they were women affected by ulcerated cancer), the sufferers were no longer perceived as a 'category' posing a social problem as such. An epitome of suffering, the women who were the focus for the mystical vocation of the Ladies of the Calvaire each represented, in the eyes of those who cared for them, a tragic destiny, the destiny of an individual led to relive in her flesh the passion of Christ.

It was only at the end of a complex process, initiated by two major innovations in the area of treatment, that it became possible, for the first time in history, to deal effectively with certain types of cancer, so that the view of this illness and of those who it affected would change. In the review of examples which are discussed below, the 'horror' will be associated with the 'number' to lend a social existence to this new scourge which the first specialist cancer structures would have as their mission to combat.

2   The first successes in treatment

The turning point in surgery

Before our generation disappears, to be replaced tomorrow by a
generation which has not *seen*, it would be useful to outline the history
of surgical practice in France, before, during and after the first two-
thirds of the nineteenth century. This practice was such that never
since written history began, in the Greek world, in ancient Rome or in
the darkest Middle Ages, have there been operations so murderous: a
serious bloody operation was a death warrant; with our services, only a
madman would have attempted even a simple remedy for hernia, and,
in the hands of our most eminent masters, an amputation cost the life
of 95 per cent of patients; the extraction of a cyst or of an ingrown nail
resulted in a disaster and the old saying 'a hole in the skin, an open
door to all ills' was pure truth. Erysipelas, hospital putrefaction,
purulent infection, tetanus, gas gangrene, all the septicaemias attacked
the wound, so much so, that terrified by these massacres, the best
surgeons put down their lancets. We can say without it being a paradox
that general mortality would have decreased by several units if the
'benevolent dictator' had got rid of all the surgeons. One doctrine was
to save everything. . . . In order to inaugurate the sovereign method
the powerful armour of an undisputed pathogenesis was needed. . . . It
will be Pasteur's eternal glory that he 'objectified' the hereto invisible
enemy and created procedures to combat it. All efforts, all research by
practitioners was co-ordinated; antisepsis came from nowhere, and
from this Lister's triumphant surgery finally emerged.

(Paul Reclus, 'Eulogy of Paul Berger'
made at the Academy of Medicine
on 16 December 1913)[1]

With emphasis proper to the situation, Paul Reclus celebrates, in the homage rendered to his friend Berger, the glory of a 'generation' which aspired to the genesis of a new age of surgery. The feeling of having taken part in a great historical upheaval doubtless led him to go too far with the argument, but all those who, like him, were involved in the fight for antisepsis, when they examined their past, said the same thing. Before it was 'sheer horror', 'the operation was carried out under conditions which would make us shudder today'[2] – operating assistants in street clothes, often coming straight from an autopsy, no washbasins, only the chief surgeon washed his hands in a little white bowl. As regards the instruments, they were jumbled together on a wooden plank. The results were so terrible, as Bernard Cuneo recalls,[3] that sometimes it was necessary to stop operating for a while.

It is true that, when they were still young students, the future pioneers of antisepsis and asepsis experienced the worst, with hospitals being set on fire in the siege of Paris and the subsequent civil war. Whichever side they were on, generally that of the *Versaillais* – the loyalists – they all had their first experience as apprentice surgeons in awful conditions. 'Hospitals', wrote Edouard Quenu, 'were still cluttered with the wounded from the war and the Commune. I lived in wards for the operated and wounded who had the yellow complexions of fever. I became familiar with pus, as all the wounds were suppurating, each bandage caused complaints and shrieks and an abominable odour of fermented poultice came from these dressings.'[4] We can easily understand the impact that the introduction of a new technique from Scotland had on them. There, a surgeon, John Lister, interested in Pasteur's work rejecting the theory of spontaneous generation, deduced from the all-pervading presence in the air of bacteria that the latter could be responsible for the inevitable infections accompanying injuries with open wounds. He used a disinfectant, phenol acid, to clean wounds and the result, published in 1867, was spectacular. Fired by his success, he decided to make its use routine in all surgical operations.[5] Lucas-Championnière was the first young Parisian surgeon to make the 'pilgrimage' to Edinburgh to be trained in the new technique; others, such as Berger, and Pozzi, were to follow him. Introduced by clinic heads, taught by assistants to their interns, asepsis was received much more reluctantly by the existing masters, such as Alfred Richet or Tillaux, who had their reservations, that is they were hostile. Edouard Quenu, convinced by Lucas-Championnière after seeing him carry out his first operation with aseptic dressings, came up against one of his patrons, Després, who praised the virtues of dirt: 'maggots', he was fond of saying 'eat the infection'.[6]

But the 'new generation' was getting organised and won several department heads to its cause; the success obtained with private patients ensured their reputation and, with the help of this competition, the whole of the surgical milieu progressively took up the new technique. At the beginning of the 1880s, 'Listerism' became established in several Parisian hospitals and some of its pioneers became departmental heads in their turn. At the end of the same decade, when other antiseptics were competing with phenol acid, a new procedure, directly inspired this time by the followers of Pasteur – asepsis – appeared. Quenu installed an autoclave in the private clinic where he was operating. His departmental head at Bichat hospital, Félix Terrier, was following a training course under Emile Roux and was converted to the notion of sterilisation. Bichat then became the favoured site for a new college of surgery. A considerable number of those who were to become 'senior consultants' after the First World War passed through Terrier's department and would identify with its heritage: Henri Hartmann, Antonin Gosset, Bernard Cuneo (all three future holders of the Chair of General Surgery), Emile Forgue (professor of surgery at Montpellier), and Paul Sébileau (future holder of the ENT Chair).

The fight against germs reformed all surgical practice and gave it its modern ritual, organised around whiteness, cleanness and sterility. Masks and gloves appeared. A number of operations, up to then unthinkable or abandoned, became possible, involving at the same time other innovations such as the perfection of vascular sutures (Alexis Carrel in 1902). Cancer surgery was turned around by these.

The most important 'great firsts' were the work of German and American surgeons. Theodor Billroth succeeded in 1881 in carrying out the first removal of a stomach cancer; William Stewart Halsted perfected in 1890, at the Johns Hopkins hospital in Baltimore, the extensive mastectomy which, for many years, would remain the point of reference for the treatment of breast cancer. Ernest Wertheim in 1900, in Vienna, published his technique for extensive hysterectomy for cancer of the womb. Paris followed this movement and, at the end of the century, the treatment of cancer in hospitals was relatively routine. The biographies written by the Academy of Medicine for the members of this learned assembly are illuminating. As we pass through the generations of 'pre-Listerian' then 'Listerian' surgeons to those trained in asepsis, the interest in cancer is confirmed and grows. Not only did mentions of work in this field of pathology increase in frequency, but it also became obvious that the 'youngest' considered that linking their name to the codification of a technique of removal was a mark of excellence. There were few members of the surgical elite who, after having succeeded the pioneers of antisepsis, did not try it. Having said this, however important it may appear, the cancer issue does not prefigure, in this context, the independence of the surgical cancer clinic. It remained within the framework of general surgery and surgical specialities which were contemporarily established.

The first wave of 'special clinics' – between 1878 and 1890 – was the result of a reconstruction of the clinical field, from which emerged two new surgical disciplines, ophthalmology and urology. During the first few years of the twentieth century, three new specialist chairs were opened, all for surgery: child surgery at the Enfants Malades (Professor Kirmisson), gynaecology at the Hospital Broca (Professor Pozzi) and ear, nose and throat at the Hospital Lariboisière (Professor Sébileau). The first divided paediatric medicine into two parts, the other two divided general surgery centred on 'local targets'. This tendency of surgery to generate new divisions was closely linked with its renewal. The growing mastery of risks of infection considerably extended the area of possible operations in both 'child' and 'adult' pathology. If, for children, surgical indications were still limited, for adults, on the other hand, versatility of technical abilities became more and more difficult to acquire. An outline 'specialisation' took place at the very heart of general surgical departments. Thus, in Bichat, Terrier and his school particularly developed surgery of the digestive apparatus and the biliary ducts. Quenu, after leaving Terrier to become department head in Cochin, continued in this direction. A process which was to become irreversible had started. The existence of specialised services tended to restrict the range of pathologies treated by general surgery, which in the end was dealing with fewer 'urological' or 'gynaecological' cases and appeared less competent to treat them. In turn, this increased their own tendency to specialise. Cancer treatment was included in this movement. Even if it remained primarily the monopoly of general surgery, points of reference by location were becoming known: Hospital Necker's urology together with Guyon, Albarran, Bazy and Legueu for cancers of the kidneys, the bladder and the prostate, Hospital Broca's gynaecology with Pozzi then his successor Jean-Louis Faure, for cancers of the womb – i.e. the most frequent location of the disease's appearance.

Of course, the new interest of surgeons in cancer would not have been so great if they had not obtained some long-term, that is definite, treatment successes. Henri Hartmann presented before the Academy of Medicine in 1898 the first two 'cures' of cancer of the pylorus and published some years later statistics confirming 30 per cent success in stomach cancers and 40 per cent in cancers of the rectum operated on in accordance with rules which he codified later.[7] It is difficult to appreciate what these data meant in practice. Hartmann, at the end of his life, quoted these results when talking about long-term survival without recurrence, but gave no further details.[8] Since we lack sufficient information, we cannot evaluate the time necessary, without relapse after the operation, to suggest that the patient was cured. In the first publications showing recovery statistics, the reversal experienced only lasted longer than two years in exceptional cases. In addition, the trend was rather to publish only encouraging statistics and details were rare. As C. Mocquot wrote in outlining the career of Jean-Louis Faure: 'In the enthusiasm of his youth, he considered it a duty to put all his energy into fighting against an evil which only a bloody operation could cure and did cure occasionally. But the disappointments were many.'[9] Hospital administrative statistics are hardly more illuminating, as they only count deaths in hospital and discharges from hospital. It seems, however, from these that cancer mortality in hospital was the highest of all the illnesses treated. At Tenon during the period 1901–6, it accounted for just over one patient in two (766/1501) and while cancer sufferers represented less than 2 per cent of the patients in hospital, they accounted for 6.5 per cent of deaths.[10] However, even if insignificant compared with reality, these few successes were sufficient to give credence to the idea that cancer could now be considered as a curable illness . . . under certain conditions. These conditions are defined very empirically. A cancer may possibly be treated if it can be operated on, that is if it is still accessible to the lancet, which leads us back to a complex connection of facts linked to its location in the organ affected, to its spread to other tissues or organs nearby and to the existence or not of metastases. Related to the vision which we have of cancer as a progressive illness, the curable–operable relationship is included in a proposal whose simplicity will be its strength and which will become the basic axiom establishing the strategy of the fight against cancer: cancer is originally a local disease which only secondarily becomes generalised, it is curable if it is treated in time.

X-rays and radium

At the end of the nineteenth century, the conditions for the practice of medicine continued to be affected by major innovations. The effects of Pasteur's discoveries had hardly begun to be felt in the approach to infectious diseases and on surgery when another 'revolution' came in its turn to pave the way for new changes. This time the movement began from the physical sciences. In four years, there were three decisive discoveries: X-rays (1895), radioactivity (1896), polonium and radium (1898). They renewed the bases of knowledge. Their applications to medicine were almost immediate. Professor Roentgen's work on X-rays had hardly been published for five months, when there appeared, from the pen of H.S. Ward, the first work on radiology. The cover page of *Practical Radiology* was adorned with an X-ray of a 'human heart *in situ*'. And it was so amazing that readers would not notice that unfortunately it had been reproduced upside-down.[11] Being able to see, for the first time, what was happening inside the body, without having to open it up, caused considerable emotion. It also motivated immediate vocations: Antoine Béclère was 40 years old when he was present at a radioscopy session, in a colleague's house. He was a doctor from the Central Office of the hospitals, constrained by having to 'support' his family and thus having to renounce preparation for the *agrégation*. This man was not on a path which led to positions of power. But he became passionately interested in the 'new sciences' and undertook a good deal of personal research into immunology. He had gone to the session out of curiosity. His host called the serving maid, who was to be the subject of the demonstration, and everyone marvelled at the beating of her heart and the movements of her diaphragm, until one of the guests, having seen a denser area on one of the lungs, questioned the woman and obtained confirmation of his hypothesis. Yes, it was a pulmonary tuberculosis scar. The story intimates that Béclère left the meeting having decided to dedicate himself to the study of this technique, which he suspected was capable of revolutionising the art of diagnosis.

Appointed the following year as a doctor in Tenon, his wish to introduce radioscopy came up against a huge problem: the hospital had no electricity supply, not even for lighting. He had to construct at his own expense what was clearly a very rudimentary laboratory installed under a staircase and, because of the lack of a generator, he had to ask for the help of a trained cyclist![12] In 1898, he was summoned to Saint-Antoine; as luck would have it, the hospital, being more modern, was equipped to deal with his project and became under his encouragement the centre of radiological training in Paris.

Let us make it clear at once that such vocations are rare in French doctors. In the first few years, X-ray apparatus was more an amusing plaything than a major weapon in the medical arsenal. Even amongst those who dedicated themselves to the investigation of the possibilities offered by the technique, enthusiasm was tempered with scepticism. Jean-Alban Bergonié, professor of electroradiology in Bordeaux, in the first article which he published on the use of Roentgen rays in medicine (1896), expressed his doubts regarding the possibility of obtaining recognisable images of tissues other than bone, as 'they only show a very slight difference of transparency to the rays with the experimental methods used'.[13] If the following year, he already showed more optimism and forecast that 'most internal injuries . . . can certainly, in the near future or later, be studied or diagnosed by these new rays'.[14] His descriptions of the disadvantages of radiography gave a good idea of the problems posed by its practical use:

> The delays inseparable from ordinary photographic processing are sometimes too long for the surgeon who is impatient to carry out a diagnosis . . . then it is often impossible to get the subject to remain still, for instance when children are involved, and this even applies in the case of adults when the pose has to be held for a long time.[15]

And a long time it was, if we reflect that he considered it a success when a good negative of a bone could be obtained 'with a posing period which did not exceed half an hour'. And what should we say about the postures imposed on unfortunate male (or female) patients whose pelvis was being X-rayed? Their body was at a right angle, their pubis supported on top of the back of an armchair, their head down, their nose on the chair, all of this of course while the patient was entirely naked.

Once the initial interest had diminished, fundamental questions arose.[16] Apart from its use in fracture surgery, the diagnostic interpretation of images appeared to be more complicated than expected in the detection of calcified tissues or foreign bodies. Radiological semiology remained to be updated, and this was to take several years.[17] In addition, acquiring proper technical competence was difficult and put doctors in direct competition with photographers.

> It was a paradox in the eyes of more than one doctor who would voluntarily have left radiology to photographers, it was a scandal for certain photographers who wanted to prevent doctors from using radiology. They would have been successful with the assent of the Academy of Sciences in the guise of a law which the Senate would have passed, if M. Béclère had not managed to abort the project.[18]

In fact, one institution played a pilot role in the large-scale use of radiology. It was the army, which included it from 1897 in the systematic health examination of conscripts. The Paris *Assistance Publique* also opted for the measure but only equipped its hospitals parsimoniously. In 1913, its general manager, Mesureur, might well have paid particular attention to the financial efforts made, since there were only five suitably equipped electroradiological laboratories in Paris, at the Saint-Antoine, Boucicaut, La Pitié, Trousseau and Laënnec hospitals. Their systematic installation came later.[19]

If Roentgen rays showed images of the interior of the body, doctors discovered, sometimes to their disadvantage, that that was not their only property. In the euphoria at the beginning, demonstrations and examinations were made without particular precautions being taken. It was not long before there were unexpected consequences for those who were subject to the experiments and for those who handled the equipment. These were in the form of accidents ranging from 'simple hair removal and skin redness to third degree burns and necrosis of tissues'.[20] These skin problems did not appear immediately; they arose after a short or long latent period, lasting from several days to several weeks. The proof of a cause and effect relationship between the phenomena was made by a New York professor, Elihu Thomson, who was not afraid to expose the little finger of his left hand for half an hour to a Crookes tube and carefully recorded the appearance and spread of dermatitis at the point of impact of the rays.[21] The proof of action on living tissues showed the matter in a new light; the idea that a new treatment tool had just been discovered suddenly took shape. In a completely empirical fashion, the experiments were multiplied with fortunate and unfortunate consequences. There were great hopes for radioscopic hair removal – the fashion was for hairless skin, and the depilatory procedures which had been used until then were painful. Alas, it was not long before the results were disastrous, 'indeed the hair fell out, but the skin came off too; in addition the hair grew again later, unless the skin was replaced by scar tissue'.[22]

Albers-Schönberg published an article in 1898 on the therapeutic use of Roentgen rays for the treatment of lupus and cited a cure of the ulcerated parts in two sufferers 'resistant to normal healing methods'.[23] A lecture delivered to the Academy of Sciences mentioned 'encouraging' results on a patient with elephantiasis.[24] Dr Despignes of Lyons was the first to attempt to treat a cancer sufferer with X-rays. From his observations (made in 1896), it appeared that a patient affected by a malignant stomach tumour, already afflicted with cachexia, had improved after eight days of treatment, the tumour had reduced, the pains had diminished, the loss of weight had stopped. But 'this wonderful observation . . ., having been published as soon as the treatment was over, loses, because of this fact alone, most of its value' – the patient was to die some time later.[25] In an article of January 1897, J. Bergonié made the point:

> Until now, the fair number of experiments that have been carried out have not given properly based results from the scientific point of view. If cultures have been modified in their virulence (he was alluding to experiments on the Antracis bacillus), if diseases, normally without remission (stomach cancer, tuberculosis) have been alleviated, all this needs confirmation by more thorough experimentation. As regards the action of the X-rays on the skin . . . the facts are already more convincing. . . [but] instead of the therapeutic effects required, we have until now only obtained so-called traumatic effects.[26]

However, interest in the new therapy began to be based on more tangible successes. Shiff and Freund confirmed favourable results in the treatment of lupus. As a result of their work, a Swedish radiologist, Thor Stenbeck, had the idea, in 1899, of using the method to heal a cancroid cancer of the skin. The cure appeared radical and the scar hardly visible. In the same year, Tage Sjögren confirmed the results. Their publication reached the United States and several American doctors began to carry out a series of experiments by extending the area of action to other types of cancer. In June 1902, Dr Coley produced a review of the whole question for the American Surgical Association. He affirmed that radiotherapy produced a clear action on neoplasms, even if the cancers were deep. Skinner brought this up again the next year in a memorandum published by *The Medical Standard*.[27]

Retrospectively, with regard to the knowledge which had to be acquired to master the treatment, the first successes were somewhat 'miraculous' and owed a lot to 'luck'. The first radiotherapists worked completely in the dark, without even knowing what the active agent was. Léopold Freund studied the various phenomena capable of producing such effects by observing the activity within a Crookes tube: heat, ozone, cathode rays, ultra-violet light, emission of particles of matter, X-rays, electrical discharges produced by a bulb, and even the existence of another type of radioactivity whose nature was still unknown.[28] Two hypotheses were principally in opposition. On the one hand, there were those who explained the new by the new; they believed in the role of X-rays, without being able even to demonstrate it. On the other hand, there were those who explained it by what was already known. They tended to believe that it was an effect of electricity. Amongst these were the first two French doctors to hold an opinion on the use in medicine of Roentgen rays. Let us follow Bouchacourt in the demonstration which he presented to his jury on 7 July 1898:

> Radiotherapy is beginning to record some successes, which must be welcomed only with reserve so as not to run the risk once again of the disastrous bursts of enthusiasm which followed Roentgen's discovery. We can ask ourselves, in all these fortunate cases, which rays were used in the complicated beam emitted by the Crookes tube. Is the therapeutic action due to the Roentgen rays? We affirm again that these rays are probably not responsible for both the advantages and the disadvantages which were attributed to them, and that they made way for electrical radiation. In all the published observations, the electricity generator was in effect the Ruhmkorff coil, and no precaution was taken to de-electrify the rays produced by the Crookes tube.[29]

Soret and Sorel had published the positive results of the action of X-rays on elephantiasis in February 1898; in March an article by Albert Weill had reported a new cure of an elephantiasis oedema treated this time by electricity alone;[30] and several authors noted the appearance of disturbances in cardiac rhythm in individuals exposed to the rays. Bouchacourt himself averred that the variations in circulation depended not on the Crookes tube but on the coil. How then could one explain electricity as the active agent, when trophic problems of the skin only appeared when the Crookes tube was active?[31] The reply was shrewd, even if not scientifically based: 'The Roentgen rays have a double nature, being formed by physical agents supplied with the power of penetration and by electrical vibrations which because of this become more penetrating.'[32] And borrowing this strong image from the thesis of his colleague Schall: 'Radiation has an electrical charge in its wake, which it leads, through the epidermal cells, which are poor conductors, and it takes the vitreous lamina to the surface of the skin where it will act at its ease in a little resistant milieu',[33] he concluded that the 'electricity generator, in radiotherapy, must always be the Ruhmkorff coil ... since [the latter] therefore seems to be only a more penetrating form of electrotherapy ... by increasing the range which the Roentgen rays lend to electrical radiation, in the same way that the choke-bored gun increases the range of the shot'.[34]

That these arguments found favour with the jury was not surprising. Only a few physical properties of X-rays were known, which in no way allowed any 'biological' properties to be justified. Extrapolation 'without a safety net' was imposed on all those who tried to understand what was happening and, everything considered, Bouchacourt's interpretative leap might appear less daring than the one made by those who claimed that it was precisely the unknown X-rays which caused the trophic problems. For the latter it was difficult to prove in that one cannot produce X-rays without electricity. A few years later, the debate was still not clear-cut, and although in 1900, Kienböck, a Viennese radiologist, could argue in favour of their action, his demonstration was so complex that few were able to grasp it.[35]

The outcome of 'accidents' connected to the handling of radium, very similar to those seen by radiologists, clarified the question. Everything began in 1900, with Becquerel. Invited to a physicists' conference in London, he took with him a tube, which he had slipped into his jacket pocket containing the precious product isolated by the Curies. A fortnight later, where his jacket pocket had been, his skin was sufficiently inflamed for him to consult a doctor friend. Suspicions fell on radium. Advised of the matter, Pierre Curie decided to 'check' the experiment and tried it on himself. 'To his great joy,' his daughter Eve was to write, 'six weeks later a lesion appeared.'[36] Other cases of dermatitis on the hands of scientists working with radium were soon noticed. There were enough facts now to eliminate the hypothesis of an effect of electricity, since a radioactive body which spontaneously emitted particular radiations and which was very analogous (in its physical properties) to X-rays managed to produce on the skin trophic problems similar to those caused by exposure to a Crookes tube. At the same time as the object of the research became clear, a new field of treatment appeared with radium therapy. Becquerel was to suggest its use, from 1901, in the treatment of cancer.[37]

In the first few years of the new century, laboratory experiments, still mainly therapeutic, multiplied 'everywhere' and so X-rays were to be used in the treatment of ringworm. The *Assistance Publique*, in order to deal with the influx of young patients, opened a school for ringworm sufferers at the Hospital Saint-Louis, and, because cures were slow, the children stayed there for an average of two years. The new headmaster of the school, Dr Sabouraud, appointed in 1899, decided to try radiotherapy against the parasites, successfully it seems, since irradiated children were cured from ringworm of the scalp within two months, and from favus in four. His laboratory, used for school inspections, was responsible for almost eradicating the illness in Paris, and having lost its boarders, the school for ringworm sufferers closed down. It is impossible to find out anything about the 'secondary effects' in the children treated.[38] The *Traité de Radiothérapie*, which Jean Belot published in 1905,[39] exhaustively lists the conditions for which X-rays were used: diseases of the pilosebaceous system, psoriasis, pruriginous dermatosis, specific microbe dermatosis (lupus, leprosy), conjunctive neoformations (sclerodermia, keloid, sarcoma, melanosarcoma, lipoma), tumours of the lymphatic tissue (lymphosarcoma, Hodgkin's disease, leukaemia, etc.), epithelial neoformations (verrucas, skin cancers, tongue cancers, breast cancers, deep cancers, intra-abdominal cancers), and miscellaneous dermatological diseases (moles, intertrigo, herpes, xeroderma). They were also tried on various locations of tuberculosis, elephantiasis, exophthalmic goitre, hydatid cyst of the liver, benign tumours of the womb, syphilis and epilepsy; that is, a total of nearly seventy pathological entities. Bergonié, in 1904, prepared the first statement of research on the therapeutic action of radium in cutaneous diseases (lupus, epithelioma, rodent ulcer), in malignant tumours (carcinoma of the floor of the mouth, cancer of the oesophagus, cancer of the tongue) and various other diseases such as tuberculosis (the idea was to use radiation to kill the germs), convulsive neuroses (by the application of radium salts on the temples), pseudo-ataxia and facial paralysis.[40]

In parallel, laboratory experiments were carried out, but therapeutic testing which was based on their results was rare. The lack of effectiveness of X-rays on bacteria, observed *in vitro,* did not prevent, for example, clinicians from irradiating tuberculosis sufferers in the name of a first principle which required things to be otherwise for the patient, and of a second, according to which, although there was no known effective treatment, it was nonetheless necessary to try something. As each time a new treatment appeared, the clinic accumulated case observations. 'We are still assembling facts,' wrote Bergonié. 'We are waiting for a rational classification to be achieved to file them in order.' But the empirical method (a test is carried out in one or more cases, the results are observed and are then recorded so that the facts can be classified rationally) here meets major difficulties.

> The technique is so badly developed that certain authors have not obtained any result, whilst others, with similar instruments, it seems, have obtained disastrous effects. It is therefore best that each person brings to this matter the results of his or her personal experience, by as closely as possible describing the cases treated clinically, and the technique followed electrically.[42]

One of the problems which haunted the first radiologists was really fundamental: how to measure the quality and quantity of the radiation? Béclère produced in 1900 a 'spintermeter' which allowed the average penetration of X-rays to be measured. In 1902, Holzknecht thought up a technique, based on a property of the rays to colour certain salts, which enabled the amount of radiation received by the illuminated surface to be determined. Being based on the fact that the colouring varied in accordance with the period of exposure and the power of the Crookes tube, a pastille containing a (secret) salt composition was placed on the irradiated surface, and its colouring was compared with test pastilles calibrated in accordance with a conventional unit called the H unit. This was perfectly arbitrary in the sense that the amount it measured was not defined, but it allowed the exposures to be compared (a patient would be subjected to sessions of three, four or five H) and links between the exposures and the clinical signs to be established (so many H units determined the appearance of an erythema or hair falling out, etc.).[43] In 1904, Béclère adapted the procedure of the 'chromoradiometer' according to the action of the radium.[44] But the use of these procedures which, although crude, opened the way to the 'rational classification' of facts, was only implemented very gradually. Belot was disappointed to note that observations indicating the amount of rays absorbed were very rare in France. In addition, there was great disparity regarding methods of treatment.

> From all that has happened, we may conclude that absolutely convincing results have been obtained by most of those who used radiotherapy for the treatment of cutaneous epithelioma. But if we compare the techniques used, we are surprised by their divergence. Some, such as Williams, preferred rays which hardly penetrated; others such as Crocker and Morton, used hard bulbs. The length of the sessions, their frequency, the times of rest periods vary considerably from one observer to another. Some count in minutes, others in seconds.[45]

Schiff and Freund used short sessions of a few minutes, repeated two or three times per week and monitored until modifications were obtained; Kienböck and Béclère preferred to use massive doses (five hours every week); whilst others left a fortnight between two sessions of five hours. 'Not only does the method of application vary according to the person', continued Belot, 'but the reaction sought is most often totally different from one practitioner to another . . . [Some] feel that it is necessary to produce a moderate dermatitis; others . . . do not hesitate to produce a violent reaction. [Others, including Béclère] have published cures without dermatitis appearing. . . . We are easily confused amongst these more or less contradictory opinions'.[46] These divergences reflect the state of ignorance of clinicians regarding the method of action of X-rays on living organisms in general, and on cancers in particular.

A principle of rational classification of facts

The treatment techniques used were based on hypotheses often made afterwards to explain the positive results obtained. The first treatments undertaken were made without the slightest standardisation and without any technique for evaluating the amount of rays absorbed by the exposed tissues. In this situation of total experimental exploration, the way in which the first successes recorded by the doctor were obtained was to influence the use of his method and inspire him with hypotheses. The nature of the hypothesis adopted directed the search for facts capable of confirming it. Thus, those who confirmed that their first cures went hand in hand with radiation which provoked radiodermatitis, without this being in principle sought, would incline towards establishing a correlation between the two phenomena. They believed that the action of the rays was similar to that of a caustic product (Newcomb, Wills) and that it induced an inflammatory reaction stimulating repair and favouring phagocytosis of cancer cells (Grubbe). If necessary, they relied on pathological studies carried out once radiodermatitis was established, showing that the cancerous islets were imprisoned by the inflammatory tissues and were progressively eliminated. The fact that they also observed that the cure was more rapid when the dermatitis was pronounced strengthened them in their convictions. On the other hand, an initial success accompanied by a very weak inflammatory reaction or without the slightest dermatitis appearing, posed other questions concerning the method of action of the ray and led them to consider the pathological tissue as a privileged target since it was 'endowed' with a sensitivity greater than that of normal tissue. Such a hypothesis could still be based upon pathological anatomical examinations carried out much earlier. Amongst others, Mikulicz and Fittig, (after studying scars left by breast cancer), Pusey ('cancroid' of the face) and Elis (cutaneous epithelioma) agreed to attribute a greater destructive effect of X-rays on cancer cells than on cells of normal tissue. Antoine Béclère, gathering together different data obtained in France, established a timetable of the phenomena: the action of the rays was first marked by cellular manifestations (swelling of the nuclei, loss of their colouring power, granular degeneration). The inflammation would thus only be a reaction caused by the destruction of the cells.

For some time these two contradictory hypotheses coexisted, even though the second was more 'forceful' and was based on facts which refuted the first, for it was still a period for collecting observations which established the effectiveness of the therapy and not for their 'rational' classification. The major challenge for doctors who used radiotherapy was, above all, to confirm the relevance and interest of each new treatment when faced with a rather sceptical medical establishment. It is only necessary to see how a man like Jean Belot, a pupil of Béclère and like him convinced of the secondary role of inflammatory reactions, presented his treatise on radiotherapy. If he criticised those theses which included X-rays among 'caustic' agents, it was only after having supported the positivity of their results in a chapter which listed examples of success due to radiotherapy. Certainly, the idea that X-rays acted as a 'resolvent' determining the remission of the cancer process expanded the possibilities of its application and notably allowed the German Perthes to invent the technique of deep radiotherapy, but the practical interest of such an innovation was not immediately evident. In fact, Perthes' invention had as its purpose the resolution of problems posed by the irradiation of cancer tissues which had invaded the deep layers and which, up to then, could only be reached at the cost of a violent irradiation of the surface tissue, giving rise to accidents and often causing treatment to be stopped. Relying on a simple equation which requires that the amount of radiation absorbed is equal to the amount of radiation emitted divided by the square of the distance to the source, Perthes suggested placing the bulb at a greater distance from the skin in order that the square of the source–surface distance would be as near as possible to the square of the source–deep tissue distance (for example, instead of irradiating at ten centimetres from the skin, he irradiated at one metre). Under these conditions, the amount of rays received on the surface and in depth are practically identical.[47] This excellent and promising idea for the future had at that time, in 1903, a major disadvantage: the weakness of the bulbs producing the X-rays meant that, at a great distance, the amount of rays received was very feeble and long sessions were required for not very thorough results.

The hypothesis which makes the cell the target of the rays went hand in hand, as we have seen, with the established fact that for the same amount of rays absorbed there were great differences of sensitivity according to the types of cell, even if it was legitimate to talk, as Béclère writes, 'of an elective action of these rays'.[48] On this point, pathological anatomical observations were abundant but were not sufficient for a coherent interpretation. In fact, upon the occasion of a publication or a paper on one case or a series of cases treated, the doctors put forward an explanation which was partly based on their observations and partly on an extrapolation which was generally based on some personal opinion. In the great majority, the explanation supplied tried to answer the question regarding the difference of sensitivity to X-rays of healthy cells and cancer cells and, in order to do this, invoked a theory of malignant degeneration. In this way, the thesis popular with several German 'radiologists', such as Perthes, von Brums or Ribbert, who borrowed Virchow's idea that the cancer cell was decrepit and weak, affirmed that X-rays only aided the spontaneous trend to degeneration which existed anyway. If this was so, as the American Skinner remarked, it did not explain why radiotherapy was not always successful and had no effect on certain patients. Skinner opted for another interpretation which also originated from another theory of malignant degeneration. This would be based on abandoning the protoplasmic activity proper to the normal development of the cell leading to a regressive development. For him, the physical properties of the X-rays could influence molecular movement to the point of overcoming the aberrant trend and re-establishing the normal function of the cell. No doubt conscious that his philosophy of rectification was too general to take account of the differences in effectiveness of the treatment, Skinner introduced another variable which he tacked on to his theory 'the individual equation for the patient as regards his/her susceptibility to the healing agent'.[49] This only displaced the problem. In addition, without this excluding a differentiating suscepti-bility according to the patient, several results led to the idea that the elective action of the rays did not affect the various healthy tissues/cancer tissues but divided the healthy tissues (some were more sensitive than others) and the different types of cancer. Scholtz, by irradiating the normal cutaneous tissues in a laboratory, found that X-rays acted by destroying only epithelial cells. Béclère found that the cells of the neoplasms 'are even more sensitive when the tissue to which they belong is softer and more juicy, that is richer in protoplasm and seeming to be at the site of a cellular renewal'.[50] On the fringe of the majority of the works which continued to deal with the anatomical study of irradiated tumours, some research in the laboratory was to take place on the sensitivity of normal cells, tissues or organs. In 1903 Albers-Schönberg wrote: 'Regarding a still unknown effect of radiotherapy on the organism of animals': irradiated rabbits and guinea pigs, 'while they are still able to mate, produce semen which proves to be sterile'.[51] He attributed this result to a destruction of the spermatozoa. The following year, Heinecke experimentally caused a leucopenia (fall in the proportion of white corpuscles in the blood). Schwartz, irradiating eggs, noted an alteration in the yolk, which he related to the decomposition of one of its constituents, lecithin. Basing his idea on the fact that lecithin is very abundant, apart from in egg yolk, in spermatozoa and neoplasms, he suggested that it was in this way that X-rays operated on the cancer cells. But he did not succeed in demonstrating whether the decomposition of lecithin was a direct or indirect effect of the action of the rays.

The principle of 'rational classification' of the facts was to be discovered by Jean Bergonié and Louis Tribondeau. In their first series of preliminary experiments, published in 1904 and 1905, they irradiated the testicles of white rats and observed with a microscope the effect of X-rays on the seminiferous tubes, that is the structure where the differentiation of the cells of the seminal line takes place leading to the formation of spermatozoa. Their results, taken together, allowed a coherent interpretation. What were these results?

- The rays had the property of destroying the seminiferous tubes. The number of tubes destroyed in a testicle was higher the stronger the irradiation. The number and duration of sessions matters little; under the conditions of their experiment, it was the total amount of X-rays absorbed by the sacs which was the deciding factor.
- The tubes which were not destroyed continued to exist in a more or less atrophied and deformed state. Amongst these, certain were rendered infertile, 'aspermatogenic'; the cells of the seminal line had disappeared, only 'Sertoli' cells which normally surround the seminal cells remained, ensuring their protection and nutrition. In the others, where there was spermatogenic activity, some of the cells of the seminal line were destroyed. Everything continued to happen as if the nearer the cells were to the last stage of differentiation which forms the spermatozoon, the more chance they had of avoiding destruction.

A second series of experiments, carried out this time on female rats whose ovaries were irradiated, supplied convergent results which led the experimenters to establish a 'law' which they called 'the law of correlation between the Roentgian frailty of cells and their reproductive activity'. Its claim was divided into three parts: X-rays acted with more intensity on cells:

1   When the reproductive activity of the cells was greater.
2   When their 'karyokinetic' future was longer (karyokinesis is the whole dynamic phenomena of the division of the nucleus ending in the formation of two daughter nuclei, which precede cellular division).
3   When their morphology and functions were less definitively fixed.

The first part of this law stated that a cell, whatever type, becomes more sensitive to radiation from the moment that it enters into the reproduction process. The second part of the law emphasised the particular sensitivity of cells which, forming a line, multiplied and became permanently trans-formed. This was the case with the cells in the seminal line and also, as Bergonié and Tribondeau noticed, that of many cancer cells. Hence the explanation of the numerous observations noting that X-rays destroyed cancer cells and spared normal cells. Finally, the third part of the law was the corollary of the first two: 'The more one cell is morphologically and physically different because of special functions, the more the multiplying function becomes secondary; and inversely, when a specialised cell is reproduced, its special functions slow down and the preponderant role returns to the karyokinetic phenomena.'[52] In the testicle, the Sertoli cells, specialised in their secretory role and whose morphology is fixed, would be almost indifferent to the action of the rays. The spermatozoon, ending the line which cannot be divided, would itself be insensitive. This would also be the case with the nerve, bone and muscle cells and the red corpuscles. As regards tumours, '[they] supply us excellent examples of very insensitive cells whose functions and morphology are properly fixed (such as lipomas) and very weak cells which are very polymorphous or which do not have a definite function other than reproduction (carcinoma, epithelioma, sarcoma)'.[53]

This work had considerable repercussions, if we remember that later it was to contribute to the regulation of the whole principle of radiotherapy. It was rapidly recognised in France, and obtained one of the highest distinctions of the Academy of Science, the Montyon prize, for its authors.

The genesis of a discovery

In the historical hagiographies which doctors are fond of producing regularly, the 'law correlating the Roentgenian frailty of cells and repro-ductive activity' is presented as the successful continuation of the observations made in 1903 by Albers-Schönberg, showing for the first time that irradiated animals – in his case, guinea pigs and rabbits – became sterile. The two French doctors found what the German radiologist had missed (he interpreted sterility as an effect of the destruction of spermatozoa) because they carried out their experiments much more systematically. Criticising, not without reason, biographers who attributed to 'genius' the choice of the testicle, a 'true physiological neoplasm', as study material, Professor Meyniel saw in this choice subservience to a weighty scientific formality: 'It emerges' he wrote 'from reading their works that they were guided by purely technical considerations'.[54] With the white rat, spermatogenesis is continuous, irradiation of the testicles is easy to carry out and, after the memorandum published by Claudius Regaud in 1901, their histological structure is perfectly described. Could Bergonié and Tribondeau have simply been less rigorous in their procedures than Albers-Schönberg? The explanation seemed a little short, if only because, implicitly, it assumed that they were trying to answer the same question. I propose to show that this was not the case at all, and to accomplish this I am relying on the analysis of an element whose consequences are never taken into account by biographers, that is that the work of Bergonié and Tribondeau was the product of a meeting and of co-operation between two individuals with very different qualifications.

What was Albers-Schönberg trying to discover when he irradiated his rabbits and guinea pigs? In 1903, in the debate on the question of the choice of the method of action of X-rays, the radiologist was considering the problem of whether the latter were capable of producing effects on 'normal organs' other than the skin, that is on the 'deep' organs. And he could, on the basis of his observations, answer yes. He had caused azoospermia, without the testicles apparently being injured. This last point was critical for him, as it meant that the disappearance of spermatozoa could not be attributed to the secondary effect on the testicles caused by a violent action on the skin of an acute inflammation type with necrosis. We can assume that he contented himself with offering as an explanation for the azoospermia the direct effect of rays on the spermatozoa, without trying to carry out an *ad hoc* experiment to prove this, because, for him, the question was secondary to the one that he had been asking himself from the beginning.

How did Bergonié receive these findings when he became aware of them? He mentioned it in an article in 1904 on 'Radium from the medical point of view', in a paragraph dedicated to various effects of radium on living organisms: 'Regarding the spermatozoa of the sea urchin, Mr Bohn saw movements weaken fairly rapidly. Perhaps we could compare this observation with the, *very odd*, one made by Mr Albers-Schönberg on the reduction of generative potency in normal individuals subjected regularly to radiation from the Crookes tube.'[55] Nothing could foretell, on reading the article, that he was on the brink of carrying out the experiment again, all the more so as he began the following paragraph, 'Action on germs and ferments' by declaring: 'More interesting for us would be the germicidal action of radium if it could be measured . . . .'[56] When his position changed a little later, the meeting with Tribondeau was decisive. In fact, until then,

Bergonié had always ignored the histological approach in his personal work. An electrophysiologist by training, he had dedicated himself to the study of emergent radiology on two levels: as a semiologist contributing to the establishment of diagnostic signs, and as a technician concerned with improving methods and equipment. Although a fundamental 'non-clinical' professor, he took the initiative several times to look after patients and he tried radiotherapy, and even radium therapy, on 'inoperable' cancer sufferers. He successfully treated in this way a 'cancroid' of the eyelid and the eye socket, a lingual epithelioma and obtained two remissions of breast cancer. A significant fact: in none of the publications where he reports his results did Bergonié resort to microscopic pathological anatomical examination to evaluate the incidence of treatment; he was content to use clinical development criteria. Nothing, in his practice, predisposed him to develop Albers-Schönberg's observations. Tribondeau was himself a naval doctor, appointed in 1902 as a histology and microbiology lecturer at the main Naval School in Bordeaux. His interest in X-rays originated with the first work mentioning their action on certain normal cells. He read Albers-Schönberg's results from a histologist's point of view and so from a completely different angle. With the testicles, microscopic analysis is coupled with microscopic physiology, in the sense that not only are the different functions of the organ individualised in cellular lines which are known, the 'Sertoli' nutritional and productive cells and the reproductive cells, but also the physiological process resulting in the production of the final 'active' product, spermatozoon, is identifiable, histologically, at various stages of its development, stages corresponding to a particular variety of cells (spermatogonium, spermatid, spermatozoon, etc.). Cutting seminiferous tubes allowed a 'photograph' to be obtained of the various phases of the physiological process. Tribondeau was very familiar with the subject. He had previously had the opportunity to study the alteration of these tubes in a subject suffering from tuberculous epididymitis and he had demonstrated that the latter had affected the seminal line, sparing the Sertoli cells. He had also read the Regaud memorandum which updated the knowledge of the histology of the testicle of the white rat and he could, therefore, on this basis, question the results of the German radiologist. The disappearance of spermatozoa did not mean that the action of the rays affected the final product, and it should have been possible, with an appropriate experimental method, to verify this. Thus he made contact with the person who, in Bordeaux, knew the most about radiotherapy. But Bergonié did not only contribute to this combined effort his competence regarding irradiation. He also brought his findings concerning the anti-cancer action of X-rays, at least as far as he was able to explain them as is revealed in a text from the same year, 1904: 'The action of X-rays on certain types of malignant tumours is today certain, but we do not know how and when the action is the most favourable during the development of these tumours'.[57] It took this meeting and this diversion to find a first coherent answer to this.

The first steps in radium therapy

> I have taken the radium from the pitchblende and I have burnt my fingers on this forbidden fire.
>
> (Aragon, *Les yeux d'Elsa* ['Elsa's eyes'])
>
> I love it, but I am annoyed with it.
>
> (Henri Becquerel)

The circumstances of the discovery of the biological effects of radiation emitted by radium were identical, or almost, to what happened with X-rays, the difference being that nearly always the first victims of 'accidents' were nearly always researchers involved in work on radioactive bodies. Warned by the precedent of X-rays, Henri Becquerel and Pierre and Marie Curie suggested to doctors that they try their substances for therapeutic purposes, and their commitment to the development of radium therapy cannot be denied.

The use of the Roentgen rays in medicine very quickly became independent of the world of learned physics. A professional group of physicist doctors mediated. This group, in competition with photographers, appropriated the applications of the discovery to turn it into a medical discipline. In France, for some time, things happened differently with radium; the relationship between fundamental physicists and doctors was much closer. If advances in radium therapy appeared directly linked to the work of scientists, the institutional development of research into radioactivity was to benefit in turn from the interest in medical applications, and the creation of the Institute of Radium would strengthen this interaction.

In 1903, Becquerel and the Curies received the Nobel Prize for Physics. These 'young luminaries' of science were enthusiastic about the medical repercussions of their discovery and contributed to their introduction by offering to Dr Danlos' department, in the Hospital Saint-Louis, a few samples of their precious product. Dermatologists immediately tried their hand at the treatment of lupus and skin cancers. The possibility thus created for the application of radium, given credibility by the precedent of X-rays, reached the attention of an industrialist, Armet de Lisle – one of the largest producers of cinchona – who decided to establish a factory for its manufacture in Nogent-sur-Marne in 1904. The entry on the scene of the industry occurred at a propitious moment for physicists as well as for doctors. In fact, research on radium was coming up against a major difficulty, that of obtaining the product itself. The situation was very different from what was happening with X-ray production. The latter initially involved only a small cost for equipment and could be satisfied with rudimentary apparatus: on the other hand, the extraction of radium demanded very arduous techniques. In order to be able to isolate a few milligrams of radium, Pierre and Marie Curie had to process several tons of a radioactive ore, pitchblende. This took place, moreover, in a cold, damp and badly ventilated shed. 'This fabulous element' Marie Curie would say later when describing the miserable conditions of their work, 'was not an advantage, it wore us out and delayed achievement.' Scientifically 'profitable' while the radioactive body was being discovered, effort was thought to be unncessary as soon as it became a matter of furthering knowledge beyond the physical, chemical and biological properties of the substance. The Nogent-sur-Marne factory was set up at the appointed time, and without hesitation the Curies and their co-worker A. Debierne communicated all the information they had to the industrialist, without trying to protect their manufacturing secrets or to collect their share of the profits. In return, Armet de Lisle put the resources of the enterprise at their disposal so that they could process the quantities of ore necessary for their laboratory.

With a price of 1.5 million gold francs per gram, radium was the costliest merchandise which had ever existed, and we can understand why on reading what a journalist of the *Temps* wrote: 'In order to obtain one gram of radium bromide at 92 per cent, we have to have 400 to 500 tonnes of radioactive ore, 150 to 200 tonnes of various reactives, 150 to 200 tonnes of coal, 800 to 1200 tonnes of water, that is a total of 1600 to 2200 tonnes of raw materials, without including the labour of 30 people employed in the factory, nor that of the miners who extracted the ore.'[58]

Philanthropists acted in their turn, also moved by medical interest in radium. Dr Henri de Rothschild and Denys Cochin financed two new factories and a fourth saw the light of day at Gif-sur-Yvette on the initiative of Jacques Danne. Alone in possessing specialised chemists, France ensured the world production of radium and processed radioactive materials from various countries. On the eve of the First World War – which would signal the end of France's monopoly and the decline of its radium industry – several dozen grammes per year were being manufactured there.

Starting with the same blind empiricism as radiotherapy, radium therapy was codified more quickly, in part because it benefited from the scientific rationalisation of the first, and in part thanks to the knowledge gained by the physicists. Between 1906 and 1914, there was a movement for the exchange of ideas and of staff between radiotherapy and radium therapy, which tended to come together under a 'radiation clinic'.

Two doctors from Professor Danlos' department, Wickham and Degrais, opened a 'biological radium laboratory' in 1906, in the rue d'Artois. They tested the first radioactive paint equipment provided for them by Armet and Lisle. The two dermatologists were joined by a young pathological anatomist, Henri Dominici, who transposed Bergonié and Tribondeau's discovery to the analysis of the biological effects of radium. From the results of histophysiological research, he drew up a law of correlation: malignant tumours are more sensitive to radium the closer their cells are to the embryonic stage. He also showed that among the three radiation types, α, β

and γ, the γ ray, considered ultra-penetrating, had an elective action on the neoplastic cells and left healthy cells relatively unharmed.[59] He therefore thought of a filtration technique which would only let the γ rays past (1909). Three years later, in Lyons, Claudius Regaud and Théodore Nogier published results of the same kind for Roentgen rays and explained the advantages (in terms of greater tolerance for the skin) of filtering.[60] Dominici adapted his filtration technique to the equipment. Contrary to the first instruments used, which were constructed with the idea of avoiding the absorption of radiation by the recipient as much as possible,[61] he invented the use of filtered radiation tubes with platinum which went straight to the heart of the tumour, thus initiating the technique of the 'curiepuncture'. These tubes considerably reduced the 'undesirable effects' on healthy tissues at the very time that the future domain of the choice of radium therapy was opening up, i.e. the treatment of the most frequent cancer of the time, that of the cervix, begun in 1907 at the Hospital Beaujon by Degrais and Rubens-Duval.

The codification of the treatment also took advantage of Marie Curie's work. The latter managed to obtain perfectly pure radium chloride in 1907 and to isolate, in 1910, the radioactive substance in a metallic state. This allowed her to update a procedure of administering small amounts of radium according to the measurement of the emanation which they produced, and so resolve the question of the amount of radiation emitted by a source. Béclère's chromoradiometer was relegated to the spare parts store, as the new unit of radioactivity (which would take the name of Curie) was no longer defined by totally arbitrary criteria (such as the intensity of colouring of the metallic salts), but by the number of disintegrations per second produced in a standard source (approaching one gram of radium). A second Nobel Prize, in chemistry this time, crowned her discoveries in 1911. If the conditions under which she worked were a little less 'romantic', they remained very mediocre. In 1903, Pierre Curie had, when refusing the Legion of Honour, called for a decent laboratory. Two years later, he had managed to obtain new accommodation in an annex of the Faculty of Sciences, in the rue Cuvier, and left the shed in which he had started for these new premises, a few rooms in a department. The Republic, wanting to honour its researchers but anxious to preserve the superiority of the husband over his spouse, had created a chair of General Physics and Radioactivity for Pierre Curie, appointing Marie as works manager. In 1906, Pierre Curie died, run over by a wagon harnessed to two Percheron horses. The Faculty of Sciences then offered the widow her husband's chair, at first as assistant professor, then in 1910 as titular professor. Of course, the University of Paris was moved by the working conditions which she had – even more so because, in Austria, Sweden and the United States, radium research institutes had been set up, emphasising the poverty of the French authorities – but, lacking sufficient funds, it contented itself in buying a building plot in the expectation of constructing a future laboratory. Things would doubtless have stayed the same for a little longer, if the Pasteur Institute had not accelerated the process, by intervening. Once again, scientists were taking advantage of the medical applications of radium.

In 1907, a rich industrialist, known as Mr Osiris, died. Some years earlier, he had made Dr Roux, the director of the Pasteur Institute, the first winner of a prize he had just created. The Pasteur Institute was included in his will as the only beneficiary of his fortune. Strengthened by this very considerable legacy, its management envisaged extending the range of the research dependent on the Institute, and building new laboratories within this field. One would be dedicated to 'normal and experimental histology' (Roux was thinking of Regaud as possible director), another could accommodate Mme Curie in as much as 'radium has already rendered service for the treatment of surface cancer tumours (where) the study of cancer is in the plans of Mr Osiris'.[62] This risk of seeing Marie Curie entering the Pasteur establishment mobilised the Academy of Paris. Its vice-principal started negotiations with Roux and obtained a reversal of the terms of the project.

> The laboratory which the University of Paris and the Pasteur Institute would build at common expense on a plot of land belonging to the University to be determined, between the rue d'Ulm and the rue Saint-Jacques, would be both for research on the phenomena of radioactivity and the study of the application of these phenomena to diseases at the same time. The part dedicated to learned research would be placed under the direction of Mme. Curie and her successors to the chair of Physics created for Pierre Curie; the part dedicated to the study of medical applications would be directed by the Pasteur Institute. If the University of Paris ceased to be involved, the whole laboratory would become the property of the Pasteur Institute.[63]

Between 12 and 28 December 1919, the essentials were settled and the birth certificate of the Radium Institute was signed. The individual who would manage the biological applications section was still to be selected. Claudius Regaud, previously contacted for a histology laboratory, was chosen by the Pasteur board of management. He had never worked on radium, but, being a histologist accustomed to experimental research on the action of X-rays, his double competence made him the man of the moment, all the more so since the man who could have been his potential rival, H. Dominici, was sick and died in 1910.

Delayed several times, the construction of the Radium Institute was completed in 1913 and the new directors officially took up their posts on 1 October in the same year.

In this very institutional period, rich in results for the future of cancerology, an attentive reader will not have failed to note a significant absence. This project which linked fundamental sciences and applications to medicine saw them represented by the Faculty of Sciences and the Pasteur Institute respectively. At no time had the Faculty of Medicine hinted at the least commitment, as if the fate of the radiation clinic was outside the sphere of its concerns.

3 Academicism and marginality

At the end of the last century and at the beginning of the present one, [a] group of eminent Parisian masters contributed to the spread throughout the world of a remedy created from this association between the laboratory and the clinic, which is still at the heart of French medicine. These great doctors were remarkable for their humanistic spirit, the extent of their culture and their lack of strict specialisation. Having been able to surround themselves with a team of young biologists whom they advised, they remained above all clinicians; their inspiration came from observing patients. Believe me, we should look for the origin and the secret of their success there.

(Eulogy of Anatole Chauffard
by Professor Guy Laroche, 14 December 1954)

We direct the faculties of medicine towards teaching, and this is excellent. But this improvement seems to have been unfortunately accomplished to the detriment of their central role in scientific research. . . . While remaining in a faculty of medicine, I will continue to endure the mediocrity of the working conditions. Personally, I dread even more an excessive teaching load. Since I want to satisfy my taste for biological investigation, I am paying very dearly for the means of working with which I am supplied; very dear, that is I waste a lot of time in weighty, thankless educational work and I have to be happy with the wages of a junior solicitor's clerk.

(Letter from Claudius Regaud to Dr Roux, April 1909)

The obvious lack of interest shown by the Faculty of Medicine in the establishment of the Radium Institute does not mean, as such, indifference from the hospital-university elite to the problems posed by cancer pathology. On the contrary, never was interest in the study of cancer so great as at the beginning of the twentieth century. It was strengthened, in addition, by the creation of a learned society in 1906, *l'Association française pour l'étude du cancer* (AFEC) [the French Association for the Study of Cancer], the first to permanently combine doctors and scientists from different specialised fields.

The initiative for this was due to three people: Charles Bouchard, professor of general pathology, Pierre Delbet, one of the future 'senior consultants' of surgery, for the time being still an *agrégé* since he had passed the lecturers' high level competitive examination, and Henri de Rothschild, without doubt the member of the French branch of the family who was the most absorbed in philanthropic aid for the development of medicine (he had, in addition, from pure intellectual interest, studied medicine and obtained his doctor's degree).

The first International Congress dedicated to cancer, which was held in the same year, 1906, in Heidelberg, prompted them to resurrect an old project which until then had not been possible to complete. In fact, Simon Duplay, a clinical surgery professor, tried to found an 'Anti-cancer league' in 1892, with the help of several of his colleagues in the Faculty of Medicine in Paris – Paul Reclus, Ricaud, Brault – and Metchnikoff, head of the Pasteur Institute laboratory.[1] The inspiration for this programme came from Professor Verneuil, one of the originators, together with Broca and Follin, who belonged to the renewed Paris Microscopy School: it was he who urged Duplay to involve himself in the project. The main idea of the project was to combine all medical disciplines capable of tackling any scientific aspect of the problems caused by cancer, because it was the only way to significantly increase knowledge in this field. Pathological anatomy had shown its limitations, '[it] had allowed a distinction to be made between the forms and origins of neoplasm, but that was all; it had learned nothing about its causes'.[2] By undertaking research into the causes, Verneuil emphasised the need to go beyond anatomical clinical attempts. Certainly, the 'clinic' continued to make an indispensable contribution, but it should have been linked to other approaches. First, epidemiological:

> as there was a need for multiple and well-noted observations; I would naturally require them from clinicians, doctors and surgeons of various states and regions, large and small towns and the country too; rural practitioners can supply precious documents on questions of environment, diet, heredity, etc. As neoplasm seems to differ considerably according to country, climate, race, I will question the army and navy doctors capable of turning it into a medical geography.[3]

Second, experimental:

> How unwise it would be to believe that laboratory experimentation and research have uttered their last word, the vivisectors, the histologists, the bacteriologists [must be] approached too . . . I will also try to create interest in the work of eminent haematologists, such as Hayem, a marvellous chemist, Gautier and clinical biologists, such as Albert Robin . . .[4]

By proposing to accept the confrontation between the clinical, epidemiological and experimental approaches to cancer, Verneuil defined an ideal structure which, in France, would have to wait until the second half of the twentieth century to be realised. At the time, this programme did not arouse the expected interest. The League 'did not survive its birth, perhaps it was too brilliant, and it disappeared after a death agony as dull as it was brief'.[5]

Duplay brought up the same complaints three years later, while trying to start from a less ambitious base. With Lannelongue (a surgeon, a professor of external pathology) and Cornil (the holder of the chair of pathological anatomy), he launched a *Revue des maladies cancéreuses* [Cancerous Diseases Review], the first French periodical specifically dedicated to cancer, which would cease to appear at the end of five years, as 'unfortunately', wrote Ledoux-Lebard, '[it] did not fulfil its promise'.[6]

Learning from these various failures, Bouchard, Delbet and Henri de Rothschild prepared their project carefully. Not being satisfied with taking advantage of a favourable context – the Heidelberg congress had rallied spirits, and the French who had attended had been able to assess the British and German achievements in this area – they systematically contacted all the individuals who might want to participate and appointed a prestigious committee of honour to support the enterprise. Some two years later, 'the forever laborious period of constitution and research [being] victoriously overcome',[7] on 15 June 1908 the AFEC had its first public meeting.

In the opinion of the number of 'first rate' individuals who met and the variety of the institutions represented, the action of our three promoters was a great success. No other specialised learned society could take pride in such a panel. The association was supported by a committee of honour which included Henri Bequerel (Nobel Prize in Physics), Henri Poincaré, then president of the Academy of Sciences, Professor Lavisse from the French Academy, the heads of the University and of the public service and the most important bankers.[8] The AFEC distinguished itself from other learned societies not simply by virtue of this committee of honour, whose function was above all 'decorative', but also because of the range of powerful positions acquired by its members in the medical field. However, to put into greater perspective the sociological analysis of this institution, its composition and its production, it is necessary to briefly review the most marked characteristics of the French hospital-university system and the strong relationships which served as its foundations.

The French hospital-university system: the rulers and the ruled

The 'revolutionary' reforms put hospitals at the centre of the French medical field. Because the 'clinic' was invented within them and not in the university precincts, hospitals took on a teaching role which tended to place the faculty second. It was at this level and through a series of competitions which gave access to the various positions of responsibility (*externat, internat, clinicat, médicat*) that the world of 'doctors' was organised into a hierarchy and from which the professional elite was selected. This organisation so greatly influenced what was correct and proper to the university that it governed it *de facto* if not *de jure*. In this way, the possession of a qualification of ex-intern was a quasi-obligation for a person who hoped to be admitted to the competition for the *agrégation*, and no-one could hold the chair who had not, before applying, passed through the various stages of a hospital career successfully and was not a hospital doctor or surgeon (i.e. department head). The only areas where exceptions existed fell within the so-called 'supplementary' sciences, such as physics or medical chemistry, which were not directly linked to the clinic.[9]

The take-over of the training system by hospital doctors tended to make the faculties of medicine a world 'apart' in the university. On the one hand, the professors were not civil servants, but private doctors working free of charge for several hours per day at the hospital, receiving a derisory recompense for teaching in the faculty and, on the other hand, earning their livelihood largely from their private practice; the elite of the medical body, they had as patients the elite of society. On the other hand, the existence of a double selection course, in which hospital competitions had a decisive influence, led to an adjustment of the value of university qualifications over hospital qualifications. The latter, because of decentral-isation at the communal level of the management and administration of hospitals, was local and non-national; therefore the system favoured the establishment of 'regional feudal systems' which, in their turn, reinforced the 'self-perpetuation' of the elites.[10]

Social medicine, which the First Republic had recognised under the same heading as clinical, saw, throughout this process, its influence constantly diminishing in the faculties. In Paris, the chair of hygiene remained isolated while the clinical chairs multiplied,[11] and after a century, it occupied, no more than a low prestige position, to the extent of sometimes regarded as being the 'waiting chair' for those aspiring to the supreme honour of being clinical professors.[12] This 'weakness' of hygiene in the universities is explained in part by the relative failure of the ambitions of social medicine. Certainly, the intense activity of the public health authorities in the large towns had resulted in a large number of improvements and had contributed to the transformation of the urban landscape;[13] but attempts to organise on a rational basis the struggle against 'poverty' and against the great 'community diseases' came up against the dominant liberalism of the state. In addition, a system for statistical data relating to mortality and morbidity did not succeed in being established. The départements which had an office of hygiene remained a minority, and where these offices existed, the hygienists were not successful in imposing their point of view regarding the upkeep of records, on private practitioners.[14] At the beginning of the twentieth century, only the Seine region possessed reliable data regarding mortality. In the absence of adequate equipment and deprived of the consequent institutional base, the hygienist movement was unable to increase its influence, both on the authorities and on the hospital–university elite.

Arising from a utilitarian point of view – that of training practitioners – and defying the aristocratic nature of the man of science, the revolutionary health schools kept 'scientists' apart. Their transformation into schools of medicine (1796), then into faculties of medicine (1808), did not change this situation which lasted until the arrival of the Third Republic. Ever since 1794, there had indeed been chairs for the 'supplementary' sciences, but they were limited to imparting elementary knowledge of chemistry, physics and physiology.

The majority of their holders seem to have been appointed because of their plagiarising activities, and not because of the originality of their research, which was often non-existent anyway. The scientists who had obtained a good reputation were kept apart or kept themselves apart,[15] in order to join very prestigious, but marginal, institutions, such as the Natural History Museum (created in 1793) or the Collège de France, the only one to have survived the Ancien Régime. The latter played a major role in the development of experimental medicine. The successive holders of the chair of medicine (Magendie, Claude Bernard, Brown-Séquard, d'Arsonval) attracted and trained young doctors who had chosen to involve themselves in basic research. But the working conditions were terrible, and the laboratories decrepit and badly equipped. It took until the Third Republic and the appointment of Paul Bert, a pupil of Claude Bernard, as minister for a change to be initiated which aimed at promoting scientific research in universities. The 'supplementary sciences', having become 'fundamental', benefited from the establishment of a few laboratories in the faculties of medicine, essentially in Paris and Lyons.[16] This change sanctioned the growing influence of the experimentalists on the intellectual level, at a time when purely clinical progress was losing momentum and where the knowledge of 'causes' appeared to be more and more decisive. It also sanctioned the impact on treatment and health of the Pasteur discoveries and it finally led to recognition of the tardiness of France when compared, in particular, with Germany and the United Kingdom. A reform in the study cycle was undertaken, which strengthened the weight of 'basic' disciplines in the training of students. In 1893, a certificate in science, the PCN (physics, chemistry and natural sciences), became obligatory for admission to the first year of medicine, and the teaching of chemical biology, physical biology, histology, parasitology and microbiology would be included and/or become more important in the course.[17]

The recognition granted to 'basic research' did not contribute, for all that, to preventing the experimentalists from being excluded, in that doctors who decided to dedicate themselves to research in the laboratory remained segregated from the hospital world. Nor did the reforms influence the self-perpetuation of the elite, and clinical medicine retained its dominant position. But establishing a body of lecturer-researchers sowed the seed of a conflicting situation, by causing two groups with divergent interests to co-exist within the faculties.[18] The distance which separated the hospital–academic from the basic research scientist was comprised of several factors. Socio-economically, it covered the differences which might exist between an important middle-class professional and a public servant, certainly 'superior', but poorly paid. Ideological factors were also involved, for on the basis of the disagreement between 'part-time' hospital–academics and 'full-time' basic researchers, opposing ideas would progressively arise between two very contradictory visions of what tomorrow's medicine would be: either remaining fundamentally based on the clinic, or becoming an applied branch of the life sciences.[19] At the time when the AFEC was being set up, this opposition was expressed, still in an embryonic form, by the difference in opinion which existed between the 'clinicians' and the 'researchers'. The contrasting pictures of the 'society man' and of the scientist with a monastic calling emphasise this.

An association representing the elite

At the start of its work, in 1908, the AFEC had sixty incumbent members. Two out of three were doctors, either surgeons in Paris hospitals, or departmental heads in post or retired.

In the period from 1908 to 1914, more than half of the chairs in the faculty of medicine in Paris would see their incumbents become members of the association. It particularly affected the most prestigious amongst them, the four chairs of general medicine and the four chairs of clinical surgery (see Table 3.1). If we add to that the participation of one of the two professors of obstetrics and the incumbents of the 'urological', 'gynaecological', 'ophthalmological' and 'dermatological-venereological' clinics, we may feel that it was practically only the Academy of Medicine which could claim a more comprehensive panel of the clinical elite. Curiously, it was amongst the 'theoretical' chairs that the most notable absences were found, since it was a question of studying cancer. In fact, neither Professor Prenant (histology) or Professor Weiss (medical physics) had joined the association. Most of the basic research scientists came from the Collège de France, the Pasteur Institute and the veterinary school of Maisons-Alfort. It is not surprising that being composed in this way, the AFEC seemed to be almost an annex of the Academy of Medicine (see Table 3.2).

A Parisian institution, the AFEC also had a network of provincial correspondents (fifteen in 1908), all or nearly all titular professors and half of them correspondents of the Academy.

Before the First World War broke out, which temporarily stopped its work, the association recruited forty new incumbents and fourteen correspondents. In 1908, the AFEC was largely dominated by clinicians, doctors or surgeons, but the arrival of new members was to alter this composition slightly. In particular, the ranks of the electroradiologists would be filled out with the support of several of the young 'radiation specialists' (see Table 3.3).

A wide generation range accompanied the diversity of the specialist groups represented in the AFEC. A gap of some fifty years separated the eldest (Lancereaux born in 1829, Guyon in 1831, Fournier and Guéniot in 1832) from the youngest (Mocquot, 1879, Ameuille and Masson, 1880).

By accepting the inherent arbitrariness of the constitution of the categories within that age range, we might conclude that the AFEC combined four large generation groups, defined by criteria pertinent to my topic. The first group was made up of members who joined the association at the end of their professional career, or even when they had already retired. The second included individuals between 50 and 60 years old who had already carried out, for several years, at the time when the AFEC was established, the responsibilities of head of department or titular professor. This generation would reach the end of its active life after the First World War, in the 1920s, that is at the time when the policy of the struggle against cancer was to begin. The third group was made up of those who, being between 40 and 50 years old in 1908, reached positions of power during the first years of operation of the AFEC. Several of them also succeeded their elders in the first group. The fourth group, under 40, were, between 1908 and 1914, in subordinate positions: young qualified *agrégés*, practical assistants in the faculty and organisers of courses at the Pasteur Institute. It is clear that the interest which these different generations had in studying cancer was not of the same order and that very marked differences appeared in their degree of active participation in the work of the society, as suggested in Table 3.4a. The tendency to publish papers, and to do so regularly (more than five times during the first six years of the association), directly reflected the generation of the members. This information can be confirmed by analysing the production of incumbent members in relation to the date of their joining the AFEC. Two-thirds of the initial members were content with a simply passive role, while 70 per cent of the new members (between 1910 and 1914) produced at least one written paper (see Table 3.4b). The AFEC, at the beginning, relied on a 'silent majority', for the most part made up of important senior consultants at the end of their career, as symbolised by the figure of Bouchard, its first president. A pupil of Charcot, a contemporary of Terrier, Le Dentu and Lannelongue, he was, along with them and a few others, one of those in post who would support the spread of Pasteur's ideas throughout the faculty of medicine.[20] Favourable to the relative reinforcement of the teaching of the fundamental sciences, it was he who finalised the reform of medical studies in 1894 by introducing the PCN. This professor of medical pathology (in 1879) stayed a generalist throughout his career, preoccupied above all with summarising the results of descriptive pathology: cancer only appeared much later amongst his preferred subjects (poisoning in diseases, diseases attributed to nutrition: diabetes, gout, obesity, gravel, etc.).[21]

It is interesting to note that the membership of Bouchard and his generation is significant of the new respect which the medical elite was beginning to have towards cancer. Without participating personally in developing the work on this pathology, they supported their successors' enterprise with all their academic power.

At the other extreme, 'young people' appeared more involved in learned work. A large number rallied to the AFEC from 1910, sometimes after having already submitted a paper, and it is clear that for them to make a name in cancer research was a good career move. Their presence in the association was very often related to that of their senior consultant who himself was from the generation in between.

Several teams were therefore involved in the AFEC. The most numerous gathered around Pierre Marie, professor of pathological anatomy and departmental head of the La Salpêtrière hospice, Gustave Roussy, his qualified *agrégé*, Pierre Ameuille and Jean Clunet, practical work assistants and some practical work supervisors and doctors in his department. Three heads of microbiology at the Institute Pasteur (Borrel, Weinberg and Le Dantec) had followed Roux, their director. Another more restricted team, whose productivity was, however, large, was that of the veterinary school, with Barrier, as director, and Gabriel Petit, who was to succeed him after the war as the head of the organisation. But the group which, without question, had the major role in the AFEC's life, both because of the number of its papers and because of its prominence in discussions, was that belonging to Necker's clinical surgery. The driving force behind this group was the chair holder, Pierre Delbet, whose personality made its mark on the directions and operation of the learned society.

Appointed to the internship in 1884, Delbet belonged to the first generation of surgeons trained from the outset in the modern techniques of asepsis which, in the course of their apprenticeship, were introduced into the area of cancer treatment. A contemporary of Henri Hartmann, his most direct competitor, he was not a pupil of Terrier. He found with Duplay, under whom he trained as clinic head, the tutelary power which was to support him in his career and direct his interest towards cancer. Qualified as a *agrégé* in 1882, a hospital surgeon in the following year, departmental head at Laënnec in 1905, Delbet became professor of clinical surgery in 1908 and took over the chair at the Necker Hospital. His involvement in the activities of the AFEC as secretary-general therefore coincided with the time when he reached the peak of the surgical hierarchy.

He was at that time 47 years old. The way in which he participated in the association's life revealed much greater intellectual ambitions than those of a simple virtuoso of the lancet. As a young student a combination of circumstances caused him to assiduously visit Dastre's general physiology laboratory at the Sorbonne. He was to maintain an interest in experimental medicine, even though, at a certain turning point in his career, he chose the 'royal path' of a clinical career. A noteworthy fact is that he was the first and, until the war, the only professor of general surgery to be interested in radium treatment and cancer radiotherapy.[22] Two of his assistants joined the AFEC: Herrenschmidt, one of his laboratory heads, and Charles Mocquot – both surgeons. Between 1908 and 1914, Necker's group presented 39 of the 178 papers published in the *Bulletin*, that is just over one in five, including 28 signed or co-signed by Delbet himself. But, even more perhaps, it was because of the latter's tendency to involve himself in the proceedings that the group directed the AFEC's work. Given the way that the learned societies operated, the 'comments' document, approving or critical, was a mark of authority as important as the range of the subjects discussed was varied. The distribution of debaters according to age groups (Table 3.4c) differed markedly from that of those who attended conferences (Table 3.4a). The occupation of a position of established power (Groups 2 and 3) clearly was a factor which led them to take a turn at speaking. The great majority of members who spoke about the presentation of a colleague were content to do so once, twice or three times. Only the recognised cancer 'specialists' became more involved.

Pierre Delbet's involvement cannot be compared with that of the other main protagonists. Chevassu, Borrel and Ledoux-Lebard spoke at four conferences each, Darier, whose dermatology department at Saint-Louis was in the forefront of skin cancer treatment, spoke at eight conferences, five less than Ménétrier, the departmental head of medicine at the Tenon hospital, who was without doubt the clinician who most focused his interests on cancer problems, and the theory which he had constructed around the idea of pre-cancerous conditions was one of the topical subjects of the time. Pierre Delbet himself spoke on 31 of the 56 conference subjects for debate, and gave advice on the most varied themes. Presentation of clinical cases, pathological anatomy papers, aetiopathogenic hypotheses, radium treatment, selenium, fulguration, surgical techniques, animal experimentation, research into a biological diagnosis of cancer; nothing, or almost nothing, escaped his notice. He dedicated himself to each meeting and imposed his authority on the society in a very personal way. 'He was fairly harsh in his manner,' his pupil Charles Mocquot was to say about him, 'his steely look, his disdainful lip, his slightly haughty attitude were disconcerting. . . .'[23] In fact, he sometimes spoke with a provocative force which contrasted sharply with the habitual stiff tone of the meetings. Author of the annual summary of work before the general meeting, he pronounced which purposes were legitimate and pinpointed the important amongst secondary considerations.

Ordinary learned production

Analysis of the work of the AFEC between 1908 and 1914 allows us to summarise the generally accepted facts on cancer in Paris on the eve of the

First World War, its favoured arguments and its major points of discussion. With the exception of publications relating to surgical treatment and work carried out in the provinces, which found a place in the regional reviews, the *Bulletin de l'AFEC* welcomed a large part of the cancer literature which, thirty years later, would be put forward as the major contribution of French medicine at that time and in that area.

It can be seen from Table 3.5 that clinical anatomical descriptive approaches dominated production. If we combine the research showing particular forms of cancer observed in the hospital (30 per cent of papers) and that regarding 'spontaneous' cancers in animals originating essentially from the veterinary school, they represent half the publications. The trend is to describe the rare forms, either according to their histological type, or according to their location. It is these rare forms which were the most often discussed. As a result, the two most common cancers (cervix, digestive cancers) were only mentioned in exceptional clinical cases. Only breast cancer was amongst the relatively widespread cancers to appear in a greater number of papers (eight in all). The interest which it seemed to arouse in several surgeons was also found in the works of G. Petit. The treatise on cancerous animals which he regularly put before the association devoted large sections to cancers of the udder in domestic carnivores (in particular the dog).

Two-thirds of the descriptive research in the human clinic was the work of surgeons alone or in association with a pathological anatomist from their laboratory. In addition, they represented the greater part of the work by the provincial correspondents. In the discussions which took place, the 'non-clinicians' only exceptionally became involved and, here too, the surgeons were the most in evidence. None of the clinical anatomical presentations of animal cancers, by which the vets made their presence known, involved the slightest discussion (Table 3.5).

The second major subject tackled, in terms of quantity, was that of treatments (a little more than one paper in five), the detailed analysis of which is supplied in Table 3.6a. Several evident facts need to be considered: there is little work concerning surgical treatment, and none dealing with radiotherapy. On the other hand, one technique is at the centre of the discussions – fulguration – which is dealt with in more than half the papers. In a society which counts amongst its members so many famous surgeons, the fact that the study of surgical techniques appears so little is paradoxical only in appearance. I have already mentioned above that the chief surgeons published articles at the time in specialised reviews about their disciplines. The only ones to tackle these questions at the AFEC meetings were the young *agrégés*, Chevassu, Renaud and a surgeon who was not a member, Vorwart. These five papers, of which three were on the subject of breast cancer and its subsequent recurrences, one on cancer of the cervix and one on cancer of the kidney, were also, and by far, the most discussed of all. Chevassu, in his account of the treatment of cancer of the kidney, managed to enlist the help of Delbet, Le Dentu, Lucas-Championnière, Picqué, Tuffier and Legueu in the discussion.

The major place afforded to fulguration was explained by the intensity of the debate which it caused amongst surgeons and electroradiologists. The electrotherapy method perfected by De Keating-Hart, forgotten today, was presented as a complement to surgery. It was a question, after removal of the tumour, of electrocuting the wound with a high frequency (several hundred thousand volts) spark. The purpose was twofold: to stimulate the repair of the wounded tissues and to activate a reactional process of fibrosis 'to replace the neoplasm by a connecting flow to the area where it was vegetating',[24] thus preventing a relapse. The surgeons were divided in their opinion. Lucas-Championnière and Pozzi appeared resolutely in favour, Jean-Louis Faure was 'clearly favourable' to this method of treatment, even if in the most desperate cases, 'fulguration aggravates the intervention to a certain extent'.[25] Tuffier was more circumspect: 'If fulguration is really a surgical progression, it is useful for possible removal of lesions which are without it inoperable, [but] until we have more information, it must be ignored in all cases of easily and commonly operable tumours.'[26] Pierre Delbet himself was fiercely against a procedure which found no favour in his eyes and had overwhelmed De Keating-Hart, after the latter had used this technique on several sufferers under his responsibility. 'Never', he was to remark during a session about a case of breast cancer operated on and fulgurated, 'do my patients die so quickly as after an operation.' De Keating-Hart defended his invention with obstinacy, supported by the electroradiologists Juge and Zimmern (with whom, however, disagreements arose regarding the indications of the technique), but its *pro domo* defendants found fewer and fewer supporters. After having enlivened the sessions in 1909 and part of 1910, the debate ended.

In comparison, radiation treatment hardly seemed to arouse enthusiasm. Radiotherapy, in spite of the presence among its supporters of Béclère, Ledoux-Lebard, Jean Belot and Guilleminot, who were all radiotherapists from the beginning, was not included in the presentations. Even if treatment by radium was mentioned more frequently, the subject, in 7 per cent of presentations, nevertheless appeared to be a minor one, and discussions remained confined to productive teams, such as Delbet's and that of Degrais, Wickham and Dominici's biological radium laboratory. A presentation about the radium therapy of a prostate cancer engendered a debate which went slightly beyond the area of the 'specialists', but it was essentially about the judgement one could make about the histological changes caused by the action of the radioactive product.[28]

The etiologic and pathogenic questions (third in importance, with 16 per cent of papers) expounded before the AFEC appeared relatively disparate. Besides three papers dealing with the hereditary hypothesis and a series of presentations on 'explanatory models' of pathogenic mechanisms, originating for the main part from non-member doctors, three problems were dealt with more insistently than others: Borrel's viral and parasitic hypothesis, the theory of the pre-cancerous state put forward by Ménétrier, and the role of physical and chemical agents in the genesis of cancers.

Starting with the impotence of the 'cellular theories' of cancer in order to explain the progressive extension of the tumour and the period of initial transformation, Borrel suggested a twofold hypothesis: these unexplained phenomena were the work of a cancerous virus and this virus was not directly transmissible from one individual to another (it cannot be inoculated). For contagion to take place, the pathogenic agent must undergo a transformation in the outside environment. Taking inspiration from the method of transmission (the discovery of which was recent) of malaria, filariosis and yellow fever, Borrel suggested the role of possible intermediary hosts inside which the virus would be transformed and would become pathogenic. He supported his argument by taking the example of spontaneous tumours in mice.

> It is remarkable to see that these tumours in the mouse occur in areas which are horribly badly maintained, dirty, full of vermin, fleas, various ticks and above all bugs; the bug seems to me to be an important factor, since parasites of this type are nearly always seen in cancerous cages and the bugs are themselves infested by mites and can transport these parasites from mouse to mouse.[29]

Epidemiology, by drawing attention to the macro- and microgeographical variations of cancer distribution, would not contradict this theory.

Pierre Ménétrier based his idea of a pre-cancerous state on convergent observations by putting forward as evidence the existence of a process of malignant transformation of benign tumours. From this he deduced that cancer was not, as had previously been thought, 'an original morbid form, but the outcome of previous preparatory pathological conditions'.[30] These conditions can be grouped together under two main headings: hyperplasias (the increase in size of the tissue of a cell line), and malformations in development, i.e. all cases where there is an 'abnormal' process of cell multiplication. In this way benign tumours, like 'irritations' of all types, could serve as a matrix for cancer. It was the experimental exploration of the relationship between irritation and cancer which originated various works investigating the role of physical and chemical agents. Pierre Marie and Jean Clunet reproduced the experiments of a German professor in Munich, B. Fischer, and injected 'Sarlach saturated olive oil' into a rabbit's ear and, with this procedure, obtained the production of a small tumour, which, however, did not become malignant.[31] Ménétrier, at the same time, published the first results where rats, subjected to weak repeated doses of radiation, showed epithelial 'manifestly hyperplastic and metaplastic' lesions. (Metaplasia is the transformation of a differentiated tissue into another differentiated tissue of normal quality but abnormal in its location.) In the doses used, the X-rays did not destroy the cells; on the contrary 'they excited their vitality and proliferation. . . . while the proliferated elements showed characteristics of a pre-cancerous state in their eyes'.[32] In the following year Clunet, with Marie and Raulot-Lapointe, succeeded in obtaining the first experimental sarcoma in a rat, following exposure to X-rays, the malignant tumour developing on an ulcerated radiodermatitis.[33] The work was important as it was the first experimental reproduction of the 'Roentgen cancer' which numbered hundreds of individuals amongst its victims, including several pioneers of radiology.

The way in which these different approaches to etiological questions were dealt with within the association throws light on the relationships between the various members. The observations, of a similar nature, of Petit and Bridé,[34] both veterinarians (one in Maisons-Alfort, the other in the provinces) and a memorandum by M. Mayet,[35] laboratory head at the Lyons faculty, which held an opposite point of view (since its author claimed to have succeeded in experimentally inoculating cancer in mice), matched the research by the Pasteur follower Borrel. The viral and parasitic theory did not provoke comments from the Parisian hospital–academics. They also remained silent before the work of Clunet and Marie, which only one article by a provincial basic research scientist echoed.[36] On the other hand, Delbet ('Observations on pre-cancerous states and their treatment'), Darier ('Pre-cancerous diseases of the skin'), Legueu ('Origin and transformation of vesical papillomas') each made a contribution to the debate on pre-cancerous states and together with Pozzi, Bouchard, Landouzy and Marie, discussed Ménétrier's cherished opinion at a meeting. It is clear that because Ménétrier's problem required clinical observations, it aroused more interest in hospital–academics than others. The result was that the various etiological debates were held in parallel by different groups, there being no interaction between them.

Other subjects examined were less important: some papers dealt with detection in the blood or in urine of specific biological signs of cancer, or with the perfection of screening by intradermal tests (the results were disappointing each time), some experimental studies dealt with attempts at cancer grafting, three were on epidemiological investigations and one article denounced the misdeeds of quackery. Only biological diagnosis gave rise to commentaries, but they were nearly always still limited to Pierre Delbet alone.

Analysis of the works published in the *Bulletin de l'AFEC* allows the broad outlines of the learned work regarding cancer to be determined and the main parts of interest and its omissions to be located. It is patently obvious, therefore, that epidemiological approaches occupied a secondary position – in all, two studies on the incidence of cancer in Morocco and an investigation from Jullierat, the head of the health services of the City of Paris, on 'cancer houses'.[37]

The 'underdevelopment' of the discipline – deprived, in France, of meaningful institutional support – has a part to play in this absence, but it does not explain everything. No voice was raised in the association to express regret at the lack of information on cancer morbidity and mortality, which seemed to indicate that clinicians, like basic research scientists, were hardly concerned about it – which was not the case in other countries. In 1900, the Komitee für Krebforschung, only just created, began investigations with the help of all German doctors to study the incidence of cancer. Each of the three regional committees of the association (Baden, Württemberg, Bavaria) carried out investigations having descriptive and etiological aims.[38] Projects of the same type were started in the United Kingdom by the Cancer Investigation Committee of the Middlesex Hospital[39] and by the Imperial Cancer Research Fund 'who, while still supporting the creation of laboratories also provided itself with a statistics department'.[40] The lack of interest shown by the AFEC members in 'medical statistics' was mirrored by that of some medical statisticians competent in the question of cancer, for only partial information on cancer mortality and its development existed. In 1906, Jacques Bertillon, the director of the Statistical Office of the City of Paris, published a major retrospective study analysing the development of the causes of mortality in the capital during the course of the second half of the nineteenth century.[41] Within this work, rich in information of all types – and which shows, for example, that cancer, the eighth cause of death in 1876, rose to fifth place in 1905 with 109 deaths per 100,000 inhabitants – the author is content to note, without dwelling on it, the fact that the number of deaths due to cancer, after having been stable until 1875, had subsequently increased, 'progressively and continuously'.[42] An ardent supporter of a rising birth rate, Bertillon was, above all, worried by decreasing fertility and the ageing population; so he reserved his comments for diseases accentuating this phenomenon. The publication of these cancer statistics 'lost in the crowd' passed unnoticed at the time; they would not be resurrected until several years later, when the theme of the 'danger from cancer' was topical.

If the epidemiological approach was unknown, experimental cancer medicine was hardly dealt with any better; on the eve of the war, cancer was above all a clinical subject. The profusion of descriptive studies and the numerous commentaries on it formed a sharp contrast to the scarcity of the contributions tackling aetiopathogenic mechanisms and the polite silence which welcomed them, even when put forward by a clinician of the Establishment. The only three to do this, Marie, Ménétrier and Delbet, did not get any more reaction from their hospital colleagues than Borrel with his acarids and his parasites, or Vidal, a provincial biologist, with his grafting attempts. Significantly, papers on 'pre-cancerous states' were discussed when they dealt with clinical examples, and not when they were about attempts at experimental creation of phenomena. And what is true for 'knowledge' is also true for therapeutic practices. With the exception, in this area also, of Delbet's ubiquitous presence, 'radiotherapists' and surgeons did not interact. It was necessary, as with fulguration and surgery, that two techniques should be united in a common practice so that an exchange between specialists could begin. Almost without exception, the similarity existing between the distribution of the different learned interests within the members of the AFEC and that of their hierarchical position meant that 'professors' debated amongst themselves or with their future alter egos, and 'ignored' the work of basic research scientists without any recognised clinical status. In this way, the hierarchy was respected, without that respect even needing to be consciously expressed.

It is also interesting to compare the ordinary output of the AFEC before the war with the significant facts or discoveries which were put forward several decades later by two qualified cancer surgeons and which they attributed to French doctors of this period. The first, Emile Forgue, regional correspondent of the AFEC since 1910, retraced, in the manner of a chanson de geste, 'Gesta Cancerologiae per Francos' the epic story of French medicine in its struggle against cancer in a long informal lecture in 1936. The second, René Huguenin, ten years later, wrote a chapter relating the major French contributions to the study of cancer in a collective book dedicated to the glory of French medicine. These two texts, not exempt from nationalist if not chauvinist ideas, both reflected the need to relate French work of this heroic period to an international context in the light of what, with hindsight, might be considered pertinent. Both make almost the same points.

Forgue said the following in 1936:

> The experimental study of cancer: this is the decisive progress which has just been made in the contemporary period . . . Hardly fifty years ago, cancer was still being studied as a *dead tissue*: all the work of the pathological anatomists . . . in the second part of the nineteenth century, was dedicated to the *morphological study* and classification of tumours. The secret which it is important to grasp, is not the *final lesion* . . . what we must observe, is the tumour in activity . . . the cancer in the *dynamic* state *from its start* and *during the growth* [emphasis in the original].[43]

France's contribution to the experimental study of cancer?

> Marie and Clunet [who], five years before the Japanese [Yamagiwa and Itchikawa were the first to obtain, in 1913, the production of a cancer by application of tar], had induced with chemical irritants the appearance, in a rabbit's ear, of metaplastic lesions. [Forgue forgets to mention that this was a reproduction of Fischer's experiments.] On the other hand, it was a Frenchman, Jean Clunet, who, from 1910, deserved recognition for his success in inducing a malignant tumour to appear by the action of X-rays.[44]

'Since then, this French discovery has been used for much research throughout the world',[45] added Huguenin. Another name mentioned was that of Borrel, forerunner to Forgue in the demonstration of the verminous aetiology of cancer, and also pioneering the unknown field for Huguenin concerning the role of the virus in carcinogenesis. (Of the two texts, the verminous aetiology theory was to misfire.) Ménétrier, on the other hand, forgotten by Forgue, was only quoted by Huguenin because of his theory which, 'after having caused general enthusiasm, dragged on bringing both good and bad luck'.[46]

Forgue does not grant any place to the clinical anatomy work of this period. Huguenin dedicates a few lines to it, only mentioning the isolation by Alezais and Peyron of the paraganglions of the renal seat (published in the *Bulletin de l'AFEC*).

Forgue's lyricism reached its peak when he called roentgen and radium therapy 'the highest point of this French work'. When referring to the work of Degrais, Wickham and Dominici, besides, of course, that of the Curies, he concluded: 'At all stages in radium therapy, as you will see, French names lead the way. *It is our country's duty to preserve these names,* as it has the right to *be proud of this work*' [emphasis in the original].[47] Huguenin himself rendered homage to the pioneer role of the three doctors of the Radium Biological Laboratory, and put them in the same league as Bergonié, Tribondeau and Regaud because of their discoveries in the area of radiotherapy.

These two retrospective views, completely determined by later development of knowledge and practices in cancerology, only contain a few vestiges of the work published in the *Bulletin de l'AFEC*, between 1908 and 1914, say very little about their authors, and the remaining publications appear to be quite eccentric in comparison to the dominant academic scientific output. If, as Forgue says in his own way, the direction of the 'progress of knowledge' regarding cancer has changed from anatomicoclinic to experimental medicine since the end of the nineteenth century, we must accept that this movement finds little place in learned institutions. The new infatuation of the hospital–academic elite for cancer pathology is expressed in literature which obeys the canons of clinical orthodoxy. Progress in clinical anatomy almost always dominates the discussions, and those who explore experimental cancerology must face the relative indifference of their colleagues. The therapeutic innovations which constitute roentgen and radium therapies have a similar fate. The way in which they are treated inside the AFEC faithfully reflects what was happening in the field.

Supplementary treatments

In 1914, fulguration was already largely unfashionable. Doctor De Keating-Hart's method met with a progressive fall from favour because it had not produced satisfactory results. It had, however, largely been tried out by surgeons. The situation of roentgen therapy and radium therapy was quite different. Even those who had been eager to experiment with 'electric sparks' were reluctant to welcome them into their departments. The surgeons were hardly explicit regarding the reason for their attitude. They did not issue particular criticisms, being content to say nothing. This silence was occasionally broken by a few lone voices pleading for their integration into the cancer treatment arsenal. The lack of interest, however, was real and was demonstrated by the facts. In Paris, radiotherapy was only practised in a few hospital departments: those of Béclère at Saint-Antoine, of Delbet at Necker, of Jean-Louis Faure at Cochin and in the dermatology departments at Saint-Louis; and one would have had great difficulty in finding a single surgery department which practised it in the provinces. Theoretical and practical teaching of these methods of treatment was only carried out in two places, in Saint-Louis, within the context of supplementary courses held by the chair of dermatology–syphiligraphy, and at Saint-Antoine, where Béclère held a series of conferences for training radiologists (8 conferences out of 53 concerned theoretical teaching of radio and radium therapy).[48]

In 1922, when asked to give a lecture on radiotherapy before the general meeting of the Franco-Anglo-American League against Cancer, Ledoux-Lebard described its state of development before the war in these terms: 'In everyday applications, it was confined to healing skin tumours, then, mainly to relieving innumerable incurable neoplasms against which it was the last conceivable resource, and to a few too-isolated post-operative preventative attempts at irradiation.'[49] His evidence was corroborated by others. Bergonié received his first patients in his electroradiology laboratory in the Bordeaux faculty, although he did not really want to. All were 'desperate', inoperable cases, and it was not without bitterness that he replied to the request from his surgical colleagues:

> Our hand is forced, so to speak, to carry out premature therapeutic applications. . . . Is there any electrical doctor today who has not experience being sent, with the usual, semi-mocking, semi-sincere, compliments, one of those cases of advanced cachexia, which the surgeons did not want or no longer wanted, on which the most powerful cancer serums have been tried, without counting all sorts of chlorates, arsenics and caustics? We can hardly refuse to try to perform a miracle . . .[50]

Radiotherapy appeared to be torn between two extremes. On the one hand, in dermatology, it was considered as a curative treatment in its own right. On the other hand, it was only regarded as a palliative method, only considered when everything else had failed. Between the two, at a time when cancers seemed to be potentially, or almost, curable by surgery, clinicians were unaware of it and remained deaf to the pleas of radiotherapists. 'We must,' wrote Jean Belot in his *Traité*, 'whenever possible, combine surgery and radiotherapy; to carry out, as Béclère said so appositely, a 'radiosurgical' treatment. These two methods should not conflict, as we have so often believed, but they should be of mutual help for the good of the patients.'[51]

It is easy to believe, as Belot's remark suggests, that surgeons remained distrustful regarding the use of such treatments on these occasions, in place of surgical removal. After all, the example of dermatology supports the suggestion that competition between techniques could prove to be very worthwhile. Belot hardly burdened himself with the bother of collaboration when he tackled the question of therapeutic indications for skin epitheliomas. He did not hesitate to review all the cases where X-rays proved to be 'unquestionably superior to the bloody procedure', in that the treatment caused no pain, suppressed the bad odour when there was any, and 'did not frighten the faint-hearted patient [who] did not need to fear the knife'.[52] But the argument for being wary would have been more relevant if, in other countries, particularly Germany, surgeons had not been motivated to develop radiant treatments. (Otto Franqué, a gynaecological surgeon, published in 1912 the first results of a cure of cancer of the womb by radiotherapy).[53] In their protests, radiotherapists did not forget to emphasise the open-mindedness beyond the Rhine, in a socio-political environment where to praise German virtues almost seemed to be a provocation:

> Originated largely due to French work, these productive methods were more recently extended, with extreme audacity, by German radiotherapists. . . . Their task has been made much easier firstly because of the passionate interest with which surgeons and gynaecologists from Germanic countries have undertaken their work in the pursuit of the elusive problem of a cure for cancer, and later by the wise attempt at constant collaboration with technicians and physicists.[54]

In the gynaecological clinic at the university of Munich, directed by Professor Doderlein, the treatment of cancers of the womb was jointly developed by surgeons and the radiology department. From 1913, the majority of carcinomas were no longer operated upon, but were exclusively treated by radium puncture. Correlatively, future gynaecologists studied radiotherapy during their training.[55]

The German example showed that surgeons could both be committed to a cancer treatment strategy, and make way for non-surgical methods without their position of power being questioned because of this.

Why did things not happen thus in France? Why was there such a contrast between gynaecology in Munich and gynaecology in Paris? At his clinic in the Broca hospital, Pozzi, who was still in charge (he was 67 in 1913), carried out only surgical treatment in cancers of the womb, sometimes supplemented, with the support of Zimmern, by fulguration. Was it because of his age? But Proust, his qualified instructor, did the same and ignored radium. Furthermore, the students were to know nothing about it.[56]

Radiotherapists cited the conservatism of French surgeons, but their point of view was too biased to be used in any argument, especially as, in their field, there appeared a certain tendency to innovate and to renew their techniques, and the example of fulguration indicates that they were not hostile in principle to every non-surgical method.

The position of French surgeons as regards radiotherapy and the place which radiation treatment more generally occupied becomes clear as soon as we look for the determining factors in the medical field before the war and in the social relationship which regulated its operation. So the description by Ledoux-Lebard of the actual conditions of radiotherapy must be related to the development of the process of specialisation and to the institutional and social division which separated 'clinicians' from 'fundamental researchers'.

Initially, medical applications of radiation were of direct interest to two categories of doctors. The first came from diverse backgrounds, but had in common the creation of a new speciality, the purpose of which was to bring together these applications. The second, clinicians specialised in skin diseases, only concentrated on the radiotherapy dimension itself. For dermatologists, the gamble which radiotherapy represented was hardly a mystery. Their recently recognised speciality was, as far as skin diseases were concerned, rich in nosographic classifications and poor in means of treatment. The discovery of a potential method of treatment opened up new horizons and dermatologists did not hesitate to frantically try out its effectiveness. In the particular case of skin cancers, the mastery of radiotherapy, even when only relative, allowed them to break free from the supervision of the surgeons to whom, until then, their patients had been restricted. In so far as they were able to argue satisfactory results by this single procedure, they were not very inclined to collaborate with their ex-partners. In dermatology, radiotherapy would only be used by clinicians for healing purposes.

For radiologists, radiotherapy did not meet the same type of challenge. Their ambition to found a specialist field was mainly based on the diagnostic contribution which physical applications might provide. They were principally involved in perfecting various techniques of investigation (radioscopy, radiography) and in the preparation of a radiological semiology linked to a clinical semiology. They regarded radiotherapy as a supplementary application, of a different order, which they approached differently because of the heterogeneity of their group. Those who were, like Antoine Béclère, hospital doctors and departmental heads, could treat patients by rays and train young clinicians in these methods. But they were in the minority. In the provinces particularly, the pioneers of the discipline were all medical physicists. 'Pure' academics, they divided themselves between teaching at the Faculty and the laboratory which was often, but not always, situated at the hospital. They had access to patients only through the intermediary of hospital staff who referred patients to them for specific purposes. The relationship which a person like Bergonié had with radio-therapy illustrates this fact. He was more inclined to attempt to base the practice on radiotherapy than to empirically test its action on patients, and did not agree to it unless compelled to by the request.

During the period with which we are concerned, radiology initiated developments in a few areas of education, of which the most important was organised under the aegis of the *Assistance Publique*. The status of radiolo-gists within the hospitals tended to unify the group as regards their being outside the clinical services. The linking of radiology laboratory/medical department which existed in Saint-Antoine was a phenomenon connected to Antoine Béclère's singular, i.e. unique of its type, trajectory. Everywhere radiology was institutionalised as an annexed hospital structure. Its function was to meet the specialised technical needs of the departments. Its laboratories were part of an arrangement for the social division of work. Its purpose was medical care for patients, entirely supervised by those who legally had the responsibility for the treatment. It was only in extreme cases, where the patient's condition was no longer within the clinician's capabilities, that a patient would be referred, experimentally, to a radiologist, for a 'last chance' radiotherapy.

The use of radiotherapy for palliative purposes was inseparably related to the position of subordination of the non-clinician in a hospital universe where the status of the clinical practice dominated. Imbued with the feeling of belonging to an elite, the surgeons' relationship with the radiologists was so distant that they hardly had any contact with each other during their training, as each mixed in very different groups. It was this social distance which, without it being necessary to mention any notion of old-fashioned opinions, was an obstacle to 'radiosurgical treatment'. On the eve of the First World War, the social conditions for practical collaboration between clinicians and non-clinicians regarding the case of patients potentially curable by surgery were not realised; the combination of lancet and X-rays or radium remained exceptional.

A few doctors engaged in basic research joined these first contingents of radiotherapists, dermatologists and radiologists. Few in number, but rich in remarkable personalities like Tribondeau, Dominici, Regaud and Lacassagne, this group retrospectively appears of prime importance in the history of radiation therapies. A common approach linked them: they all encountered radiotherapy when they were devoting themselves to updating their original discipline (pathological anatomy or histology) through the intro-duction of the 'experimental method'. Major contributions to the study of the biological effects of radiation, which would contribute to founding new treatments on rational bases, originated from these meetings.

Dominici, because he died young, and Tribondeau, because the Navy took him away from his research to re-appoint him to the post of overseas health officer, would not have the chance to pursue in the long term their scientific activities in this field.[57] On the other hand, Regaud, and later, Lacassagne, who was to succeed him, were to make their impression on developments in French cancerology. The path which led Regaud, a typical experimental doctor, to become involved in radiotherapy and then to leave the Faculty of Medicine in Lyons to manage the biological section of the Institute of Radium, deserves a short biographical sketch. My objective here is to evaluate those elements which are capable of clarifying the nature of the challenges which occupied him throughout his career.[58]

The faculty of law at the Institute of Radium: the complex career of an experimental doctor

Born on 30 January 1870 in Lyons, Claudius Regaud experienced the ordinary destiny of a child of the urban middle class, which was both little inclined to be encumbered permanently with the presence of its offspring and anxious to ensure him a perfect education. Entrusted to an 'excellent' nurse 'from the mountains and brimming with health', he spent his first few years in Bauges. On returning to Lyons, after spending a short interval in the family home, he continued his primary studies as a boarder at a secondary school. In 1882 his parents entrusted him to the Institution des Chartreux on the plateau of the Croix-Rousse, the epitome of good education for polite society, so that he could take his final examinations there. His father, Félix Regaud, an official receiver, directed him towards law, with the intention that he would eventually succeed one of his unmarried uncles as the head of a well-known office of solicitors in Lyons. An obedient son, Claudius resolved to enrol in first year law, but at the same time decided to attend lectures at the faculty of science. He then performed a perfect parapraxis, failed his legal studies and passed his science examinations. Encouraged by his results, he imposed on his father his wishes to enter the Faculty of Medicine. All went smoothly and he was only 21 years old when he passed the competitive exam to be an *interne* in 1891. His first choice was Joseph Renaut's medical department. His future chief, anatomy and histology laboratory professor at the faculty of medicine, advised him to then attend microbiology lectures at the Pasteur Institute before taking up his post. He was a brilliant student and during this short stay in Paris he was noticed by Emile Roux. He had, that year, the outstanding honour of being appointed as pupils' representative for the ritual visit of homage to the aged Pasteur. On his return to Lyons, the young intern divided himself between clinical activities, laboratory work, where he was taught the techniques of histology, and mountaineering in which, as an experienced climber, he excelled. At the end of his internship, Regaud abandoned his hospital work preferring to complete his scientific training. He studied for a certificate of higher studies in physiology and took lessons in German so that he could familiarise himself with the biological literature from across the Rhine. In 1897 he obtained his doctorate, made his last climb (an unfortunate attempt to climb to the top of the Elbruz in the Caucasus), and became engaged to Marie Crozet, the sister of a colleague from 'Chartreux'; in short it was a decisive year which marked his passage from studying to working. Regaud became an assistant in Renaut's laboratory and took the path of what seemed to him to be a future which was already mapped out: the career of a professor. Several works regarding colouring of the nerve cells by methylene blue (1895) and on the origins of the lymphatic vessels in the breast (which gained the Portal prize of the Academy of Medicine in 1896) assured a beginning to his fame. It was not long before this was confirmed after a series of studies on the cytology of the testicle.[59] Asked by Renaut to produce, on this subject, a chapter for a treatise of practical histology, Regaud found himself confronted with a thorny problem, i.e. to make clear and coherent a wealth of complex information in a field still in full development. He took to the task with relish and began to summarise the existing work, which he assembled in a subsequent document (340 pages of *Archives d'Anatomie microscopique*, illustrated with numerous drawings and plates). This enterprise was his opportunity to discover new horizons, that of the relationship between the structural histology (of the seminiferous tubes) and the physiological processes (of spermatogenesis). This was the report on which Tribondeau and Bergonié based their first experiments.

In 1901, Regaud entered the *agrégation* examination in anatomical and physiological sciences. Supported by Renaut and encouraged by his advice, the jury appointed him to the vacant post in Lyons. As an *agrégé*, he had to train the students, give a large part of the lectures and, in addition, take responsibility for the organisation and operation of the laboratory. In the free time which these heavy duties of teaching and administration left him, he developed his own research in a direction which led him away from the work his chief had been doing, and for which he had been trained.

For Renaut, histology was a descriptive science, a microscopic pathological anatomy which allowed progress in clinical anatomy to be defined. Regaud himself turned resolutely towards a physiological histology, inspired by the experimental approach itself 'to enrich the study of forms and structures and throw light on the problems of life by observing changes provoked intentionally under exactly defined conditions'.[60] 'It is likely,' he wrote to Roux in 1909, 'that histology is going to become more and more important, as it seems to be the essential basis of biology. Until now, the science of cells and tissues has been particularly morphological and descriptive but it is becoming physiological, chemical and experimental.'[61]

The divergence of ideas between the master and the pupil did not originate solely from the classical 'quarrel between the ancient and modern', it also included more fundamental differences of attitude and direction.

Renaut's histology was rooted in a hospital clinician's practice and supplemented it. Regaud's science of the cells and tissues rejected it to search for replies to his questions concerning the laboratory animal. Here too, the undertaking was suited to the choice of career. The requirements of experimentation combined with the constraints of teaching were incompatible with hospital work.

It was as a convinced histophysiologist that Regaud received the first notes published by Tribondeau and Bergonié at the end of 1904. The reaction provoked by the reading of this work so in accordance with his new creed, and which took advantage of his own analysis of the cytology of the testicle, was immediate. 'Regaud realises,' wrote Lacassagne, 'what an incomparable experimental instrument radiation represents in the research which he is carrying out, and he is resolved to tackle this new field.'[62] Nogier, a radiologist friend, taught him the rudiments of the technique and allowed him to use the X-ray equipment in the hospital laboratory where he was working.

Then research began on the differentiated radiosensitivity of the seminal cells, in part parallel with that of the Bordeaux doctors. He then researched the ovary and other organs not involved with reproduction phenomena, the thymus, the mucous membranes of the gastrointestinal tract and the skin. With these, the emphasis of Regaud's work shifted from the histophysiological subject itself to the study of that 'incomparable instrument'.[63] It was very logical, since it was also necessary to understand its working more precisely in order to master it properly. In parallel, Regaud and Nogier were determined to perfect the equipment and improve irradiation techniques. In 1906, they succeeded in carrying out a homogenous irradiation of the testicle of the rat (which Bergonié and Tribondeau had not been able to achieve); later, they obtained the same result on the much bulkier testicle of a ram. In the meantime, since funds had been obtained for the purchase of X-ray equipment, irradiations were being carried out in the histology laboratory, and the study of their biological action became a subject of research for the young researchers who frequented it.

> With this instrumentation which was used to irradiate dogs, cats, rabbits and rats, Regaud began in 1911 to apply to his patients the principles of radiotherapy which resulted from his experimental observations . . . He asked surgeon friends to send to his laboratory patients suffering from inoperable cancers and, consequently, inevitably destined to die from the progress of their disease. These were mainly extensive epitheliomas of the face, carcinomas of the breast and sarcomas. The technique considered suitable was applied, always with the same patience and meticulousness. Regaud, in a corner of the laboratory, himself applied and removed the dressings before and after the irradiation sessions. He kept up to date all the details of the changes which he was making in each case, noting all the modifications

of the tumours in the course of treatment. Often he went through periods of hope . . . But it was only a transitory improvement and the cancer was soon showing evidence of relapse. Manifestly, the root cells of the cancerous tissues were, for the most part, less radiosensitive than those of the testicle. . . . Although unable to cure, at least Regaud could make interesting observations. It was in this way that he noticed an important fact . . . : the decrease of radiosensitivity of malignant tumours treated by successive and too infrequent doses of X-rays. Therefore, certain ways of administering the radiation could be harmful. In this case, not only is the cancerous tissue destroyed, but in a way it becomes autoimmune to the rays.[64]

The progression to therapy is the outcome of a coherent scientific development from the moment when the instrument for the histophysio-logical research became, via questions concerning the biological activity of radiation, a subject for study in itself. But the therapy used was, in its conception, very different from dermatological practice. Its referents were clearly situated alongside the experimental medicine of Claude Bernard. The treatment of the patients was undertaken as an extension of the study of X-rays on normal tissues, the pathology testing the facts which had been established experimentally. 'It was not the same problem in the case of a malignant tumour as in the case of the testicle, it was, in both, a question of obtaining the selective sterilisation of the root elements, considered as more particularly radiosensitive.'[65] In addition, experiments on the patient raised new questions and allowed improvement in the knowledge of the multiple biological properties of rays (such as radio-immunisation). Finally, it was morally acceptable because the patients were 'cancerous incurables'. There was therefore no bitterness on Regaud's part in seeing himself entrusted with hopeless cases; on the contrary, this time the demand for treatment came from the researcher and not from the surgeon.

These early clinical tests very shortly preceded Regaud's departure for Paris, since it was in 1913 that he took on the post of director of the biological section of the new Institute of Radium, an event which Lacassagne interpreted as a chance occurrence 'which changed Regaud's life and allowed him to envisage the realisation of his dream of scientific treatment of cancer'.[66] Nothing, in fact, allows us to foresee that at the time Regaud thought of his new work in this way. The proposition to which he was responding was the result of a process which owed little to chance. The *agrégé* at the faculty of medicine had wanted, for several years, to leave the university in order to dedicate himself fully to his research, and his appointment to the Radium Institute satisfied an ambition to join the Pasteur Institute, to which he had been committed since 1909, with the support of Roux. Regaud was stifled in his job in Lyons. He was suffering from the inflexibility of the university organisation to the requirements of research activity. To the derisory funds, to the disproportionate teaching tasks there was added a miserable salary which reflected a profound injustice: 'You in fact know' he wrote to Roux when asking him to get him out of trouble, 'that there is an inequality of treatment in our faculties which is causing the most severe, as it is the least apparent, injustice: the same fees are paid to the practitioner who in addition dedicates a small part of his time to teaching and to the man of science who does not leave his laboratory.'[67]

Having heard about the Osiris inheritance, Regaud pleaded with Roux to create a normal and experimental histology laboratory, which he would organise. In his reply, the director of the Pasteur Institute told him that he approved of the idea, but that the project was still premature. A few months later, negotiations began between the University of Paris and the Pasteur Institute. Both parties were favourable to the installation of a Radium Institute covering two sections, a laboratory for Marie Curie and a laboratory for the study of the biological effects of radiation and their applications to medicine. Roux, who could put forward as an argument the work on X-rays already undertaken by Regaud, seized this opportunity to obtain his entrance to the Pasteur Institute. The *agrégé* from Lyons would be, at one and the same time, both the director of the biological section and the professor of histology at Pasteur. Thanks to this combination he would receive two salaries and could therefore properly support both his needs and his family. In his opinion, this departure for Paris would finally allow him to realise his ambitions. He would be in a position to continue his experiments on radiation and, if necessary, to use its applications, and take up once more histophysiological research, which, because of the lack of funds, he had been forced to abandon temporarily.[68]

When, Regaud took up his new job, followed by the young Lacassagne who he had asked to join him, he felt that he had taken an important step at the institutional level, by correcting a path which did not suit his ambitions as a man of science. But he saw his future career as an extension of his previous activities. The true 'turning point', which would lead him to total commitment to the 'scientific treatment of cancer', was to come later. This was to be at the end of the First World War when, after having been demobilised, he returned to his post at the Radium Institute and decided to radically change the direction of his laboratory and turn it into a 'cancer centre'.

> I am, regretfully, abandoning my microscopic anatomy and histo-physiology research as I must dedicate the greatest part of my work to the study of X-rays and radium rays on tissues, to medical application of these rays and finally to the organisation and development of a centre for radiation treatment of malignant tumours.[69]

The man who in this way gave up following the path of fundamental research was a man transformed by his war experiences, who found a greatly changing medical field. The cataclysm had shaken a certain order of things, overturned the visions of the world and caused new problems to emerge . . . amongst these a 'social scourge' which was gaining in strength. Still minor in comparison to tuberculosis and syphilis, but promised a great future, the danger from cancer had surfaced.

4 War and the birth of the Anti-Cancer League

On 14 March 1918, Robert Le Bret's reception rooms at number 6 Avenue Marceau had trouble in accommodating the crowd of guests. The master of the house, a descendant of an old family of *intendants* [administrators] of the kingdom,[1] a lawyer by training but living on his private income, and his wife, Alice Le Bret, née Chauchat, daughter of a member of the Council of State, were regular guests at society receptions. But this time the reception was out of the ordinary. The hundred guests who were crowded in had come to sign the birth certificate of a new association. A single aim was the cause of their enthusiasm, until then a too neglected social peril against which they had decided to fight: cancer. The assembly contained a number of prominent personalities, known for their charitable opinions and their commitment. Baron Henri de Rothschild, already involved in the Association for the Study of Cancer, was present, as well as Baron Edouard and two other Governors of the Bank of France, Félix Vernes and François de Wendel and several merchants and businessmen. They rubbed shoulders with several of the faculty masters, the dean, Roger Hartmann, Achard, Jean-Louis Faure, Maurice Letulle, Ménétrier and Mesureur, the ex-director-general of the *Assistance Publique*, who could not be excluded from this type of initiative. Roux was also there, with Claudius Regaud who, some years earlier, could not have been imagined in this company. As far as ladies were concerned, there were many who, like the old Duchess of Uzès, took a personal part in the organisation of the care of the wounded.

The British Ambassador, his American counterpart and several nationals from both their countries gave their support to the initiative. In any case, the Anti-Cancer League, which was intended to be Franco-Anglo-American, was christened under the auspices of the alliance sealed on the battlefield.

At first sight, it may seem surprising that a project to establish an association against cancer, which had been dreamt about before the war several times but had never been achieved, in spite of the efforts of Ledoux-Lebard amongst others,[2] was finally attained now that the intensification of military activities was at its height with the resistance to Ludendorff's armies' offensive. The presence of the man who, because he had accepted the management of the League, was the central character that evening, led one to ask what this event owed to the change of context caused by the tragic events of the world conflict. In fact, this person was none other than Justin Godart, the ex-Secretary of State for Health of the armies, just leaving the post in which he had distinguished himself for several years. The relationship between the war and the crystallisation of social concerns for cancer was complex. The basic movements influencing the new attitude of the state regarding scourges and the transformations of medicine combined with events, which although fortuitous, nevertheless played a decisive role, at the time.

The state looks again at social diseases

With 1,300,000 deaths, 1,100,000 wounded, of which nearly 400,000 were disabled, the French army was the one which, among all the belligerent countries, had most suffered the murderous madness of the conflict. With 10.5 deaths for every 100 active soldiers, its losses were greater than those of the defeated Germany (9.8 per cent) and much greater than those of the United Kingdom (5.1 per cent).[3] The question of the permanent renewal of combatant strength was, during those years, crucial. But it came up against such difficulties that the authorities were forced to take another look at the population's state of health. It was known that tuberculosis was a 'social scourge', but the absence of reliable statistics on morbidity and the taboo surrounding its declaration did not allow a quantified vision. The extent of its influence was then discovered, which shed some light on this partial figure: 110,000 discharged soldiers who were within the age range which could be recruited.[4] In addition, it was impossible not to take account of the disaster to which the state policy of non-intervention had led. Since the law of '16 *vendémiaire* year V' (7 October 1796), the administrative and financial administration of public health establishments had been entrusted to councils who decided when they should be set up. Delegation of power concerning health equipment to local communities who were unequal in their response to demand had brought about a situation of almost total shortage. If France was saturated with anti-tuberculosis charitable works of all kinds, it had in 1914 one hundred times fewer clinics than Germany.[5] Its health stations, at the beginning of 1916, had a total capacity of fewer than 2,000 beds.[6] The 'medicine men' of the Rockefeller Institute who supported Alexis Carrel's action were bemused and fiercely critical of the state of health of 'Pasteur's country'.[7]

This brutal confrontation with reality forced a radical change of perspective to come about. The recriminations of the hygienists against the inertia of the authorities were finally recognised. On 5 April 1916, Léon Bourgeois had a law passed which engaged the state in taking responsibility for the installation of a network of preventoriums and sanatoriums. The beginning was slow; at the end of hostilities, the military hospitals and health stations could not accommodate more than a tenth of the discharged soldiers – themselves privileged compared with the women and children. But the impetus was there. In addition, the Bourgeois project would benefit from American aid directly aimed at supporting the French war effort. The Rockefeller mission contributed financial support and particularly methods of organisation, involving itself in training in its techniques men and women capable of operating in the field.

Venereal disease, another scourge, had not, until then, given rise to any health action, apart from what was local and specific. God knows, however, that fear of syphilis haunted the Belle Époque, crystallising around its name the anguish at the degeneration of the race.[8] Faced with this great reaper who was seen at work everywhere, standardising and horrifying speeches took the place of policy. Now, with the armies in the field, the phenomenon took on proportions unknown until then. The figures established from the military population speak for themselves. The rate of primary syphilis in the army grew sixteen times between 1915 and 1919; at the end of the conflict, 2 per cent of soldiers were infected, that is nearly 50,000 men. In addition there were 130,000 cases of gonorrhoea and 60,000 cases of simple chancres.[9] This information did not even include civilians, for whom no exhaustive census was possible. If, in the population of registered prostitutes, the percentage of recent syphilis was low, it was not the same with the unregistered ones who tended to grow in number. Appeals to virtue, 'Chastity only makes fools laugh. Keep yourselves unsullied and healthy to start a family and to increase its number on your return' were only relatively effective.[10] After a period of non-intervention, the civil and military authorities collaborated to organise the suppression of 'clandestine' prostitutes, health monitoring in brothels and systematic examination of soldiers on leave. A little before the war started, the *Assistance Publique* had created several clinics and this time the Army Health Service and the Department of Assistance and Public Health decided to increase the number of these establishments. In 1916, the *Institut prophylatique* was set up in Paris. It consisted of a central clinic in contact with local offices in the capital and the suburbs. In the same year, in the provinces, in Bourges, the first example of a new category of clinics called 'ancillary departments' was set up (the name was sufficiently neutral so as not to stigmatise those who went there for examination). They gave daily free consultations and were equipped with several beds to accommodate patients who were 'a danger to their family'.[11] As with tuberculosis, the idea was to considerably reorganise preventative action with encouragement and supervision by the state. Eighteen dermatology centres were to be opened in this way between 1916 and 1918.[12]

It was in this context of attention being given to the health of combatants that the fate of soldiers suffering from cancer would be taken into account. The need to mobilise several million men '*has transformed the age range of the army*. The latter is not merely made up as in peacetime of young men remote from the period of life when cancer is rife, *it includes older people*, some nearer fifty, who are thus *near the age when the frequency of cancer is high.*'[13] The incidence of cancer lost its rarity to the point where it was a problem to the military medical authorities. Its extent was impossible to evaluate, due to lack of information from the military authorities. The only figures available come from files which gave rise to requests for compensation from widows imputing the death of their husband to his military service. Of 17,220 files on widows, 479 concerned the death of husbands suffering from cancer.[14] This number only gives a very vague idea of the reality as it does not take into account either patients in the course of treatment, or deceased cancer sufferers who were discharged because of their illness, as 'it is rare for expert doctors to put them forward for compensation because of the absence of original documents'.[15]

Whatever the case, the phenomenon led the Secretary of State for Health to take steps. At the end of 1917, three 'specialised services for army cancer patients' annexed to the general surgery departments of civilian hospitals were to be created in Paris (Professor Hartmann's department at the General hospital), in Lyons (Professor Bérard's department) and in Montpellier (Professor Forgue's department). Although far from having the social influence of the measures undertaken to combat tuberculosis and syphilis, the inauguration of these three departments marks a turning point for several reasons. For the first time, the authorities intervened on behalf of cancer, which meant that the particular conditions caused by the war situation had changed the social visibility of the disease. The fact that it affected the whole army, i.e. a non-medical institution containing a large part of the population, mostly male and 'active', contributed to the outline of a collective pathology. The effect of this incidental view also led the Secretary of State to wonder about a possible increase in cancer morbidity due to the war. He asked the Association for the Study of Cancer, which resumed its meetings in 1918, to give its opinion on the possible relationship between traumas and cancer and clarify to the authorities the liability of the state regarding soldiers suffering from cancer. The association's office entrusted the study to nine of its members. Their reports, presented on 22 July 1918,[16] emphasised the great complexity of the problem, the extreme difficulty in establishing with any certainty a connection between cause and effect and concluded that, under these conditions, the soldiers should be given the benefit of the doubt.

For the first time, too, special organisations for the treatment of cancer patients appeared. Certainly, they could not deal with anyone except soldiers, but a precedent had been set when, peace having returned, the methods of organising the 'fight against cancer' would be in dispute. But the importance of the Secretary of State's initiative was not confined to this alone. It comprised the treatment of cancer as a clinical subject coming under *ad hoc* structures, because it recognised that it had specific needs which were not catered for by the 'ordinary' services, that is the need to combine surgical healing with treatment by radiation. Collaboration between surgeons and radiotherapists was established in each of the three departments created. The changed status of radiotherapy, which was visible also in the deliberations of the Association for the Study of Cancer as early as 1918, became part of a more global process of transformation of the medical field.

The war imposed a different way of practising medicine and involved reorganisations of the health system. It blurred the divisions between groups, modified relationships between the protagonists, created new loyalties and overturned 'civil' hierarchies to establish others. It also gave a new generation of young university and hospital doctors the opportunity of exercising responsibilities which would not have been the same in peacetime.

Medicine in wartime

The belligerent countries all thought that the duration of hostilities would be short and they were not prepared for its long-term continuation. 'Trench warfare' took the Army Health Service attached to Headquarters by surprise. It was incapable of facing the problems created by this new form of combat. Certainly, to the surprise of the doctors themselves, the measures taken against the epidemics which had drained the armies in the nineteenth century proved effective. The mass vaccination against smallpox, taken as a measure of urgency at the start of hostilities, was a success. The action of the Permanent Epidemic Prevention Commission, supported by the people of the Pasteur Institute, allowed a typhoid epidemic to be checked at the start.[17] On the other hand, army medicine was completely overwhelmed by the extent of the fighting, the number of wounded and the problems caused by their evacuation and treatment.[18] The government decided in 1915 to entrust the reform of the Health Service to an authority coming directly under political power and created an Under-Secretary of State, the management of which was entrusted to a deputy of the radical party, Justin Godart. A professor of political economy and a barrister at the bar of Lyons, Godart started in politics at the beginning of the century. In 1904, he was assistant to the mayor of Lyons, Dr Augagneur, alongside Edouard Herriot, and specialised in public health and labour regulation problems. Elected to a deputy seat in 1906, he occupied the duties of vice-chairman of the Labour Commission in the Chamber and had just founded the 'Social Democracy' group ('to prepare the reforms which are due to the people who have saved the country'), when he was appointed to be the Under-Secretary of State for Health.[19] A convinced hygienist, but with little understanding of genuine medical problems, J. Godart surrounded himself with a group of experts. At the risk of upsetting the feelings of the Headquarters doctors, he chose them from amongst the doctors of the supplementary staff. Thanks to parochial solidarity, all of them were to be, as he was, from Lyons. It was in this way that Claudius Regaud, who had just been appointed to the Radium Institute, was called up and sent to Gérardmer as head doctor of the evacuation hospital, and suddenly found himself promoted to a post of political responsibility. Godart, writes one of his biographers,[20] thought of him when he recalled a discussion which had taken place the previous year, when the deputy, mobilised as a simple stretcher bearer, found himself at Gérardmer. The two men from Lyons had, during their conversation, discussed the question of the evacuation of the wounded. The slowness of their transfer to medical units had had dramatic consequences. When it was not directly responsible for deaths, it had too often entailed amputations which an earlier intervention would have avoided. Godart would have been influenced by the ideas of his deputy regarding solutions to bring an end to existing negligence.

In the vast programme which the Secretary of State set himself, Regaud was entrusted with the publication of documents regulating the operation and organisation of surgical teams working with the armies, the setting up of a 'Medical–Surgical Research Centre' ensuring a triple activity, clinical, scientific and educational, and the preparation of related surgical conferences.[21] These tasks were included in a global perspective which had two aims: to restructure military medicine and render practicable its collaboration with the civil medical and scientific institutions and the various Red Cross associations.

The first reform undertaken upset military tradition. It consisted of promoting to a grade corresponding to their institutional 'civil' position the doctors and surgeons mobilised as reservists. Because of this, *agrégés,* professors of faculties or hospital doctors who had neglected to undergo periods of instruction in peacetime which led to officer rank, and who had been enlisted as simple nurses, became commanders overnight and saw themselves allocated to the management of military hospitals.[22] Since he wanted surgical activities to be supervised by recognised authorities in the profession, the Under-Secretary of State obtained the creation, in 1917, of consultant posts in each of the ten armies, instituting in this way a hierarchy above that of the military doctors, who were chosen from the body of the reservists.

At the same time as care centres for tuberculosis, venereal disease and cancer sufferers were being set up, efforts were being made to increase speciality services (orthopaedics, maxillo-facial surgery, stomatology, ophthalmology), bacteriology laboratories and legal medical centres (among other things responsible for research on the effects off asphyxiating gases) with the help and support of the Academy of Medicine, the Society of Surgery and the Pasteur Institute.[23] The stalemate reached in the conflict was not only to reveal the inadaptability of military medicine. It would bring to light the need to co-ordinate the three Red Cross societies (The Society for Aid to Wounded Soldiers, The Union of Frenchwomen and the Association of French Ladies), all anxiously competing with each other. The huge influx of wounded and suffering forced the installation *ex nihilo* of auxiliary hospitals, particularly since the occupation of territory by the German army had caused the loss of 64,000 beds. Several hundreds of thousands of new beds were provided, for which it was necessary to ensure nursing training.[24] In the patriotic enthusiasm which accompanied the start of hostilities, civilian goodwill was not lacking. It was still necessary to provide this 'army of good women' with the necessary rudimentary training.

Justin Godart's team also started to carry out basic reforms here. It organised a Red Cross military office supervising the three societies, created a corps of temporary nurses, reorganised the status of Red Cross nurses and supported the start of an 'Edith Cavell' school, directed by a female doctor, Dr Girard-Mangin.[25] Once carried out, the organisational work was to exceed the aims targeted. The adjustment of the Health Service to military 'needs' also determined the social conditions necessary for receptiveness to the medical innovations which took place during this period. The progress of medical knowledge, and particularly know-how, are largely attributable to wars. And the 1914–18 war was to have a much greater importance than the conflicts of the previous century. The whole field of bone, nerves and gut surgery was perfected because of it, not forgetting bacteriology and serotherapy. 'Shock' medicine was being invented, psychiatry was enriched by the 'discovery' of war psychoneuroses, radiology was being perfected and developed.[26] Because of the extent and duration of the conflict, civilian doctors were also much more directly involved than during the Franco-Prussian War. The commitment of the medical elite did not just cause the involvement of the various specialities in the particular pathologies engendered by the conflicts. All the chair holders, department heads, laboratory managers, their *agrégés* and their assistants, now outside their normal working environment, were confronted by another universe which upset their habits. Faced with new problems they had, in order to respond effectively, to find another way of living and working, and forge new relationships with each other. Confronted with the war-wounded, with their forever dirty dressings and shrapnel lodged in their bodies, medical practice had to be based on a new active collaboration between the various specialised abilities. 'Individualism' was not appropriate, treatment meant teamwork in emergencies which caused surgeons, bacteriologists and radiologists to pool their knowledge. The physical and social distance which separated the clinical service from the laboratory inside the hospital was reduced to a minimum in the field, and minds adjusted themselves to practical needs. The Bouleuse camp school is an illustration of this, since even the idea of it would have been unthinkable a few years earlier. This school was created to deal with the 'permanent training' needs of practitioners and medical students who had been mobilised, once more, on the initiative of the Secretary of State; and its management fell to Claudius Regaud.

The dreadful crowd of wounded had supplied a varied and practical medical teaching aid. It was important that the whole of the health corps in the armies should become more familiar with the new knowledge on the treatment of war wounds and fractures and the radiolocation of projectiles and gas poisoning – among other acquisitions. For this reason, a proper faculty of medicine at the front was set up at Bouleuse, in Champagne. Treatment services received the wounded . . . Laboratories for the main disciplines were attached to it. In turn, army ambulances and health groups came to Bouleuse for training, in order to receive theoretical and practical education on the most recent discoveries in emergency surgery and prevention of diseases.[27]

Evacuated and destroyed in May 1918 because of the advance of the German armies, the Bouleuse camp had become, in its short existence, a 'pilot' centre for the teaching of medicine. It had approached the reforming ideal advocated, before the war, by certain divisions of the university body. The close links, on one site, between teaching and research and clinical activities were comparable to the 'faculty of the future' of which Bergonié was dreaming in 1908,[28] when he rebelled against the administrative and spatial division which separated the laboratories from the health units. The Bouleuse experiment was the most complete institutional expression of this change of mentality, without which the installation of the first services for cancerous soldiers or the philosophy that after the war would influence the organisation of the future network of cancer centres, could not be understood.

Regarding responsibility for cancerous soldiers and the creation of the Anti-Cancer League

Nothing, in principle, seemed to predispose the total commitment of the country during the war to becoming a decisive contextual element in the birth of a movement to fight cancer. Surgeons, doctors, researchers, all were required to commit themselves to the war effort. The Radium Institute closed its doors. When Regaud was called up, Marie Curie dragged an order out of the War Ministry to organise the army radiological service. She persuaded women to lend their cars for the purpose of organising a fleet of radiological vehicles. So twenty 'little Curies' went into circulation.[29] She undertook the training in the field of future radiologists who would work at the two hundred fixed posts situated behind the lines, then, when the 'Edith Cavell' school opened, it was she again who would teach young girls how to handle radiological equipment.[30] Most of the 'pioneers' of radiotherapy were keen to organise an army radiological service which Béclère directed, and strove to adapt the equipment to make it suitable for troop movements. Ledoux-Lebard invented a piece of equipment allowing mobile radiology and Belot perfected a 'universal radiological table',[31] whilst Bergonié, too old to be called up, involved himself in setting up an 'agricultural hospital' at Martillac, in the Bordeaux region. The hospital was for the rehabilitation of the wounded. Its name came about because its boarders were put to work in the fields, and Bergonié was convinced that the recovery of the muscle and joint functions due to this activity was more effective than when mechanotherapy was used. He perfected a rehabilitation programme tailoring a specific agricultural activity to each individual injury.[32] But Bergonié, too young for the 1870 war and too old for this one, was also a true patriot behind the lines. He took over the task of supervising respect for discipline and, above all, sincerity when working with the wounded. 'To get results, it is necessary for the wounded to consent to the proper use of the injured part. Treatment through agricultural work requires a man to be totally genuine. . . . No work to rule would be permissible!'[33] To avoid the patient, 'obsessed by the idea of discharge', using subterfuge so as not to recover, Bergonié invented a check based on analysing the hardness of calluses, which led to the frauds who were not very anxious to return to the front being flushed out.

The surgeons who were members of the Association for the Study of Cancer were obviously very great contributors. During the first few years of the conflict, the youngest, such as Gosset, Proust or Marquis (a provincial correspondent), were enlisted as medical majors and were employed in surgical vehicles;[34] Jean-Louis Faure divided himself between his gynaecology department and the care of the wounded in various Paris hospitals;[35] Tuffier, president of the Surgery Society in 1914, acted as consultant at the General Headquarters until 1916.[36] Quenu was called to the Val-de-Grâce Hospital to manage a department there and organise the allocation and evacuation of convalescent wounded to secondary hospitals.[37] Delbet and Hartmann occupied key posts within the Higher Consultative Commission of the Army Health Department, while being responsible for technical surgical advice. Finally, when the Regaud orders aiming at the appointment of consultant surgeons to the various army corps were endorsed by the government, Justin Godart appointed Faure, Tuffier, Walther, Gosset, Proust and Marquis to these posts.[38]

We would be correct in thinking that the presence in the armies of a certain number of doctors involved in the treatment of cancer had some effect on the problem of soldiers suffering from cancer. Moreover, when this question was put to the Secretary of State, it not only found a favourable ear in an authority sensitive to widespread diseases, but also in men who, within it or closely linked to it, were particularly interested in cancer treatment. The idea of creating specialised clinics was suggested to Justin Godart by Henri Hartmann[39] who, himself, suggested accommodating one which would be annexed to his department at the General Hospital. In an effort at decentralisation, the other two were installed in the provinces. Hartmann thought of Forgue, professor of surgery at

Montpellier, whom he had met at Terrier's house and who was famous for various works on nephrectomy in kidney cancers and treatment of cancers of the womb. It was impossible to avoid choosing Lyons. The centre for cancerous soldiers was to be accommodated in the General Hospital in the department of Léon Bérard, who was a surgeon in touch with the Association for the Study of Cancer. For this project, which recognised radiotherapy as a discrete skill, Hartmann found a willing collaborator in Sonia Fabre. French by marriage, Sonia Fabre was one of those ladies of polite Russian society who had come to study medicine in Paris.[40] Once a pupil of Marie Curie, she was familiar with the handling of radium. She agreed to practise curietherapy in the department and contributed, for this purpose, all the radium which she personally possessed.[41] At Montpellier, it was Dr Pech, head of the radiological laboratory at the hospital, who carried out X-ray treatment. Léon Bérard accepted the assistance of Dr Malot, himself also a radiologist, and Auguste Lumière. The photographic industrialist – whom posterity has mainly remembered for his invention, with his brother, of the cinematograph – was also passionately interested in biology, pharmacodynamics and therapy. Director of a polyclinic, he had a laboratory for his research built by its side. This self-taught 'scientist' (he still refused to become a doctor) had connections with Léon Bérard through their common commitment in the fight against tuberculosis. When the war broke out, Lumière, free of any military commitment, became involved in the organisation of radiology in the General Hospital in Lyons. He financed the equipment from his own funds and put his photographic ability at the disposal of the surgeons. In addition, he was even more ready to collaborate with the cancer service as cancer was for him an important subject for thought and he intended to change the approach to it.[42]

In this way, the pattern for the future cancer centres was mapped out. However, operating conditions and equipment still remained very rudimentary, the radiotherapy apparatus was too weak to allow deep radiotherapy. There were only a few radium needles and a staff which was partly voluntary.

But very quickly the idea prevailed that it was necessary to go further and to conduct the experiment on another level, and in order to do this, it had to be supported by a change of opinion. For the project investigators, cancer had changed status. Everyone, on a more or less conscious level, perceived that its 'social dimension' must now be taken into account. Therefore, when Sonia Fabre suggested to Henri Hartmann that he bring together several well-chosen personalities to set up an association for fighting against cancer,[43] the surgeon's agreement was immediate. They approached Regaud and Justin Godart who, without any hesitation, lent their support to the initiative. The moment, for them, was appropriate. Justin Godart, tired of parliamentary intrigues and in a minority on a secondary question in the Chamber, resigned his post as Secretary of State on 2 February 1918.[44] Now, being much more available, he accepted the presidency of the future league. Having been, for some years, at the centre of an organisation which was to mobilise the health system, Godart, Regaud and Hartmann found no difficulty in bringing together a hundred founder members.

The origin of this association, based on the inspiration and assistance of a charitable society woman and that of a government sanitarian, a clinical surgery professor and a basic research scientist, was rich in symbols: it only lacked a Puvis de Chavannes to be able to leave behind a charming picture for posterity of this association and its fruit. From that moment, the movement to fight cancer and the institutions specialised in the treatment of the disease were partly linked. The concept of a treatment based on collaboration between several specialists could only happen in France thanks to the exceptional circumstances which made it possible for this improbable meeting between society and the clinic, social medicine and experimental medicine, to take place. It was a decisive meeting – I must emphasise this point – as collaboration between surgeon and radiotherapist was only possible and lasting because of the involvement of hygienists and philanthropists. The cancer centres which are outlined here owed their existence and their durability to the politico-social plan which supported their establishment. It was thanks to this state of affairs alone that they were able to provide opportunities for the resolution of conflicts and the maintenance of a balance of power between the recognised clinicians and the 'non-clinicians' involved in clinical work. Autonomous organisations which had relative administrative independence within the public hospital sector, the cancer centres remained places where the concept of 'medicine in wartime' was perpetuated; when peace returned, the medical field gradually retrogressed to social relationships which became ever more similar to what they had been before the war.

As the vehicle of this politico-social project, the Anti-Cancer League played a role which went well beyond the publicity and the organisation of the social action which it undertook. It was formalising an alliance between all the various partners and giving it the permanence proper to every institutional structure. By striving to achieve this project and by contributing to updating it as the situation developed, the League was at the same time modernising this alliance which originated from the contingency of a historical moment, and it was in this way perpetuating it for the future, and ensuring its continuity.

We cannot understand the origin, the development and the role of an association for combating cancer without the changes which, with the coming of the war, appeared in the charity world. The emergence of social concern regarding the danger of cancer took on meaning and form in a context where the reorganisation of charitable works and their connection to public health became a major challenge for the theoreticians of social medicine and for all those who earnestly wished to improve the defects of the French health system.

A modern concept of charity

> The fight for survival in the world of charity is harsh and difficult. Since the war, the excessive restriction of our legislation against associations has been relaxed a little and, faced with the need to help unfortunates of all types, many associations have been created and have appealed to public charity. An extreme competitiveness is the result and only the most able are successful. Finding an idea attractive to the public, obtaining the support of all those could contribute to its success, booking halls, motivating people, these are difficult skills, which require much work and devotion. A whole treatise could be written about charity days; on the cover there could be a sketch representing pleasure coming to the aid of charity. Inside would appear all the topographical, administrative, literary, society, scandal, psychological and other gossip. By adding to this flair, presence of mind, social skills, kindness, diplomacy, a wide Paris location, generosity, authority and a little temerity, you will have all the elements necessary for good publicity . . .[45]

This is what the first secretary general of the League, Robert Le Bret, said very pertinently, and humorously. He revealed a side of charity neglected both by the apologetic historiographies of 'great works' and the analyses which aimed to discredit them. Defining what was at stake concerning the charitable associations while keeping to the study of relationships which link rich and poor, ruling and ruled, reduced the phenomenon to its most explicit. It caused people to be unaware of what this eagerness for charity meant internally for the ruling classes. In French society in the second half of the nineteenth century, charitable commitment was one of the constituent attributions of a 'society' position. It made sense in a system of values where wealth was not confused with the external signs of fortune, 'being rich' was to assume duties towards the poor which went with the position. Carrying out 'charitable work' was one of the 'compulsory criteria' for a 'nouveau riche' to earn his place in a world to which one gained entrance by co-option. In addition, 'society' did not have a uniform structure, it was subdivided into multiple hierarchical areas structured around salons and circles, access to which was governed by complex regulations, all the more difficult to understand for the neophyte as they were tacit. Charitable investments quite 'naturally' became part of the strategies engendered by these different competitive levels in order to preserve or increase their legitimacy. As a result, we can understand this trend towards institutional proliferation of charitable movements. The accomplishment of the duties which Wealth owes to Poverty took place amidst disorder and conflict. Experiencing the social opposition within the ruling classes and the political quarrels which raged around the secularisation of the public hospitals, the charity market was influenced by the competitive battles which were waged by very numerous 'small independent producers' who, in order to gain recognition there, permanently tended to invent new 'good deeds'. Besides several large associations (such as Red Cross societies), most of these good deeds had an influence which was only local (in a district, a suburb, a town), had a limited objective (assistance to a clinic, an orphanage or a nursing school) and aimed at succouring a particular category of unfortunates (orphans, released prisoners, young incurables, people from Alsace-Lorraine who remained French, the blind, children brought before the courts, etc.).[46] The smallest cause, even if futile, could give rise to a committee patronised by a celebrity: the charity (in Nancy) for the loan of sheets, the 'French lace' (who organised annual competitions to encourage the production of hand-made lace),[47] 'Health by example' (which suggested installing a washbasin and a shower room as an experiment, in a rural community school[48]). When reorganisation took place, as in 1890 with the setting up of a Central Charity Office presided over by the Marquis of Vogüe (the founder of the first Red Cross society), or as in 1902 and 1905 with the creation of the French Anti-Tuberculosis League and the National League against Alcoholism, it could only be a case of forming a federation at the head of disparate and relatively independent institutions. If the conflicts between the *Assistance Publique* and private charity lost, on the eve of the 1914 war, much of their bitterness and, because of this, allowed one to hope for a possible co-ordination between the various organisations combating social diseases, the outcome of the conflict revealed the mediocrity of the achievements. There were many charities (Paris had 500 in 1914),[49] too few clinics and too few 'charity graduates' (there were less than 7,000 girls and society ladies who had acquired a Red Cross nursing certificate).[50] At its peak, patriotism caused the number of charitable associations to increase. The 8th district of Paris alone was to contain 51 new soldiers' charities in 1915, and a 100 two years later.[51] Faced with the extreme confusion which ruled over French charities, the idea that at all cost there must be an end to the incoherence and dispersion of efforts acquired a new meaning. For the hygienists in the government, for the leaders committed to the development of tuberculosis and venereal disease clinics or for the founders of the Association of Welfare Officers of France, a plan was taking shape: defining a health policy worthy of the name and giving the country a true 'social service'.[52]

Justin Godart, who was directly concerned in this project, was employed with his friends in the creation of the Anti-Cancer League according to these directions. It is enough to read the first two articles of its regulations to understand that the new association was setting itself objectives similar to the definition of a national policy for fighting cancer:

> Article 1: The aims . . . of the Association are:
> 1. To establish treatment centres for patients, primarily for serving and discharged soldiers and refugees suffering from cancer.

2. To carry out research on the causes and nature of cancer, and the means to combat it.
3. To disseminate amongst the public elementary notions on cancer, to describe its first signs, in order that it may be dealt with in time.
4. To create teaching centres.

Article 2: The methods used by the Association are to be the founding of hospitals, scientific research laboratories and clinics; financial support or allowances to organisations related to cancer; all forms of publicity, teaching, encouragement or reward; and the organisation of local committees.[53]

For the charitable institution, the question was not so much to be aware whether such a programme was or was not 'realistic' in relation to its means; there is every reason to believe that its directors were not tempted by the illusion that they could be its project managers. Their ambition was rather to inform the state on the direction to follow and to play in some way the role of political adviser as well as being a pressure group. On the other hand, in so placing itself in the political field, the League intended to appoint itself as an institution for the preparation of a consensus between the various groups which comprised it and which were represented on its board of management.

Justin Godart's association also expected to be involved in the construction of this famous 'social service', the cornerstone of which had to be the creation of a new profession, that of district nurse, the French counterpart of the British and American 'public health visitors'. In article VI of the external regulation dealing with the local committees of the organisation, it was stipulated that 'they must participate in the training of nurses and organise visiting Ladies and nurses in hospitals and at home'.[54]

A modern charitable organisation, gaining a foothold in the charity market by opening up a new field, the League, in order to realise its ambitions, had to occupy the whole area from the outset. In order to do this it was necessary for it to monitor local initiatives regarding cancer, by starting them or taking part in them. For this purpose, it formed itself into a centralised organisation similar to the one which had proved itself in the political field.

The executive power was concentrated in a board of management elected by secret ballot for a period of six years in a general meeting of the members. The board of management adopted a consultative role, to deal with questions of a scientific nature which concerned the subject of the League, and a scientific committee, of which it appointed the members. It had, in addition, the power to create (and dissolve) local committees, who were legally minor authorities. In fact, these committees 'do not legally have the power to hold, acquire or collect donations and legacies themselves. Only the League (being recognised of public utility) has these rights. It exercises them for the benefit of the committees, by appointing them as agents to collaborate in the management of a part of its assets, and also to collect gifts and legacies made especially in their favour'.[55]

But principles of organisation, however efficient the internal regulations, were not enough to gain the monopoly of a cause; in addition the managers of the League were to do everything possible to attract the support of the principal medical authorities and the collaboration of the most extensive panel of influential individuals in the charity world. It was here that the wealth of relationships accumulated by Justin Godart, Claudius Regaud and Henri Hartmann, and the 'tact' which they could show, were to prove decisive. As regards doctors, a delicate problem arose. The League was not in any circumstances to attract the hostility of the Association for the Study of Cancer; it had, therefore, to eliminate possible points of conflict. The Association for the Study of Cancer; even if it was up to then exclusively concerned with the activities of a learned society, had also included in its articles of association undoubtedly vague but nevertheless explicit ambitions regarding 'organisation of laboratories, clinics, hospitals, etc.' In January 1919, after an announcement by Anselme Schwartz of his plan 'to do something to combat the ravages of cancer', that is forming a 'league' occupying itself with the education of people and doctors,[56] Pierre Delbet replied dryly that he 'regrets that Mr Schwartz has not been aware that the social fight against cancer has been, for at least ten years, one of the main preoccupations of the association of which he is a member'.[57] During the course of the same meeting, Delbet announced the installation of a commission responsible for organising 'public information'. Negotiations would therefore be started between the two associations, facilitated by the fact that several founders of the League, Hartmann himself and also Roger, Mesureur, Roux, Achard, Faure, Gilbert, Mme Girard-Mangin, Letulle, Auguste Lumière, Ménétrier and Baron Henri de Rothschild were members of the Association for the Study of Cancer. (Claudius Regaud would waste no time either in putting forward his application for membership.)[58]

It was even suggested that the two institutions should merge into one. The principle was passed by the Association for the Study of Cancer in a meeting on 23 May 1921,[59] but the matter was not finally decided. After several months of discussions, a *modus vivendi* was found, which assigned a well-defined territory to each.[60] The Association for the Study of Cancer would continue to be involved in 'science' and the League would keep itself strictly within its limits of political and social action. Its scientific board (all members of which were also members of the Association for the Study of Cancer) would confine itself to keeping the board of management updated and would not carry out any learned work, except that for public information. As a result, the Association for the Study of Cancer would not take any action regarding the social fight against cancer which was not carried out in collaboration with the League.

The recruitment of individuals to the world of charity posed fewer tactical problems. Godart, Regaud and Hartmann took advantage of the network of relationships which had grown up around the Secretary of State. Having influenced the reorganisation of the Red Crosses, they could easily attract officials: the Countess of Haussonville, president of the Society for Assistance to Wounded Soldiers, the Countess of Terray, daughter of the Marquis of Vogüe (founder of the Society for Assistance to Wounded Soldiers), the Marchioness of Montebello, honorary president of the same society, Mme. Barbier-Hugo, general president of the Union of French-women, Mme. Ernest Carnot, president of the Association of French ladies, as well as Mlle de Caters, founder of the Mutual Association of Red Cross Nurses.

It was when visiting her to compliment her on her work that Justin Godart made the acquaintance of the Duchess of Uzès.[61] The latter had put her chateau at Bonnelles at the disposal of the army and this had become the annex of the great Rambouillet surgery hospital, and, at the age of seventy, she had taken the examinations to become head nurse. When a year later the ex-Under Secretary of State asked her to become a member of the League, the Duchess accepted, all the more willingly since she had been interested in cancer sufferers for a long time. Widowed (in 1878), she joined the ranks of the Oeuvre du Calvaire and dedicated herself to the care of patients on a regular basis.[62] This unusual character, who made her mark on the history of the Third Republic by having been at the centre of the monarchist intrigues and by financing the campaign of General Boulanger, the 'Jaune' [strike-breaking] trade union movement and several anti-Semitic newspapers,[63] before realistically deciding to compromise with the republican authorities, was a great asset to the new association. Because of her rank, her family and her varied activities – she founded the Women's Automobile Club, she was vice-president of the Aeroclub Ladies' Committee, president of the Union of Women Artists and Sculptors – and because of the hunting which she organised at her Bonnelles estate where she welcomed 'kings, princes and presidents of the Republic', the duchess was at the heart 'of society'.[64] She contributed to the Anti-Cancer League a wealth of relationships accumulated throughout the years, comparable only perhaps to those of the Henri de Rothschild family. The baron, the administrator of the Northern Railway Company, was a partisan of all medical causes, but was particularly in favour of everything connected with cancer (he was treasurer of the Association for the Study of Cancer). A great lover and organiser of hunting, his reputation in this area was equivalent to that of the Duchess of Uzès, and the *battue* (hunting party) held in 1905 in honour of King Carlos of Portugal was remembered by everyone.[65] Baroness Mathilde divided herself between the life of fashionable Paris (it was she who 'launched' Coco Chanel before the war)[66] and encouraged charitable works (for tuberculosis sufferers and sick children); when she took on the publicity committee of the League she was putting at its service charitable experience inherited from an already proven family tradition.

Baron Edouard de Rothschild, head of the French family, was without any doubt less involved than Henri in social chit-chat, but he exercised a considerable influence over financial matters. A director of the Bank of France, a member of the board of management of Assurances Générales and of the Wassy Railways at Saint-Dizier, president of the Northern Railway Company, the man was a benefactor to the sciences, both in his office in the Institute and also on the committee of honour of the Association for the Study of Cancer. He was to remain, until the fall of France in 1940, a member of the board of management of the League, with two other governors of the Bank of France, Félix Vernes, head of the bank Vernes et Cie, and François de Wendel, chairman of the Committee of the Forges from 1918 to 1940. The latter also pursued a political career. Regularly elected deputy of Meurthe-et-Moselle, he was affiliated to a group on the parliamentary right, the Republican Federation (presided over by his friend Louis Marin), which he had contributed to forming.[67] The co-existence, at the heart of the League authorities, of sections of society 'who, before the war, would never have mixed with each other' and who were bitter political adversaries here also bore witness to the profound changes induced by the conflict: the spirit of sacred unity ruled over the enterprise.

The active participation of these 'great Parisian names' increased the potential for relationships within the initial core. The League was developing quickly and went from a hundred founders in 1918 to 330 members in 1922, 400 in 1925, and more than 500 in 1927.[68] The nobility of the Ancien Régime or Empire, the great financial, industrial and trading upper-middle class, the politicians, the army, the high administration and, of course, medicine, i.e. all those who made up the ruling classes, would be present to make their financial contribution, but often they also lent their active participation – through the Ladies' Central Committee – to the fight against cancer.

The many different social positions of its managers and its campaigners allowed the League to become linked with a number of public and private organisations (Red Cross, tuberculosis charities, charities for mothers' and children's protection, anti-alcohol charities, etc.) which took part in the movement to reorganise health and social action, started during the war.

Being encouraged, as secretary to the Health Service, to collaborate with the charitable representatives of the allied countries on French soil, Justin Godart wished to prolong the collaboration which had begun and which also gave an international dimension to the association over which he was to preside. It was because of him that the Anti-Cancer League became 'Franco-Anglo-American' and was, on 14 March 1918, christened by Lord Berthies of Thames (the British Ambassador) and William Sharp (the US Ambassador), thus marking by their symbolic commitment the Allies' support to the enterprise. The international organisation's ambition was to misfire; the American and British 'native' cancer associations did not in any way appreciate the competitive initiative, and it was to take other routes. But the presence, on the board of management and in the Ladies' Committee, of British and American philanthropists (Sir John Pilter, the honorary president of the British Chamber of Commerce, president of the charitable and educational institutions of the British community in France; Walter Berry, the president of the US Chamber of Commerce and president of the charity for the rehabilitation of the wounded; Bernard J. Shoninger and Bernard Flurscheim, American businessmen and philanthropists who started many charities; Laurence Bennet and his wife, who started the American Red Cross) strengthened its influence. Not only did they put 'their Anglo-Saxon know-how' of the organisation of social work at the disposal of the League, but they also gave the association an international dimension and reinforced its right to aspire to the monopoly of the fight against cancer in France.

Strengthened by these trump cards, the Franco-Anglo-American League was to impose itself on the market as the only organisation for combating cancer and was to profoundly influence not only the cancer policy of the state, but also its health policy.

5 The beginnings of a policy for the fight against cancer

First outlines of an institutional framework

The defeat of Germany released energy for new struggles with a more uncertain outcome. 'The mysterious, cunning, murderous and exquisitely cruel evil against which we are trying to organise an effective fight in France is an enemy of such magnitude that it seems madness, or at least singular presumption, on our part, to attempt to overcome it.'[1] In this post-war atmosphere, where speeches still resounded with the raised voices of warlike rhetoric, the Anti-Cancer League officials liked to appear in the guise of 'combatants', whose 'generous' bravery had 'the excuse of being absolutely necessary, in the presence of danger'.[2] But behind the deliberate melodramatic exaggeration of the proposals and the eloquence of a secretary general who had not forgotten his training as a lawyer, the situation which Robert Le Bret depicted was not so far from reality. The contrast between the enormity of the ambitions, the condition of the cancer organisation and the means which the League had to carry out its programme gave it the right to speak of 'singular presumption'. When the armistice was signed, everything was still to be done: structures to be invented, the necessary competent staff to be provided, early diagnosis to be made, patients to be monitored, all this on a country-wide scale, at a time when the funds of the association were barely adequate.

The first thing was to consolidate what had been achieved by ensuring the durability of the cancer centres created by the Secretary of State for Health, that is their transformation into 'civil' structures, whilst ensuring them a minimum of equipment. Delving into its meagre funds, the League made its first donation (40,000 francs), to the *Assistance Publique* in 1919 for the purchase of a few milligrams of radium for Hartmann's department.[3] For several months, all efforts were concentrated on the Hôtel Dieu Hospital. Hartmann's wife and Le Bret's wife were active in the service of the patients and organised an embryonic social service. Regaud himself was employed for a few afternoons a week in the therapeutic application of radon. A 'non-clinician', he had obtained authority to carry out therapeutic tests indoors from the management of the *Assistance Publique*.[4] But, very quickly, the Radium Institute director decided to intervene on another scale and to involve a maximum number of surgeons in the affair. The war had very noticeably changed his position in the medical field and it would have been difficult to recognise in him 'the modest provincial whose arrival in Paris had passed unnoticed'.[5] Having been able to establish personal relationships with the clinical elite and to treat surgeons 'as equals', he assumed authority and suggested direct collaboration with them in the treatment of cancer. Antoine Lacassagne thus recounts the actions of his chief:

> He left by bicycle in the morning, carrying radioactive tubes which he was going to place on the patients himself. I was appointed to help him in this task. He took me in turn to Tuffier's departments, in La Pitié, Lecène's at the Dubois house, Delbet's at Necker, Lenormand's at Saint-Louis, J.L. Faure's at Broca, Wiard's at Tenon and Rouvillois' at the Val-de-Grâce. When I was sufficiently experienced, we practised our task of radon peddling independently. He was demanding, tactful and fearsome, in the eyes of the neophytes that we were, when demonstrating the possibilities of a therapeutic agent to surgeons, who were certainly curious, but diffident.[6]

The immediate effects of the treatments were to make a favourable impression on the surgeons as, in a short time, the 'radon peddlers' were swamped by the influx of patients with whom they were entrusted. Forced to make more and more frequent journeys, they could no longer ensure timely checking of the results obtained and turned to Emile Roux to arrange for a 'hospital clinic' which could accommodate the patients. He made an agreement with the manager of the Pasteur Hospital to provide a small ward of six beds for them and the use, two afternoons per week, of premises for outpatients consultation;[7] the service started in July 1919, with Regaud at its head and an entirely co-opted team. Because of its director's wish, the biological section of the Radium Institute seemed to take a different direction to that originally expected. What should have been a basic research laboratory applied to the biological action of radium, linked with a histology laboratory at the Pasteur Institute, became an institution including in its aims an entirely separate clinical purpose. This new requirement for practical links between the areas of the fundamental (research on the biological action of radiation), the applied (updating treatment methods using radiation) and the therapeutic (preparation of radiotherapy treatment methods and use on patients) went hand in hand with Regaud's choice to give up his histological research. This choice between two directions which were equally coherent and non-contradictory was seen by the director of the biological section in terms of economy of personal effort; very prosaically, he could not lead all his activities from the front, when he knew what the creation of a care structure involved in 'political' and administrative commitment, a situation all the more difficult when the latter was outside the control of the *Assistance Publique*. Several elements combined to explain the turn in Regaud's career. When in 1913 he went up to Paris, his relationship with histology was already a little strained, not only because he was focused (temporarily in his mind) on the study of X-rays, but also because he needed to prepare his departure and take care of his new tasks (and his new premises). He may still have been considering a return to histophysiological research when the war broke out, and it imposed very different duties on him for four years. This long break came for him at an age when it was liable to weigh heavily on him. At the time of his discharge from the army he was nearly fifty, and it was even more difficult for him to return to a position in an area where he had fallen behind, while during these four years he had had an experience from which no person remains unchanged, that of power. Not having had the time to practically exercise his duties as director of the Radium Institute, Regaud passed almost seamlessly from the status of *agrégé*, to that of head doctor of a military hospital, only to find himself one year later in the position of an organiser of war surgery, a co-ordinator of inter-army war conferences and a chief in the Bouleuse camp. His climb up the social scale had been considerable. To be convinced, it is enough to reread what Regaud himself declared in 1912, in front of his peers, at a dinner for *agrégés* in Lyons. 'You are suffering,' he said to his companions, 'from the absurdity of our status, you would like to be more closely associated . . . with the decisions and responsibilities which education involves; given that the development of an individual's faculties does not increase by leaps and bounds, you find it excessive that we are made to pass seamlessly from the condition of a simple *agrégé* where we are almost nothing, to that of a professor where we are almost everything.'[8] What would he have said, then, about what was to happen to him? If the transformation from the almost nothing *agrégé* to the almost everything professor happened within the same local discipline, the hazards of war and of politics took Regaud to a higher level within the social space which P. Bourdieu called the field of power. Here he was in direct contact with a 'statesman', in a position to deal on an equal footing with the cream of the medical elite on questions regarding the organisation of health policy itself. A social climb of this type, even if temporary, has many consequences. A person who experiences it is brutally restricted to dedicating himself to a new type of social role and can only withdraw with panache if he has completely subscribed to the stakes of the current game. Regaud adopted the aims of the Secretary of State: that is to make medicine in wartime more operational and, for this purpose, to redefine the relationships between doctors, surgeons, scientists, voluntary nurses, charities, etc., and to commit the state to a policy of fighting against epidemic diseases. He could adopt these aims because he was no stranger to at least one aspect of these problems, having endured them (and rather 'badly') at his own level in the Lyons medical environment (his position as a relative rebel predisposed him to becoming involved in a reformist project dealing with the organisation of the health system). But by changing his social position, he also changed his point of view of the medical world. Before the war, Regaud did not have any particular interest in transforming this world, being 'unsuited' to the development of scientific knowledge, because he felt 'trapped' there, without having any real means of action; hence his strategy of leaving for the Pasteur Institute. On the other hand, having become actively involved in its transformation, he saw this world, which he had believed fixed, develop at the same time as he was acquiring intimate knowledge of the organisation which had power and where decisions producing results were taken. Involved in the reform of medicine in wartime, Regaud was drawn into the game and intended, when peace returned, to continue in that direction, at the price of 'sacrificing' his histological research. The aim which he set himself, 'to prepare a scientific treatment of cancer' was, for him, closely linked to a plan of organisation of anti-cancer medicine, which was founded on the close connection between fundamental, applied and clinical research, for which the institution which he directed was to serve as a model. His departure from the university to the Pasteur Institute became under these conditions advantageous to his plan. The independence which he had as regards the *Assistance Publique* and the Faculty of Medicine allowed him to put into practice a concept of 'scientific medicine' which would not have found a place in the hospital–academic world, being too heterodox for the current practices. His turning point was not, therefore, a break with his 'Bernardian' ideal of the 'experimental doctor', but rather a different way of conforming to it. Claude Bernard tried to define this ideal in the final chapter of the *Introduction à la médicine expérimentale*, by anticipating that the toing and froing between the laboratory and the patient's bedside must take place in a socially organised plan of the division of work.

> Experimental medicine, as we perceive it, includes the medical problem in its entirety and covers theoretical and practical medicine. But by saying that each individual must be an experimental doctor, I did not want to establish that each branch of medicine must cover all experimental medicine. There must always be doctors who will concentrate on physiological experiments, others on normal or pathological anatomical investigations, others on surgical or medical practice, etc.[9]

After the war Regaud changed his tone. He deserted 'physiological experiments' for experimental medical practice, i.e. a clinical practice which rested on research on what was the 'initial determinism of phenomena'.[10] One objection immediately comes to mind: is cancer not a particularly bad choice for such a purpose, since its cause is unknown? In fact, Regaud bypassed this obstacle by giving himself an intermediate aim.

Aetiology and pathogenicity of cancer are unknown phenomena. On the other hand, however, the action of radiation on the cells itself appears accessible to knowledge: irradiation destroys certain categories of cells. As regards such cells, then, irradiation can be made part of the 'initial determinism' of a pathological phenomenon. An 'experimental medical' approach is possible, as long as it takes as its subject not cancer physiopathology, but the physiopathology which affects the irradiated (normal or cancerous) cells. In so far as the scientific mastery of this pathology provoked by cells allows supervision of their destruction, it becomes conceivable that the cancer (or at least the histological types of cancer sensitive to radiation) can be reduced without one understanding the psychopathological mechanisms. We should, however, be aware that this hypothesis implies implicit loyalty to the cellular theory of cancer and its reductionist axiom, which requires that the 'initial determinism' of the cancerous disease is completely within the malignant transformation of a normal cell.

The cancer clinic which Regaud intended to establish from the Radium Institute was therefore significantly different from what had been achieved until then. Contrary to the empirical medicine of the dermatologists, it had its origins in the fundamental knowledge acquired in the laboratory and tended to be presented as an applied science. To fulfil this project, Regaud was to surround himself with collaborators who shared his vision of what the 'scientific treatment of cancer' should be. The initial core of the 'Pasteur clinic' had been recruited by co-option; all its members had personal connections with their 'boss', their 'chief', as they called him. With the exception of Lacassagne, the pupil from the histology laboratory in Lyons, they would have made the acquaintance of Regaud at one or other of the various stages of his 'military career'.[11] Henri Coutard, the roentgeno-therapist, was the Gérardmer military hospital radiologist in 1914. Octave Monod, whom Regaud 'converted' and trained in radium therapy, was at his side in the staff of doctors from Lyons who were with Justin Godart at the Secretariat of State for Health. Three ex-members of the Bouleuse camp completed the team. René Ferroux, a young physicist from Grenoble, who prepared radium tubes and who had been incorporated as a 2nd class nurse, carried out the task of technical assistant in the radiology laboratory. Jean-Louis Roux-Berger, a hospital surgeon, managed one of the clinical departments in the camp, with Mary Thurneyssen as nurse. Roux-Berger carried out consultations at the Pasteur clinic and was responsible, at the Hospital de la Charité where he practised, for patients needing treatment by curietherapy and surgery. Mlle Thurneyssen agreed to become head nurse, on a voluntary basis. This daughter of a manufacturer of radiogenic tubes was immediately involved in the 'fight against cancer'; a founder member of the League, she became one of its 'lady visitors'.[12] The team at the Pasteur clinic still had the advantage of the support of an influential person in Antoine Béclère. The 'father' of the Paris radiological school who, during the war presided over the technical commission for radiology at the Secretariat of State, became friends with Regaud. On the eve of his retirement (he left the service in 1922), he espoused the cause of the 'scientific treatment of cancer' and suggested to Regaud that he should take part in consultation activities. He supported the enterprise by directing several of his young pupils towards it. Amongst them,

> Dr Béclère suggested Dr Georges Richard who became our radium therapist at the Pasteur hospital, until the disappearance of our clinic when the Curie Hospital opened. This radiologist was at first helped by another of Dr Béclère's pupils, Miss Juliette Baud, particularly qualified as she was a pupil of Mme Curie at the Radium Institute. Soon Richard took on his friend, Dr Jean Pierquin.[13]

The service was then able to begin its work, partly due to a gift of a ½ gram of radium made by Henri de Rothschild. The baron behaved as if he were the appointed patron. At the end of 1919 he allocated to the clinic all the funds from a scientific foundation which he had just created (i.e. 200,000 francs). The large number of patients, however, soon revealed the precarious nature of the installation. The following year, the Pasteur Hospital provided an extra nine new beds for the service, but the improvement was only temporary. Marie Curie and Claudius Regaud then decided to formalise appeals to charity and suggested that a 'foundation' be set up to receive donations and legacies. The project was accepted by the supervising authorities. Once again it was Henri de Rothschild who supplied the initial legal funds. Roux, very influential in the Tote commission, granted financial aid which allowed the amount of radium to be increased by 200 mg. Rector Appel persuaded the board of the University of Paris that a strip of unoccupied land, situated near the rue d'Ulm between the Chemistry Institute and the Convent of the Ladies of the Adoration, be conceded to the Institute for ten years. On 27 May 1921, the Curie Foundation was recognised as a public interest institution. It received several donations at once: two grams of radium (one offered by Henri de Rothschild, the other due to the generosity of the 'American women' who had organised a collection in favour of Marie Curie, following a journey she had made to the United States),[14] and a sum of 500,000 francs granted by the authorities for a purchase of radium. Rapidly started, the construction of two wards comprising consulting areas, a hospital department of fifteen beds, four laboratories (histopathology, haematology, serology, bacteriology) and rooms for roentgentherapy treatment was completed on 29 November 1922. During these four years, the most 'advanced' French cancerology institution was to take shape, and between the wars would become one of the international reference centres. Its particular situation in the medical field, the plan which it put forward, the ideology which motivated it were some of the many elements which contributed to making it a cancer centre 'apart', unique in its field. The name of Pasteur ensured that it had the necessary independence from the hospital–academic world, so that it could be what Regaud wanted: the institutional expression of his ideal. The directions of the Curie Foundation, and also its method of operation, the individual involvement of the team members, their collective relationships and their relationships with the 'boss', all of which contributed to create what one would crudely call a 'team spirit', appeared motivated by a willingness to attain this ideal. Hence the permanent tension which Regaud himself revived as soon as he felt it weaken, a sign of which was that astonishing speech made at the time of a ceremony where he presented his new year's wishes to all his staff, the peroration of which ended with the words which were, in the true sense of the expression, those of a visionary. 'Of course, by admonishing you collectively, I blame no-one, but I see clearly before me *that imaginary being who is the perfect worker, the great scientist which you should all be and which none of you is.* My dear friends, to a better 1925 than 1924' [my emphasis].[15]

The realisation of its director's project, the Curie Foundation was, as a collective institution, to give substance to the ideal which was his. But the prophetic aim which supported this whole creation could only be at odds with the bureaucratic reasoning inherent in the existence of an institution, a conflict which was clearly revealed in the content of the 'admonishment' in question:

> *Never consider us as civil servants* scrupulously carrying out the task assigned to us, and closing down as soon as the work is no longer there. We must regard ourselves as the *extreme opposite* of civil servants. *When we do not have enough work, let us create some, let us ask for some.* I am always able to give you some. Let everyone find in himself what in soldier's language is called an 'adjutant'; not only the guardian of discipline, but the perpetual motivator. Do not search for this person outside yourself, or somewhere in the team, we do not have him. Therefore let us always find more work, spontaneously created [my emphasis].[16]

The injunction made here to each one is not to be found in the Courtelin style of criticism of 'pen-pushers', it was not the parasitism of the civil servant which was under examination, but the incompatibility of the two kinds of relationship with work. Contrary to the public service official having only to perform his task, scrupulously and competently, within a calculated and regulated period, the scientist does not begrudge work ('still more work') nor, because of this, the time which he dedicates to it. Regaud had no need to be more explicit, as he was certain that he would be 'understood' by his collaborators, who were all aware of the 'existential' nature of the difference between a civil servant and a scientist. The civil servant had a defined social identity, visible and recognised by everyone, which was conferred upon him by the 'public' nature of the post which he *filled* (the expression is used figuratively) in the name of the state. He had a time for work (which was public time) followed by 'private' time according to fixed timetables. On the other hand, the 'scientist' was never really assured of being a 'true scientist'. How could he be so when the ideal to which he aspired was posed as inaccessible to the individual ('this imaginary being . . . that none of us is'). Acting out his very identity through his work, he dedicated his life to his work and as a result could not count the time spent in doing it. (The edifying descriptions of 'lives of scientists' always emphasise this 'sacrifice' of private life.)

By referring to these shared values, Regaud knew that he would be understood, but his 'call to order' was not just a formality for all that. It demonstrated an acute perception of the risks inherent in the development of social conditions for the practice of a science which, in this particular case, placed a strain upon the institutional practice of a scientific medicine. As long as a division of scientific work was established and was socially involved in differentiated administrative tasks and, in this way, 'publicly identified', the 'civil servant' could take precedence over the scientist. To keep this risk at bay, Regaud appealed to the ego of his collaborators, to that internal 'adjutant' which, let us wager, must have its say and its attributes. Since the 'great scientist' can only be a 'collective entity', it is necessary to avoid both the risks of bureaucratisation and the pitfall of individualism, inevitably doomed to failure by clinging to an 'old-fashioned' mentality. Neither a 'machine' – an image of bureaucracy with its 'administrative moving parts' – nor a broken-down body in which each member would work for his own ends, the Curie Foundation would need to create a concrete whole out of harmoniously united complementary elements. In short, a living organisation of which Regaud was the head (the chief in the first sense of the word).

> The aims which we are pursuing are too difficult for any one of us to achieve on his own. Don't wait for someone to unite you, band together. Don't work in a vacuum. Don't hide away. There are no secrets between us because no deviation of purpose is to be feared. Trust each other. Help each other, offer your services. I am still there to establish links and I want to know about everything you are doing so that I can maintain the necessary harmony.[17]

This entire speech by Regaud clarified what we could call the metaphysical basis of the Institution. The Curie Foundation, as a fictitious entity, was identified with the 'great scientist'. The name chosen was, moreover, particularly relevant. Regaud, doubtless because he was unsure in himself that he was a 'great scientist', did not create any institution bearing his name. Curie was at one and the same time a recognised (by a Nobel prize, among other things) 'scientist's' name and also part a 'learned set' (a married couple). This effect of naming symbolically registers the independence of the fictitious person in relation to the one who created him. In the eyes of his collaborators, Regaud did not claim to be the 'great scientist', but more the guarantor of the 'spirit' of the institution ('the adjutant in everyone's head') and its protector (as is said of the king who is the protector of the crown):

> I am at your disposal at any time, and you don't even need to knock at my door. Use it. I am very busy and too variously occupied with overwhelming tasks which are unfortunately nothing to do with science, to give all of you my very active attention. Never mind, ask, take the initiative, act, nothing is impossible.[18]

So in order that this 'great scientist' which he had created could live, the creator had to sacrifice his own scientific work on the altar of administrative–political 'needs' necessary for an institution to be able to function. The commitment which he required from his collaborators had to equal the gift that he made of himself. Because of this, membership of the institution involved total adherence to the values of the 'chief' and a behaviour and a participation in the life of the team which matched these values. Recruitment by co-opting achieved the essence of its meaning here; to enter the Curie Foundation was to commit oneself as regards Regaud on an existential basis, returning the gift with an equivalent gift. In short, in addition to the question of knowledge, ability, spirit of invention, there was also the question of love; as certainly everywhere, or nearly everywhere, 'love' had a functional role in the institution.

In 1921, a small cancer department was set up in a hospital in Villejuif, the Paul Brousse hospital, on the initiative of its head doctor, the *agrégé* of pathological anatomy, Gustave Roussy. A few beds and a minimal laboratory, which were the first steps towards what later was to become one of the largest (if not the largest) of the medico-scientific anti-cancer structures in the world, were not really much to look at. At this moment in time, its initiator himself did not know, in all likelihood, that he had just committed himself to an enterprise which was to lead him to a major turning point in his career. Swiss by birth, born in 1874, Gustave Roussy came to France at the beginning of the century to perfect his medical training at La Salpêtrière. An intern of Déjerine, he was instructed by the latter in the pathological anatomy of the nervous system. According to Jean Lhermitte,[19] the training was difficult, and the work tedious, unpleasant and often discouraging, but the field was expanding, and the school of La Salpêtrière, still influenced by the figure of Charcot, was a prestigious place. Roussy dedicated his thesis to the study of the 'optical layer' and made himself known by associating his name with the clinical anatomy description of a syndrome (connected to a lesion of the optical layer), the thalamic syndrome (called Déjerine-Roussy). Soon, however, he began to abandon the 'pure anatomical' tradition of his masters in order to take a direction which was not unlike that of the histologist Regaud.

> If the school of Salpêtrière has early established itself as fond of clinical anatomy research . . . it seems that we were, at the beginning of the century, much less eager to take the path of experimentation and it was not without surprise, in 1906, that we saw Gustave Roussy pursuing, in spite of the deficiencies of experimental surgery at the time, the study of thalamic destruction caused in animals.[20]

For a time head of operations at the École des hautes études [School of Higher Studies], he was appointed in 1910 as *agrégé* in pathological anatomy at the faculty of medicine in Paris, and joined Pierre Marie's team, which he assisted in its attempt to reform the practical education provided for the students. Although he was one of the 'irregulars' who, according to Bernard's ideas, thought that medicine should be made part of the range of biological sciences, Roussy nevertheless did not neglect pursuing a hospital career. But his repeated attempts in the hospital medical examination resulted in failure, and he had to content himself with the subordinate position of Head Doctor in a hospice, and once more found himself, in 1913, managing the 'Paul Brousse' which had just opened in Villejuif.[21] It was possibly surprising to see him assume a function traditionally limited to the hospital supervision of poor, old people. Charitable concerns were not without influence on his decision. This man, endowed with a large fortune from his family and marriage (he married a Nestlé daughter), whose 'allure of a grandee, in behaviour, attitude and words'[22] made an impression on his contemporaries, had a 'social conscience'. 'Being very compassionate to humble people, he wanted them to be as well treated as those whom fortune had favoured.'[23] By taking on the management of the hospice, Roussy managed to combine his charitable concerns with a scientific project. He organised the operation of the hospice so that it was a clinical area adapted to his research. Patients, grouped according to diagnosis into 'pathological families' would supply material for a 'set of important publications, impressive because of the variety of their subjects and the rigour of the clinical and anatomical descriptions which they contained.'[24] Having to suspend his activities when war broke out, he became an ambulance doctor at the front, then chief neurological surgeon for the Tenth Army and responsible for the neurological centre of the Seventh Region in Besançon. His clinical experience was enriched by dealing with a whole series of pathologies resulting from the fighting: the multiple wounds damaging the nervous system and the psychic traumas affecting soldiers. Together with Jean Lhermitte, the neurological doctor of the Eighth Region, he wrote two outstanding works, the first on the 'nature and development of injuries in the spinal cord and the cauda equina', the second on 'war psychoneuroses'.

Then life resumed its normal course, and Roussy returned to Paul Brousse where he joined Roger Leroux, one of his assistants at the Besançon Centre. The hospice doctor was then enjoying a solid reputation as a pathological anatomist and clinician for afflictions of the nervous system. Moreover, he had established himself in the psychiatric field, being a forerunner in the subject of psychopathology of traumatic origin. Now Roussy, who until then had shown only a relatively secondary interest in problems connected with cancer, agreed in 1921 to succeed Jean Darier as secretary general of the Association for the Study of Cancer. He had, like several other collaborators of Pierre Marie, joined the learned society shortly after its creation, but very little in his participation in the Association's activities for the study of cancer allowed such a commitment to be foreseen. With a few morphological studies of rare forms of cancer based on the most classical descriptive pathological anatomy, his papers reflected his circumstances: the experimentalist Roussy found his chosen subjects elsewhere, in the analysis of hypothalamo-hypophyseal disturbances. Then, at the beginning of the 1920s, the idea of cancer treatment centres took hold and were favourably viewed by Paul Brousse. Given the age of the patients in the hospice, the method of classification by pathological families could not fail to cause a 'family' of cancer patients to emerge, sufficiently large in number for its head doctor to decide to open an *ad hoc* surgery.

> It was in a modest room in the hospice that Roussy received this crowd of patients worried by the idea that they could catch this feared disease. He himself examined each patient, palpating the most repugnant neoplasms with his gloved hand, exploring the organs and analysing the biopsy which was presented to him.[25]

A shrewd politician, he saw the opportunity to increase the prestige of the hospice, tried to give substance to the therapeutic infrastructure and, in order to do so, gained the support of the Seine département council, which wished to open a cancer treatment centre in the suburbs. In 1922, the existence of the centre was made official; the board passed a first credit for the purchase of radium.[26] At the same time, the team was enhanced by new appointments of staff and started work in several research areas. Roussy, Leroux and Edmond Peyre (a young histologist) successfully reproduced the first work of the Japanese Yamagiwa and Itchikawa (the production of an experimental cancer in a mouse by painting it with tar).[27] In addition, the arrival of Simone Laborde, one of Marie Curie's pupils, allowed Paul Brousse's doctors to start curietherapy of cancers of the womb.[28] If, like the Curie Foundation, the Villejuif cancer treatment centre intended to develop fundamental and clinical research, its structure did not have the same coherence. Work on cancer pathogenicity and therapeutic research centred on the evaluation of treatments, and the adjustment of protocols were not directly linked. The various activities were carried out in parallel, without there being any interaction at team level. Here the institution did not completely centre around a unifying project of 'scientific cancer medicine'. The cancer centre only comprised, within the hospice, one sort of activity amongst others, certainly more and more important but in no way exclusive. Gustave Roussy himself – and this was significant – continued to favour in his personal work the study of the pathologies of the nervous system, pursuing animal experimentation and clinical observation of hospital patients.[29]

There is much less to say about the small cancer centres which, in the wake of the Hartmann service, were born from the *Assistance Publique*, except that they functioned under a classical hospital system. At first, two centres were created, annexed to general surgical departments, one in the La Salpêtrière hospital (Professor Gosset), the other in the Tenon hospital (Proust). Gosset had just inherited the chair of clinical surgery, and Proust began work upon the retirement and departure of Wiard.[30]

During the war these two 'young' chiefs had been consultant surgeons in an army corps, at one time being part of the network of medical officials working with the Secretary of State for Health. They were titular members of the Association for the Study of Cancer, and also members of the Anti-Cancer League, taking part in the activities of its scientific council. Ledoux-Lebard was Gosset's radiotherapist, De Nabias was Proust's, and both acted as assistants. Here, there was co-operation between surgeons and radio-therapists, and so the relationship between the two methods of treatment were part of a hierarchical relationship.

In 1921, the management of the *Assistance Publique* decided to extend this type of structure to three other surgical departments in Necker, Saint-Antoine and Lariboisière. The project was supported by the Paris Municipal Council which, after a report from Dr Calmels, the assistant in health matters, granted 2.5 million francs for the purchase of radium.[31]

On the eve of the direct intervention by the authorities in the organisation of the fight against cancer, an outline of a specialised institutional field was set up in Paris and its suburbs centred around three structures differentiated by their administrative status, their position in the medical field, their organisation and the relationships of the various 'specialities' within them. The Curie Foundation and the cancer departments in the *Assistance Publique* were opposed to each other on all of these points. The first was a private law structure linked with the Pasteur Institute: clinical activities figured there as the extension of research work on the biological action of radiation; surgery was only involved as a supplementary technique, subordinate to radiotherapy. The second belonged to the public sector; operated as annexes of the general surgery department, the links with research were distant (if not to say non-existent) and here, it was radiotherapy which was subordinate to surgery.

The cancer department of the Paul Brousse hospital was in an inter-mediary position. It belonged to the public sector, but shared with Curie a certain marginality as regards the hospital–academic elite. There was a place for basic research alongside clinical activities, each developing in a relatively independent manner. The coherence of the research was not driven by a clinical purpose, but was much more likely to be in response to the system of a 'disciplinary' project: that of a pathological anatomist wanting to update his expertise via experimental approaches (and, supplementarily, to accede to the chair of the Paris faculty, which would take place in 1925). The creation of the cancer centre was a strategic opportunity for this project. Because of this, the various treatment techniques, surgery as well as radiotherapy, neither being of major importance for Roussy, were initially on a relatively equal footing.

These three structures comprised the cancer centres which were available to the authorities, until they themselves were able to decide on the line of direction for the construction of a network of specialised structures in the fight against cancer. The commission set up by the ministry to define this line was clearly not to opt for one or the other of these alternatives, but was to be won over by the proposition of a combined structure, going to look elsewhere, in the provinces, for the person who was to be the promoter, Jean-Alban Bergonié.

The Cancer Commission and the Bergonié Project

At the time of its creation, the method by which the Franco-Anglo-American League wanted to combat cancer consisted of an outline programme for a specific health policy regarding cancer, and this during a period when the authorities seemed to have nothing to offer. Four years later, in 1922, the establishment of a Cancer Commission at the Ministry of Health, Assistance and National Insurance raised the fight against cancer to the rank of national causes. The Commission took the League's ambitions as its own and, following the proposals prepared in a report by Jean-Alban Bergonié, recommended to the Ministry the construction of a network of regional centres specialised in the treatment of cancer, the country-wide organisation of early diagnosis and the use of advertising to educate the public.

The arrival on the scene of the authorities, although apparently displacing the League in its supportive role, was greeted as a very positive action by the managers of the association. 'Rest assured that we will be at your side, under your orders, as auxiliaries and scouts, good soldiers for the battle in which you are leading us,'[32] replied Justin Godart to the presentation made by Minister Paul Strauss, and speaking of the first decisions taken by the Commission at the General Meeting of the League on 8 May 1923. He was followed by Robert Le Bret: 'Last year's great movement, the start of which we forecast, was developed with remarkable energy and took off even surpassing our hopes.'[33] Satisfaction was not feigned. The directors of the League claimed that they had taken advantage of having significantly influenced the government's decision to involve the state. The steps taken by Paul Strauss, who came personally to preside over the General Meeting of the League in the previous year, managed to convince it that it was necessary to treat cancer as one of the great scourges. It is true that, as a hygienist of consequence, the minister was predisposed to accept the arguments of Justin Godart and his friends. He came to believe that the 'cancer peril' could not be reduced by the mobilisation alone of charitable work, however active, and that the country-wide organisation of the 'social and scientific struggle' required the authorities to take action.

As with all ministers who have any self respect, Paul Strauss initiated the process by putting into place an *ad hoc* commission, and allocated to it the task of 'co-ordinating work and efforts relating to aetiology, pathogenicity, clinical study, therapy and prevention of cancer'.[34] It had an exhaustive programme and a considerable structure: the Cancer Commission, chaired by Professor Quenu, had no less than five vice-presidents (Calmette, the vice-president of the Pasteur Institute, and Dean Roger, Professors Maurice Letulle, Pierre Delbet and Henri Hartmann) and seventy-one members who were supported in the work by three secretaries and two assistant secretaries. It was divided into five sections each dealing with a large number of the problems mentioned in its objectives.[35] As in all ministerial commissions, its composition depended at one and the same time on concern for representativeness (in terms of the sector of activity relating to public health, political groups, large institutions), and on weighting (between the various specialists, professionals, politicians and administrators). The lecturers at the faculties of medicine, the doctors and/or surgeons of the hospitals comprised the largest group, including at least half of those holding office (16 clinical doctors, 12 surgeons, 6 radiologist–radiotherapists and 3 basic researchers). The remainder was divided between the members of various scientific institutions, such as the Pasteur Institute (7 members), the Radium Institute (Marie Curie and Claudius Regaud), the École des hautes études, the Veterinary College of Maisons-Alfort, the faculty of pharmacy in Strasbourg, the faculty of science in Paris, the Museum (represented by Bécquerel), the chief officers of higher education (the rector of the Paris academy, the director of higher education), some representatives of the administration and of military medicine, a few members of the minister's cabinet and elected representatives (5 senators, 4 deputies and 2 councillors).[36]

The purpose of this type of commission was not so much to collectively prepare a policy but, by the weight of its representation, to sanction and legitimise the projects which were submitted to it The great diversity of the positions occupied by its members made of it an authority predisposed to ratify the proposals and to bring about a large consensus. The first text adopted, 'Principles according to which a regional centre to fight cancer should be organised in order to be recognised by the Ministry of Health and to receive financial support', perfectly illustrates this concern to introduce something 'new' while respecting 'the old order'.

It was to his personal (and political) friend, Jean Bergonié, that Paul Strauss entrusted the work of thinking about the organisation, its operation and the equipping of future cancer centres. The physical condition of the spokesman certainly gave the matter a pathetic dimension. After many years, Bergonié had been affected by the 'X-ray disease'. Successive amputations of his fingers had not been able to prevent the progress of an epithelioma 'provoked by radiation' and that same year, 1922, he dislocated his shoulder, for which he knew that there would be only a palliative treatment.[37] But none of this was reflected in his text, which could be read as an appropriate and perfectly accomplished 'work' of detachment from his own situation.

The entire programme developed by Bergonié derived its coherence from the basis initially set by the surgeons. Cancer was curable, because, from the start, it was a local disease, accessible to different treatments: surgery, X-rays and radium. It only became generalised secondarily and then grew insensitive to treatment. This representation of the sequential development of cancer, in two stages, allowed a strategy of intervention to be suggested, in spite of the 'enigma' posed by the aetiology of the pathological phenomenon. Even if 'science does not have a remedy which can make the cancer cell gripped by this anarchically spreading mysterious disease respond',[38] the characters involved in the natural history of the disease enabled the setting up of an effective system to be planned, at least partially. Mastering the 'scourge' was possible, but it was difficult in that it imposed two absolute conditions: diagnosis must be established very early, and treatment perfectly carried out. Screening too late, or incomplete destruction of the tumour, would condemn the patient irremediably to a certain death. Two main aims must therefore be at the basis of the policy in the fight against cancer: create the conditions to facilitate early diagnosis and provide the country with suitable equipment for treatment. Bergonié's text surveys this prospect by clearly situating it within the theme of the health rules for the fight against social diseases. 'Cancer has become after several years a fearful illness . . . which it is necessary to fight with *social organisations* similar to those for tuberculosis, syphilis and children's diseases which are the main examples.'[39] With reference to these examples, the 'notion of social organisation' related back to two complementary ideas. It emphasised, on the one hand, the need to create – in the image of the clinics and sanatoriums – structures specialised in the treatment and care of patients who, because of the peculiarities of the pathology by which they were affected, only found a very unsatisfactory place in ordinary establishments or departments – either because their co-existence with other patients created problems, or because these establishments or departments were not equipped to deal with them. It affirmed, on the other hand, the need to put in place – having taken notice of the social dimension of the illness – institutional cover throughout the nation, the setting up of which would involve the guiding hand of the state.

Considering what existed in reality in the field of anti-cancer structures, the project was obviously voluntarist. Apart from the few Paris centres, where the equipment was still very rudimentary, the departments opened during the war in Lyons and Montpellier, and the civil hospitals in Strasbourg equipped by the German administration with three deep radiotherapy machines (because of which they became the best equipped in the country), the network imagined by Bergonié had to be built from nothing. In addition, Bergonié did not neglect to go along with the daily (not unfounded) rhetoric about France's delay as compared with the United States, England and particularly Germany, where there were 'victors' laboratories' while France had only 'laboratories for the defeated'. Proposing to reverse this course of development, his programme had one overriding ambition: that of setting up a regional organisation to fight cancer 'which will be the first in the civilised world, here in France'[40] and in the first part of his report his concern was to try to demonstrate its advantages.

The social benefits of the 'healing factories'

> So that a centre for the fight against cancer may produce results and have a return which is not too small compared with costs which – let us say immediately – will be, in the present circumstances, considerable, there must be: patients, instruments and experienced staff who will benefit from this agreement.[41]

The financial cost of the programme was one of the major problems which could affect the project. Bergonié, in his report, echoed the declaration made on 4 April 1922 by Robert Le Bret to the League campaigners:

> The fight against cancer is both social and political. It is also costly. . . . Costly, because large financial means are needed to create modern methods requiring more and more expensive apparatus, to maintain laboratories with the necessary animals and to pay staff.[42]

In fact, in spite of its still rudimentary nature, the amount of necessary equipment required investment from the start and the maintenance costs would be much heavier than those that the caring institutions had previously been used to. Before the war, the director of the *Assistance Publique* had been making financial efforts, which were considerable in his opinion, to equip hospitals with radiology material.[43] But with the therapeutic applications of radiation physics, the problem now changed. The treatment of cancer provided the conditions for the beginnings of a new age, that of high technology medicine, and of 'big medicine'. Several elements combined to make the future cancer centre the most costly structure in the hospital. First, the deep radiotherapy equipment, which the Gaiffe company had just put on the market for 100,000 francs but which could produce 200,000 volts (or four to five times more than the equipment which, for example, C. Regaud used in his laboratory in Lyons).

Then radium, which was still the most expensive product in existence in the world, even though its production had increased and been remarkably simplified (with the discovery, in the United States, of deposits of carnotite, a radioactive material much richer than pitchblende). During the war, American industry, being capable of manufacturing radium, imposed artificially low prices, causing the cost of the product to fall to 200,000 francs a gram, so stifling French production. Once they had reached a monopoly position, the Americans raised the price to its previous level. The discovery in 1920 in the Belgian Congo of a new source of radioactive material pushed prices down temporarily, as the main area of production became once more Europe (the Belgian factory of Oolen). But this factory, set up with American capital, had an understanding with industrialists on the other side of the Atlantic. When Bergonié issued his report for the Cancer Commission, a gram of radium was once again being traded at between 1 and 1.5 million francs and was to be kept at this level during the whole inter-war period.[44]

'Under the present market conditions for radiotherapy equipment and the price per milligram of radium-element, the first purchase of equipment and the supply of radium for the centre to be created cannot be expected to cost less than 400,000 francs.'[45] Even this figure only took into account the minimum ambition of allocating to each centre two radiotherapy apparatuses and 200 mg of radium. 'It would be advisable,' suggested Bergonié 'if the basic equipment was to become fairly rapidly three apparatuses and 500 mg of radium'.

To these costs were added those relating to the fitting out of the premises. 'The healing factory which is the centre for the fight against cancer should be able to comfortably afford its installations, as limited premises lack security'.[46] It needed to have at least one radiotherapy room, one for the use of radium, to which was annexed a smaller room for the deep applications of needles and tubes containing radium, a site for surgery, consultation and waiting rooms, a laboratory for calibrating the equipment and a repair shop. The annual operating budget was evaluated at 200,000 francs, an amount which was particularly high for the period, as it was necessary to provide for the frequent renewal of a fragile material 'the price of which goes up each month'.

The figures – which today would make us smile – shocked the commission members, as they were not accustomed to including in their view of the hospital world any idea of investment in material. We only have to consider the fact that a few years earlier Belot had thought that the cost of test discs for the calibration of the Holzknecht chromoradiometer was high, because they were 2.50 francs each.[47] So Bergonié felt he had to argue very seriously that the operation was profitable, all the more so since it was not directly financed. In fact, given the relationships which governed the division of the patients between the public hospital and the private sector, the cancer centres could only take non-paying patients. The spokesman, anxious to make allowances for the reactions of private doctors, did not hesitate to reaffirm it:

> You won't be short of patients. I mean patients from the impoverished classes: all are poor and unfortunates, whether or not they are registered for free medical assistance, as the others, the fortunate ones, can always go to a specialist of their choice, and it is not for them – let us be clear on that – that we wish to create public laboratories for the fight against cancer, since they have private laboratories at their disposal just as well but not better equipped.[48]

However, even under these conditions, the costs for the construction of the cancer centres were not a useless investment, because they could prevent financial loss and still have a social value.

> Of course, we surgeons and specialists, all have our poor. We will always have the ashamed poor with us, which we always wish to have; but there are the others, the ones who do not approach us that must be considered. They are legion, we can see this when an outpatients department is opened where they know they can get help. Cancer sufferers whom we see in those outpatients departments . . . are normally full of life. *They sometimes have considerable relative social value:* they are fathers or mothers of a family, able workers, still robust farmers, women some way past the menopause, etc. Clearly, this social value is often even greater when they are cancer sufferers from the moneyed classes, but, whether they are one or the other, we may say that a cancer patient at the beginning of the disease or even for a fairly long period afterwards, *precisely the period during which he may be cured by present methods, is not a social waste, far from it. And if we save him, it is not an unproductive asset that is recovered for society. In a word, from a social point of view, the fight against cancer may pay* [my emphasis].[49]

Within the normal range of the arguments put forward to justify the operations funded by collective welfare measures, the themes are new in that they make explicit reference to the effectiveness of treatments. It is not a question of 'children in danger', where we must take measures to prevent the production of future delinquents,[50] nor as with tuberculosis or syphilis sufferers is it a question of introducing measures to control contamination. Here it is a question of the potential healing qualities of medical practice which are put forward as a factor concerning social profitability. To preserve for society values which it could lose. Bergonié knew that here he was dealing with a subject which had every chance of being understood. The country was just coming out of a war in which, including deaths and disabled, it had lost two million men from the working population, and the subject of 'depopulation' was at the centre of the concerns of the ruling classes.[51]

This line of reasoning had several implications which expressed without any euphemism 'the image of the healing factory':

> The cancer centre must not become a hospital for incurables. Every patient for whom the present treatment is recognised as ineffective must therefore be removed from the centre to *ad hoc* establishments (Calvaire, Saint-Michel Hospital . . .), so as not to take up the place of a curable or improvable cancer sufferer. In addition, most patients will be capable of walking and the centre will function actively as a clinic. The patients examined and treated will be sent back to their families to be recalled later after a fixed period. . . . Fifteen to twenty beds will be sufficient for hospital cases.[52]

The outline of the social structure for the fight against cancer was taking place. The centres were crucial: the healing function was more important than the rest, the patients only stayed there for the time necessary for operations and supervision of the immediate outcome. There was no question that they should convalesce there, beds were to be freed as quickly as possible, the factory must be productive. Upstream was the publicity work, supported by the Anti-Cancer League, to whom fell the difficult task of influencing the public and the town doctors and educating both to recognise the early symptoms of the illness (this problem, also crucial for the efficient progress of the project, was the subject of a second report entrusted to Regaud). Downstream, finally, were the charitable institutions which were to receive the 'social rejects', those whose advanced illness could no longer be treated, and which were to care for them until their death while bringing them consolation and comfort.

But the requirement for profitability, which gave coherence to the social, technical and institutional division suggested by Bergonié still involved something else. In order to be completely effective, the cancer centre had to be able to count on the presence of competent specialists mastering new techniques. 'Let us see the men who will manage it: that is the most important thing. . . . If there is no-one to apply the treatment judiciously or with the minimum of technical errors, nothing will work. Even worse, instead of benefits, this healing factory will only produce disasters.'[53] The relative dearth of surgeons experienced in the difficulties of cancer removal, and, even more, the few doctors able to practise radiotherapy correctly, had a particular influence on the development plan of the centres. The division of the national territory had to be made according to demographic and geographical criteria alone, since 'with a few fortunate and too rare exceptions, it is in the universities, within the regional faculties that there is the greatest chance of finding these invaluable abilities.'[54] Hence the first of the 'principles' held by the Commission, included under the heading 'headquarters' (of the centres): 'The large town in which the regional centre for the fight against cancer will be organised must be the headquarters of a faculty or a school of medicine.'[55] This was further justified by three arguments. As long as the centre recruited its staff from the faculty it was not necessary for a new post to be created (which would reduce by as much the costs of regular operation). Situated in a faculty, the centre contributed to the training of students, the instruction of future doctors and so, in time, to the improvement of conditions leading to an early diagnosis. Finally, its integration into a university meant it would also be a research centre, and would in this way make 'its contribution to the deepest and clearest knowledge of the aetiology, nature and development of cancer'.[56]

A fourth requirement was added to these three, relating to the question of premises (second principle):

> We can and must find, in the physical medicine laboratories, in the attached premises of clinical surgery, or in all the other premises belonging to the School or to the faculty, or even in a hospice administration wishing to take part in the fight against cancer, a place to site the deep radiotherapy and radium therapy equipment, as well as annexes: waiting rooms, document examination rooms, hospital wards, etc.[57]

This would allow the centre to operate without having to await the construction of independent premises. This saving in time had as its consequence the avoidance of extra investment from the start in terms of 'walls'.

But, because of this fact, neither Bergonié nor the Commission could make headway in the preparation of the development plan. More precisely, they could make no proposals on either the number of centres which were to be created, except for saying that they would be 'very few', or on their sites. The counterpart of the savings made in the hiring of staff and the construction of *ad hoc* buildings was paid for by limiting the decisive choices which remained dependent in the first instance on the policy of the local authorities. In fact, the setting up of the centres was to imply as a prerequisite the commitment to the project of the faculties, or of the civil hospices, as well as local communities, towns and regions, in so far as the latter would have to agree to provide a large part of their annual operating budget.[58]

However, at that time, the uncertainty concerning the number of centres enabled the spokesman and the Commission to avoid having to fix in too tangible a fashion the budgetary requirements needed by the authorities. This same vagueness meant that it remained uncertain whether there was a possibility of setting up a network of centres sufficiently large for it to cover the 'needs' of the country. Selection and exclusion criteria regarding potential patients – the centres would only receive 'curable' poor – were enough to make the plan credible, even though no-one was in a position to know exactly what this would involve in terms of patient population.

Presented as a harmonious adjustment between what was necessary, what was technically possible to do (taking account of human resources) and what all the various constraints allowed one to do, Bergonié's programme did not meet any opposition. Taken over again by the Commission, it was adopted by the Parliament which, without reluctance, passed a law (30 June 1923) granting financial support from the Tote for the purchase of deep radiotherapy and radium therapy equipment. Two accompanying budgetary measures of 5 million (in 1924 and 1925) were more specifically destined for the purchase of radium.[59] The consensus surrounding the initial policy for the fight against cancer was that, by satisfying the interests of some, it should not directly alienate anyone. The Anti-Cancer League could only applaud the start up of certain measures which meant a great deal to it. In addition, its role was recognised both by a 1923 decree giving its local committees charity status and legal personality, by which they could serve as tutors in training centres and receive grants and financial aid for them,[60] and by the place it was granted by the publicity organised for the population and the 'education' of non-specialist doctors. Radiotherapists saw interest in their clinical tools become official – it was largely due to this that the centres were created. They also took advantage of restrictive clauses for the setting up of the centres which they perceived as guarantees that their speciality, in gestation, would not be harmed by 'barbarian' practices. The clinical hospital and university elite were entirely involved and its legitimation was not at any time doubted. The authorities, principally engaged in the organisation of the fight against tuberculosis and syphilis could, at a relatively small cost, be prevailed upon to make an original intervention and so improve the status of a health policy often censured, inside the country and abroad, as archaic and improvident. Finally, 'the fight against cancer', although opening up a new field of medical practices, began to mould itself into the system, respected the privileges of the private sector as regards paying patients and seemed less threatening to them because it was not so ambitious concerning organisational structures.

Receiving a unanimous vote, thanks to the limits which it imposed on itself, the project was concerned that the ambitions of the new policy should take into account the realities of potentially contradictory interests. This wish to neutralise sources of conflict was also found in the definition of principles aimed at the different specialists involved in the centres and in the hierarchical structure of their relationships.

> All disciplines should collaborate to achieve the direction for the treatment of each patient which will be the most effective, given our present knowledge. The disciplines will be as follows:
> 1. a pathological anatomist will decide by preliminary examination the nature of the cancer to be treated;
> 2. a surgeon will be responsible for healing or palliative operations which are necessary;

3. an electrical doctor who is very familiar with deep radiotherapy and curietherapy will direct these applications;

4. a physicist may contribute, continuously or from time to time, his advice on the operation of the instruments for treatment and measuring.

The Management of the centre for the fight against cancer will belong to one of these disciplines, without this being able to lessen in any way the importance of the advice of the collaborators consulted in difficult cases [my emphasis].[61]

Of the three kinds of pre-existing centres (Curie Foundation, *Assistance Publique*, Paul-Brousse Hospice), the text kept the idea that the complementary nature of the disciplines was necessary. On the other hand, by not appointing anyone in principle to the director's discipline, it did not favour anyone, preferring a genuine diversity. On taking a close look, the decision was, however, bolder than it seemed. On the one hand, the Commission made the existence of a completely original hospital structure official, since it instituted the idea of organic co-operation between specialists. The cancer centre had no equivalent in the hospital world where each department dealt with a single type of 'discipline' and tended to constitute a care unit which was very independent in relation to what was around it. On the other hand, the equivalence accorded to the radiotherapist and the pathological anatomist in the eyes of the surgeon put fundamental researchers and clinicians on an equal footing. These were rather 'subversive' ideas if we consider what had been up to then the dominant hospital–academic ideology. There was now an ideology which referred itself to the recent past, to war medicine. As Regaud explained to the meeting of the campaigners:

> There cannot henceforth be a serious organisation of cancer therapy without a concentration of resources and without co-ordination of disciplines. *Like war surgery used to be, cancer treatment is a matter of team therapy.* The number of staff put to work in such a case condemns the individualism which is dear to our habits. In order to correctly treat a cancer, whatever it may be, even if operable by classical surgery, from now on several people must take part, a histopathologist . . . a surgeon . . . a radium therapist and a radiotherapist . . . a bacteriologist. . . . In this team, there must be a chief with authority, who is familiar with the various methods of treatment, but who does not allow his opinion to be bound by habits of a different technique [my emphasis].[62]

The time was surely right for adopting such principles – in so far as they were applied to a sector which was still undeveloped, since the experience of war surgery was still recent. What was more – and this is not negligible – a certain renewal took place within the elite with the arrival of 'young' heads of departments or clinical surgery professors directly involved in army medicine, the ones who, like Antonin Gosset and Robert Proust, were to be found at the head of the Paris cancer centres.

This constituent nonconformity of the centres was to have long-term consequences on the development of cancerology in hospitals. The putting into practice of the principle of equivalence was more and more to come up against the powerful return of that logic that underlay the implicit hierarchy of those disciplines at the heart of the hospital–academic system. The fact that it is called into question for the benefit of the primacy of clinical surgery was to become one of the main points of conflict in the development of the policy of the fight against cancer.

6 The policy for the fight against cancer

First contradictions, first reorganisations

General mobilisation

> Official activity was such that no-one asked themselves whether there was still a place for the League and if, after having started the crusade, it should not hand over to others the torch which was now aflame. As far as I am concerned, I have the opposite opinion. For a work as colossal as the fight against cancer, all the forces of society would not be too great to attain serious results.[1]
>
> (Report by Robert Le Bret
> to the general meeting
> of the Anti-Cancer League on 8 May 1923)

> It goes without saying that the role of associations such as your own should not be minimised because a parallel effort is going on in the hospital world for the treatment of operable and curable patients.[2]
>
> (Speech by M. Paul Strauss
> to the general meeting
> of the Anti-Cancer League on 8 May 1923)

The 'publicity' section of the Ladies' Central Committee went to work and increased their efforts to make the public at large sensitive to the issue of cancer whilst making the association famous and raising some funds.

> At the beginning of June 1921, Mme de Rothschild gave the League the first profits, at the Renaissance theatre, from a pretty play by Félix Gandera. Again at her own expense, that year, on 25 February, she organised a collection in theatres, hotel-restaurants and cinemas. From the Ritz headquarters, a bevy of elegant ladies and charming girls came forth, on behalf of the most horrible of scourges, to solicit their donation for our League from the inexhaustible charity of the Paris public. A good income was the happy outcome of this beneficent initiative. On 25 March, Mme. Laurence Bennet informed us of the

gracious offer of the manager of Romano's to hold a tea-concert, with Fyscher and some of the best players in Paris attending. This party was also a great success. How can we thank all those who supported our work? The very word 'cancer' has had the magic power to open all doors, attract all membership applications and unite all support.[3]

The total profit thanks to these cultural events (18,000 francs from the gala at the Renaissance theatre, 60,000 francs from the collection at the tea-concert), together with miscellaneous donations (22,000 francs in 1920, 74,000 francs in 1921, 57,000 francs in 1922), allowed a few advertisements (small posters, blotters) to be financed, the purchase of a few milligrams of radium and support for several research projects.[4] The main beneficiaries of this were Regaud, Dr Peyron for his embryology work on tumours, and Bothelo, who tried to perfect a method of serum diagnosis of cancer.[5]

At the same time, Mme Hartmann co-ordinated the enthusiasm of the Visiting Ladies. Forty members were divided into two groups, some visiting patients in hospitals, others monitoring them at home. The support committee was able to attend the Hôtel Dieu, Lariboisière, Beaujon, Broca, Cochin, La Salpêtrière, Tenon and Necker hospitals, the Curie Foundation and the Paul Brousse Cancer Centre.[6] The 'Ladies' attended consultations and prepared individual cards which mentioned the 'site of the disease' and dates of operations, as well as 'all social and family details which appear to be of interest from the point of view of the spread or prevention of the disease'.[7] In addition, they made efforts to monitor and place with private charities all those incurables who did not 'require' hospitalisation. Finally, in each district, a campaigner was responsible for liaison with other charitable institutions grouped together within the '*Union des oeuvres*' [Charities Union].

The role of supervising future regional cancer centres devolved upon the League by the authorities stimulated the creation of provincial committees. The Association in Lyons for the fight against cancer had preceded the movement by being formed on the day after a conference held by the Paris headquarters in the great amphitheatre of the faculty of medicine, in January 1922. The town from which Regaud and Justin Godart originated, the cradle of the Oeuvre du Calvaire, which the war had endowed with one of the three cancer charities, was favourable to initiating the policy of setting up regional institutions. Supported by a committee of honour bringing together several important personalities from the town (Edouard Herriot, his deputy mayor, the president of the Chamber of Commerce, the prefect, the rector of the academy, the president of the civil Hospices, the military governor-general, the British consul, a deputy and a senator), the board of management on which illustrious representatives of Lyons' high society such as Francis Sabran sat was run by an office which counted amongst its members Jean Lépine and Professor Léon Bérard, the surgeon director of the soldiers' cancer centre.[8] It had only just been set up, when the Lyons association made a grant to the hospital, the two 'Calvaires' for the townsmen and women,[9] and for 170,000 francs bought radium which it made available to Bérard's clinic at the General Hospital.[10]

This example was soon followed by the inhabitants of Dijon, with the establishment, on 15 December 1922, of a Burgundy Cancer League. In 1923 it was the turn of Alpes-Maritimes, Loir-et-Cher and the départements in the West to welcome the provincial committees, followed in the next year by Algeria, the Bordeaux and Toulouse regions, Gard and Maine-et-Loire, the spate of openings coming to an end between 1925 and 1928 with the committees of Hérault, Ardennes, Loiret and Seine-Inférieure. These structures did not all attempt to have the same type of influence: eleven were départements, four – the Leagues of the West, Burgundy, Bordeaux and Toulouse – were regional. Sitting in Rennes, the committee in the West had correspondents at Mayenne, in Manche, Côtes-du-Nord, Finistère, Sarthe and Morbihan.[11] The Toulouse League extended at first over Ariège, Aveyron, Gers, Haute-Garonne, Tarn and Tarn-et-Garonne, and then was to attempt to cover fourteen neighbouring départements; local committees which had a certain financial independence were set up at Mazamet, Castres, Albi, Montauban and Tarbes.[12] Installed in a smaller geographical area, the Burgundy League operated with representatives in Beaune, Montbard, Semur and Chatillon:[13] the South-Western League remained centralised in Bordeaux and in practice was only involved at first in the affairs of Gironde.[14]

The articles of the League – stipulating that local committees were not legal entities and therefore could not on their own account receive gifts legally – appeared poorly suited to the new situation. In order to avoid tension with the provincial structures which were starting up and which claimed the right to manage their own funds in order to benefit specifically the potential cancer centre of their own region, the Paris managers accepted the idea of a new formula. Those associations for the fight against cancer which wished to, could establish themselves on an independent basis, and ask the authorities for recognition as being of public benefit (and so acquire a legal personality) and keep close links with the League by a procedure of affiliation. By renouncing direct control over local groups, the League managers wanted principally to avoid the break-up of the movement into potentially competing associations. Robert Le Bret affirmed:

> We have only one wish', that is. to see the birth of groups for welfare publicity, support, therapeutic organisation and scientific research, inspired by the ideas which we have put into practice. . . . We have never thought to divert any part of their local resources in order to employ them for our own benefit. We only think that it is necessary to have an organising body, centrally placed where we are . . . ensuring essential communication. . . . We have decided, in order to create a stable group, to publish a periodical bulletin where each one will be

included. We accept with the same philanthropic spirit the formation of a committee of the League or an association affiliated to the League.[15]

But this greater flexibility in operation, brought about by giving less power to the central board of management (i.e. Paris) over the decisions and actions of the provincial structures, was not going to prove without consequences for the future.

Development plan and local dynamics: controversy on a question of numbers

Taking up on his own account the recommendations of the Cancer Commission, Paul Strauss set in motion the prefectorial apparatus by means of a circular dated 15 November 1922. Cancer, he in effect wrote, has today become a scourge to be feared as greatly as tuberculosis. It can be combated thanks to early diagnosis and appropriate therapeutic methods, methods which must be used together under the direction of competent people in regional cancer centres. These centres may be created in towns where there are faculties or schools of medicine. They will treat the needy people of the département, and also those of neighbouring départements, on the condition that the latter ask for their incorporation into the centre and contribute to its finance. It was therefore the prefects' responsibility to assist the minister in this organisation and to take every initiative with the various university and hospital institutions to accelerate the process.[16] Paul Strauss was questioned in the Chamber by a deputy who criticised the circular for its imprecise conditions regarding the incorporation of the neighbouring départements, '[it being understood] that the expenses can only rarely be met by a single département, and that if a département is deprived by a neighbouring one of the financial support which it could expect, there is every reason to believe that it will abstain'.[17] These fears were without foundation, but the proposals to the minister were so numerous that it made certain people anxious. In an article written in 1923 where he set out the 'guidelines for the fight against cancer', Claudius Regaud, while congratulating himself on the interest aroused by the cancer centres, had some reservations concerning the somewhat disordered zeal for the operation.

> It's going well! Let's however be careful not to overstep the mark! We would overstep the mark if organisation and effort were fragmented. The treatment of cancer is difficult, its new methods require competent laboratory workers and doctors, very costly materials and provide little income. Now it seems to me that I can see departmental centres growing, in the wake of the regional centres, and I am afraid that they will soon appear in the sub-prefectures, favoured by generosity which only wishes to benefit its own locality.[18]

Between 1923 and 1924, ten centres were created by ministerial decree in the towns of Bordeaux, Lyons, Montpellier, Strasbourg, Lille, Rennes, Nantes, Rheims, Caen and Toulouse, adding to the structures already in existence in the Paris region. In their first meeting, the directors of the early centres echoed the fear expressed by Regaud, even suggesting that they should not go any further. 'There is no need to increase the number of centres for the moment, as this might produce inadequate treatments which would prejudice the sufferers'.[19] The League did not wish to encourage the creation of centres insufficiently equipped or lacking in adequate specialisations. The authorities of the League, of which Regaud and several centre directors were members, kept unreservedly to this vow. Robert Le Bret's reply was unambiguous on this point: 'Everything induces us to advise against more centres... [and] the League has never encouraged such an idea.'[20] But the secretary-general knew how to dissociate the two items. Although the number of centres was to stay limited, the League nevertheless had every interest in the increase of its local subsidiaries, as

> it has a role to fulfil which is very different to the foundation of centres. Its mission is to educate the public, to make it aware of the need for early diagnosis. . . . Its duty is still to organise support, to help the unfortunate to receive care, to have incurables taken into hospital. . . . It is very clear that [such] a programme can only be accomplished by an increase of committees and subsidiaries which, through local and independent action, will have the maximum power possible to act in the interest of sufferers.[21]

Now, there was the problem, for even if the association's board of management shared the point of view of the centre directors, the position of the local subsidiaries was often less definite, if not openly divergent. The dissociation operated by the Paris managers between the question of the treatment structures and the role of publicity, education and support devolved to the committees was perceived by the campaigners in the field as a contradiction. In fact, in so far as the 'call for tenders' procedure chosen by the ministry left open to discussion the choice of places for setting up future regional centres, the local associations for the fight against cancer were all, or almost all, inclined to support the candidacy of the medical institutions of their own town. Where the choice was favourable to them, as in Lyons, Toulouse, Bordeaux or Montpellier, the idea of a strict *numerus clausus* was not a problem; on the contrary, it was strongly challenged. The relative independence enjoyed by the associated subsidiaries of the League left sufficient freedom of manoeuvre for them to put pressure on the authorities by the *fait accompli* method. In several areas, the local associations increased initiatives to equip the hospital with radium and with radiotherapy equipment. The Alpes-Maritimes League set up a subscription which allowed the planning of an electrosurgical department at the Saint-Roch hospital.[22] The Burgundian League managed to procure 100 mg of radium from the surgical clinic of the Civil Hospices in Dijon and contacted the Côte-d'Or council to give financial aid to the cancer department which was set up there.[23] In Nîmes, the Gard committee was created specifically to support the efforts of the administrative commission of the hospitals, which was trying to establish a 'radiosurgical department for cancer treatment of poor sufferers'.[24] The process was the same in Orleans[25] and Montargis,[26] the département of Loiret almost caricaturing the dynamics of the establishment of 'departmental, that is sub-prefectural, centres'. The power of this 'campaigning spirit' was evident even in the regional leagues who were, however, able to take up the cause of an official cancer centre. Although the 'sub-committees' of Albi and Montauban played the Toulouse regional game by gathering funds for the Toulouse centre and occupying themselves in directing sufferers and assisting incurables,[27] the sub-committees of Tarbes and Rodez, on the other hand, dedicated the essential part of the action towards the hospital of their town so that a cancer service could be set up there.[28]

This trend to increase the number of centres can be explained. The decentralisation of the hospital sector and the municipalisation of its management left a large proportion of the action to local arrangements, and in addition they caused care institutions to become an important issue in city life. From now on, wherever the 'fight against cancer' gave rise to interest, the creation of a treatment centre tended to become the priority which motivated campaigners' enthusiasm. Inclined to favour the development of groups over the whole of the territory in order to respond to its publicity and educational aims, the board of management of the League was relatively unable to block the initiatives which were part of a policy of local political issues, and saw itself forced to let things happen. In addition, this phenomenon also occurred in certain towns, independently of the existence of a committee for the fight against cancer. In Limoges, it was the département council which proposed to finance the equipping of a surgery.[29] In Besançon, it was the hospital surgeon who purchased a few grams of radium out of his own pocket, 'lent' them to his department and, supported by the département health inspector, asked for its recognition as a cancer centre.[30] In Rouen, the initiative was taken by the board of the medical school professors,[31] who were later imitated by their colleagues in Le Havre.[32]

The balance sheet which could be drawn up of the situation for the year 1925 was eloquent. Apart from the ten officially approved centres, the ministry had to deal with fifteen or so demands which, for the most part, could take advantage of fulfilling the conditions of being located in a town having a faculty or school of medicine. For applicants, the moment could appear favourable for the satisfaction of their requests since from June 1924, with the victory of the Coalition of the Left, the new minister in charge of health affairs was none other than the president of the League,

Justin Godart. But illusions were soon dispelled, Godart entrusted Regaud with the task of taking stock of the construction of the cancer centres. His report, presented to the Cancer Commission on 4 April 1925, was a judgement without appeal: 'We must not create in Continental France' [Regaud was expecting a centre to be set up in Algiers] 'other centres than those which already exist.' Regaud explained that it was not a question of preventing doctors or communities from organising special cancer departments (a prohibition which in any case would have no legal value); 'the unfavourable opinion which I am expressing only concerns the centres which the state would wish to establish under its authority, with its financial support and, consequently, under its responsibility'.[33]

Deprived of the authority to supervise the increase of cancer departments, Regaud suggested making a clear differentiation between the structures which belonged to the state and others, a differentiation in his eyes all the more necessary as certain prefects, who had misinterpreted the directives which had been given to them, had supported by decree the creation as departmental (not regional) centres several of these services, mainly at Orleans and at Besançon. The adoption of Regaud's report by the Commission marked a serious halt to the process of state recognition. Only three new 'regional centres' were to be set up, in Angers (1925), Nancy (1927) and finally in Algiers (1928) and it would be necessary to await the end of the 1950s, for those at Limoges, Nice and Dijon to be recognised, but in a completely different context.

The pressure applied on the Chamber of Deputies by certain elected representatives did not result in changing the decision. However, the arguments put forward were appropriate with regard to initial ambitions. In considering the setting up of official centres, France was far from the idea of a structural network to fulfil the needs of the country. The inconsistencies were clear, the imbalance between the regions was obvious. Emile Vincent did well to bring before Parliament the apparent arbitrary nature of their choices and the injustices which resulted from this:

> You will note that the central plateau region, the East and South East regions are the least favoured. The inhabitants of the regions of Limoges, Tours and Poitiers have to go to Paris, Lyons or Bordeaux . . . I do not understand how the centres were organised in the beginning. There were some at Angers, Nantes and Rennes. They are grouped around the same area, while whole regions are deprived of them. This is what my protest is about. In the end it will be necessary to create the centres I am mentioning.[34]

In the conclusion of his report, Regaud, anticipating criticism, held that he would consider it preferable to pay for the transport of poor cancer sufferers from their homes to the centre, even if they were two or three hundred kilometres away, than to set up specialised structures in all regions. If they were too numerous, the latter would be 'condemned to be powerless or to operating in a barely satisfactory manner'.[35]

The solution which he recommended was slightly unrealistic, which in his case was quite unusual. Many obstacles hindered the transport of patients. On the one hand, the geographical distance considerably reduced the attraction of a centre, if only because doctors in the adjacent areas did not know they existed. Professor Marquis, the director of the Rennes cancer centre, was to explain, in a 1937 report, that ten years would be necessary before the recruitment of patients would improve, 'thanks to the installation in the départements in the West of young general practitioners, who had graduated from the Rennes school and had benefited during their training from teaching at the cancer centre'.[36] On the other hand, district councils very often frowned on financing travel and accommodation costs for their poor, but conversely, pressures were exerted so that the poor originating from a département where a centre was located might benefit by being considered a priority for hospitalisation.[38] It is not surprising that in such a context, the regional centres suffered to a large extent from competition from the 'unofficial' local structures, which succeeded in attracting patients from the département, aided in this by the League committees where they were situated. A statistic established for the year 1928 shows the weakness in the total activity of the regional centres, including the Paris region: hardly 10,000 consultants, less than 4,800 hospitalised patients . . . and only five centres (the Curie Foundation, Bordeaux, Strasbourg, Nantes and Nancy) shared 70 per cent of the population needing care.[39] 'Departmental' centres, such as those in Besançon, Tarbes, Nîmes or Dijon, were sometimes equal or superior in recruiting patients for the cancer centres in Rheims, Rennes, Montpellier, Angers and Marseilles.[40]

However, the neither foreseeable consequences of the *numerus clausus*, nor the knowledge of these statistics, which showed the gap between the number of patients treated and the incidence of the illness (mortality from cancer was estimated at 40,000 cases annually and its morbidity at more than double),[41] were taken into account. Everything happened as if these inadequacies were only of a secondary importance: in fact, Regaud's report in 1925 was not only a negative reply to the question of increasing the number of the centres, it also redefined the strategy of the whole fight against cancer and the place of these centres in that policy.

The necessary review

One can firstly ask oneself whether the number of sufferers legitimises the organisation of new public treatment centres. It seems not. *What was the purpose of these centres?* It is mainly the administration of special treatment procedures: roentgentherapy and curietherapy. Surgery does not require the centralisation of resources and patients to the same degree. How can the number of patients be estimated who have been able to or who could have been able to benefit from roentgentherapy or curietherapy, amongst the 30,000 to 40,000 who die each year in France of cancer? A precise answer is not possible; but I estimate this number at half at the most, or perhaps only a third of the total, perhaps even less. Because, very nearly, all types, all locations, all degrees of extension and all particular cases of cancer are not suitable for treatment by X-rays or by radium. Among the number of cases which are treatable, how many of the poor are there who are patients of the existing or possible centres? Perhaps half. The great number of persons suffering from cancer is not therefore a reason to increase the specialist treatment centres, because these treatments are applicable to only a relatively small number of people [my emphasis].[42]

The relative offhandedness which Regaud showed in juggling with these statistics can only convince those who are already convinced. That is to say those who were ready to accept the revision of the criteria which he put forward for the selection of the patients. At the same time as making his ideas appear obvious, the director of the Curie Foundation's suggestion was no more nor less than to renounce the initial idea of making cancer centres the place of treatment for poor curable cancer sufferers and to replace it with something else. By putting forward the *raison d'être* of the centres as being the application of roentgentherapy and curietherapy, he revised the Commission's initial project on two major points. In the first place, he suggested that the specialised network should be considered a simple care system, and no longer the institutional basis for the fight against cancer. The centres were only an important and necessary supplement to surgery which continued to deal with patients excluded from X-ray or radium treatment. His report was aimed at explaining the organisational peculiarities of the fight against cancer, too hastily assimilated to pre-existing models. For tuberculosis, syphilis and children's illnesses, the large number of local facilities was necessary, since continuous supervising of patients was a condition of their effectiveness. Nothing of the kind was necessary for cancer, the prevention of which – given present knowledge – was without basis, and if frequent monitoring of patients was necessary, the town doctors were enough. The improvement of early diagnosis – a crucial point – did not depend on increasing the number of centres, as suitable structures already existed (these were the general and specialised surgeries); it depended on better training for doctors in noticing symptoms of cancer.[43]

The second point made was the redefining of the purpose of the centres around more modest aims, which was linked to a change of outlook modifying the role of radiotherapy and the other disciplines within the centres. Regaud remained loyal to the principle of multidisciplinary teams, but he assigned a privileged position to treatment by radiation: it was in accordance with the particular requirements of its function that it was necessary to think about and foresee the growth of a specialised network.

His resolute opposition to any increase in the number of centres therefore signified that he saw there a threat to the future of radiotherapy, at least in the way he envisaged it. The danger was even sufficiently real in his eyes for him to actually regret, if we read between the lines, the policy undertaken. The measures which he advised would only, according to him, be the lesser evil, a method of 'damage limitation'.

> Were we wrong to create cancer centres? Certainly not! . . . I only think that we have created too large a number and that they have increased too fast. We have thought to make common practice, easily producing constant results, of something to be kept, for a time, to a small number of large well-equipped centres devoted to both scientific research and to practical application. The concern to tell what I believe is the truth obliges me to say that that was a gross error – an excusable error, because it was well intentioned and noble.[44]

Why did the reservations expressed in 1923 give way, two years later, to deep unease? How did the policy undertaken risk putting into question once more 'scientific cancer medicine', of which the Curie Foundation wished to be the model?

To answer these questions it is necessary to go back a little, and abandon for a short while the line of argument developed in Regaud's report in order to be able to return to it and clarify its obscure areas.

Learned disputes, professional interests and political challenges

The 1923 text quoted above, 'The guidelines for the fight against cancer', was written by Regaud in the midst of a dispute which he was having with Professor Jean-Louis Faure. Started several years before, but confined to the world of learned societies, the controversy began again, brought to public notice by the gynaecologist of the Broca clinic at the general meeting of the League that same year. By putting forward his point of view on the 'surgical treatment of cancer', Faure knew that he would dissipate the illusion with which his listeners deluded themselves: faced with cancer treatments, there was no consensus of opinion, the medical elite was divided between opposing trends.

> We have witnessed and we witness each day, in the fight against cancer, such prodigious events, we have seen such strange things, which in days gone by we would have believed to be miracles, if we were amongst those who still believe in miracles, that it might seem rash, after everything that has been said about the almost supernatural virtues of the tube with marvellous emanations and the phial with the enchanted rays, to come here today, like an ancient knight in his old armour, to support the cause of bloody surgery, which finds, precisely

in the battle against cancer, both the highest expression of its power and the all too frequent cruellest of disappointments.[45]

Without abandoning this florid style which made him, at the Academy of Medicine, the most popular speaker at funerals, the surgeon developed a long *pro domo* plea with the

> deep conviction that the cause of surgery must be defended because the encouragement of new ideas and practices, especially when they are seen by the patient as being without the legitimate anguish which is part of every operation, goes too far and discourages from having surgery so many sufferers who would find in it a more certain cure, as they most often find only a temporary relief with radiation treatment and sometimes, alas! an aggravation of their ills.[46]

The charge is harsh and is directly aimed at the Curie Foundation team which recommended the privileged use of curietherapy in the treatment of cancers of the womb. The knight of the olden days did not wage a solitary battle, he became the champion of all those who were exasperated by Regaud's and his collaborators' wish to make the rules regarding the treatment of certain cancers instead and in place of the surgeons. The polemic started in 1920 during a session of the French Association for the Study of Cancer, concerning a presentation to the Radium Institute, 'On the technique of curietherapy in cancer of the cervix'.[47]

In this long memorandum, the authors developed a series of arguments leading to a conclusion which, without too many formal precautions, affirmed the superiority of treatment by radium:

> the surgeon who amputates the clearly invaded area or at least the area affected [by the cancer] cannot, however extensive his operation, be certain that the whole affected area has been dealt with. Radiotherapy tries to do and perhaps does do better: if it is true that, in an area of a certain diameter, it selectively destroys all the cancer cells growing among the healthy ones, the distance over which it is effective is often greater than that covered by possible surgical removal.[48]

Discussing in detail the curietherapy techniques available for use and their adjustment to the various forms taken by a developing cancer according to its location and extent, the article deals with several 'burning' issues:

1. We believe that curietherapy *used alone* is capable of curing the most advanced cases of cancer of the cervix.
2. When it is a question of treating inoperable cases or even those which are barely operable, . . . curietherapy is necessary, it is the only treatment (hysterectomy carried out before or after curietherapy only causes difficulties).

3.   When it is a question of clearly operable cases . . ., we can wait until curietherapy has proved its effectiveness and harmlessness. Concerning its effectiveness, let us have no more doubts. Who can do the most achieves the least. The *local cures* which are constantly obtained cause us to discount the *total cures* . . . the cases most suitable for surgical removal are also the most suitable for curie-therapy. We cannot unfortunately be sure of its harmlessness for several years. . . . While we are waiting, the combination of curie-therapy and surgical removal – *in the same order in which we mention these two methods* – seems to be a very wise line of provisional conduct. In this association, we think that *the aim of surgical removal should only be to get rid of an organ which has become useless and which is suspected of a predisposition to cancer* [my emphasis].[49]

The relegation of surgery to the rank of a simple extra treatment made Professor Delbet react violently and he disputed Regaud's assertions, his personal experience adding weight to the argument. He himself had operated on women for breast cancers considered inoperable by others, and the results obtained by surgical removal, although incomplete, were beneficial to the patients, as if the 'organism fought more effectively against a smaller tumour than a larger tumour.'[50] On the contrary, he sometimes noted the harmful effects of curietherapy, just like his friend Jean-Louis Faure, whose information on the comparative effectiveness of surgical treatments alone and combining radium with surgery should lead the partisans of radiotherapy to be more circumspect. Tit for tat, Delbet suggested that radium, when it does not destroy all the cancer cells, could contribute to the acceleration of the neoplastic process. 'Having thoroughly reflected on the seriousness of my proposals, I say that if after radium therapy we frequently observed a compensation of neoplastic growth by the rapid development of a new neoplastic mass, I would be led to attribute it to the treatment'.[51]

Three years later, it was precisely about his negative experience of curie-therapy that Faure spoke to the people of the League who had come to listen to him.

I resolved, in 1910, to combine the two methods and to monitor the application of radium, the good results of which seemed to me to be absolutely certain, and which, I was convinced, would be the perfection of the operation. . . And when, at the end of ten years of this practice, I looked into what had become of my patients, I had the painful surprise of finding out that those who had been treated by radium had relapsed in the proportion of 50 per cent, while those whose only treatment had been the operation . . . had a 40 per cent relapse. . . Since 1920, when I discovered these very worrying facts, I have never again applied radium after operations, and I am not about to start again.[52]

The gynaecologist's attack pushed to its logical outcome the hypothesis sketched out by Delbet. For him, there was no doubt that radium could act as a stimulant to the neoplastic process.

> This paradox no longer exists, if we admit, *which seems to be proved by innumerable examples,* that radium, if it has a destructive effect on cancer cells, diminishes the intensity of its action inversely to the square of the distances, as in all natural forces, and in the end has, on the distant cells, instead of a destructive action, *an influence of excitement which might aggravate the cancer* [my emphasis].[53]

Regaud was well able to reply to these 'accusations': by disputing the relevance of Faure's statistics, arguing that radium treatment carried out before the war was technically obsolete and no longer of value, and opposing them with foreign statistics and the results obtained by the Radium Institute Team in 1919, 1920 and 1921 'with very inferior techniques to those used at present' he was obliged to place himself in a defensive position.[54] One did not have to be a genius to see that the learned controversy was clearly not limited to the technical level and that the mastery of the treatment technique was at stake, and led to the question concerning the direction of treatment. The existing points of view were irreconcilable; Faure claimed supremacy for surgery in the case of curable cancers and abandoned inoperable patients to curietherapy:

> Surgical treatment of cancer of the womb, which I have used here as an example, as it is the one with which I am most familiar – *but the same could be said of all the others* – . . . is therefore a certain, even common, fact. It is the usual treatment in hopeful cases when cancers are still only at the beginning. . . . When we find ourselves with such cases, we have *the duty* to operate *without* subjecting them to radium. . . . Radium must therefore at present be kept for inoperable cases, where it works miracles and gives a marvellous services. Or it could be used in doubtful cases, which it always improves, often enough to make the operation possible [my emphasis].[55]

For Regaud, this concept was erroneous and backward-looking. Yes, formerly, when faced with a cancer diagnosis, the alternative was simple. Was it operable or not? The surgeon was then naturally in a position to order treatment. But circumstances had changed a great deal.

> When faced with cancer, the first question is no longer: is it operable, but: is it better to operate, treat with radium, treat with X-rays, or combine these methods in a certain order? The surgeon no longer decides the treatment of cancer sufferers as the one who operates. He

will only be able to do so if he adds to his operating art the knowledge of other methods of treatment.[56]

Although many surgeons used radium, only a few, and this was very understandable, managed to follow the progress of the techniques of curietherapy and roentgentherapy, as they were too rapid and too insufficiently publicised. The masters of contemporary surgery had only seen the results of yesterday's radiotherapy and young people still had a lot to do to assimilate the advances of the surgical art. 'Is it even to be desired that surgeons should add to their work the considerable task of the effective management of specialist services, where treatment by radiation is taking on a rapidly increasing importance?'[57]

Conscious of the potential conflicts in which the insurmountability of the two positions loomed large, Regaud had in addition other reasons to worry. The scientific cancer medicine which he practised was a discipline still in its infancy which cruelly lacked institutional support. In addition, eager to have the advances of their first work recognised, the Curie Foundation, partly through tactlessness, had alienated some of the precursors of radiotherapy instead of winning them over to their cause. A few papers and speeches in the debate at the French Association for the Study of Cancer were enough for Regaud to deeply shock several of his colleagues because of both the form and the basis of his suggestions. His criticism of doctors' routine therapeutic empiricism provoked this violent reaction from Degrais:

> When reading his work, it would really seem that the early radium therapists, in everything that they did, lacked medical sense as well as conscience. . . . I quote M. Regaud: 'Is radium not applied haphazardly, or as a rite the consequences of which are not favourable, without us knowing exactly why?' To act as M. Regaud says would conform very little with the sense of duty which animates the medical profession, and in addition would only explain with difficulty the result obtained after so many years.[58]

When the technique perfected by the Swedes of radium puncture by needles was imported, Curie's team evaluated the advantages of its use, relegating the previous use of tubes to the accessory stores, to the great displeasure of Degrais himself, who saw in this the mere expression of a new-fangled fad and the disrespectful rejection of a French 'tradition'.

> The desire to attach greater value to what comes from abroad than to what is French caused this event to blow up out of all proportion. . . . It would seem that our work should deserve more magnanimity from M. Regaud's school, a school which has not hesitated in greatly admiring

the work carried out abroad, although this was no more than a repetition of the work which began in France.[59]

Underlying the argument of ancient and modern, what was at stake was much more than the simple question of a recognition of affiliation. The animosity between Degrais and Regaud tallies with the main principles regarding curietherapy. For the former, the techniques of treatments which he contributed, together with Wickham, he evolved and systemised made up a stable state of knowledge and practices. For the latter, curietherapy was still in a phase of permanent revision, and the toing and froing between fundamental research on the biological action of radiation and the clinical applications to treatment was manifested by a frequent renewal of rapidly obsolete techniques. The practical consequences of these two points of view were of a crucial importance. If curietherapy techniques were stable, they could be assimilated, without too many problems, by a good number of doctors, as long as they had the rudiments of knowledge regarding the use of radiant products. On the other hand, if curietherapy was still at the experimental stage, only doctors engaged in the process of research were capable of practising it with the maximum benefit for sufferers.

Within the context of these different controversies, where he comes up against both surgeons and radiotherapists, we can understand Regaud's reservations more easily, faced as he was with the profusion of plans for the creation of cancer centres and also his worries in the face of localist dynamics which no-one seemed able to control. In fact, the increase in the number of centres tended to strengthen the influence of those surgeons (in the provinces) who were barely in touch with the advanced techniques of the radiation clinic. From he entire group of twenty-five provincial towns which, between 1922 and 1925, applied for a regional centre for the fight against cancer, sixteen supported a project based on a general surgery department in civil hospices. The phenomenon was not in itself astonishing, as the provinces were suffering, even more than Paris, from the shortage of radiotherapy equipment and training opportunities. Apart from Bergonié, his pupils and a few doctors who arrived in Paris to follow Béclère's teaching, individuals with even the slightest knowledge of radiation were non-existent. On the other hand, the country was not short of radiologists in search of outlets and ready to involve themselves in a field which was opening up to them, but of which they more or less had no knowledge. In fact, the demography of the speciality exploded during (and because of) the 1914–18 war. The 175 doctors, listed in 1916 as having carried out a supplementary training in electroradiology, proved insufficient to meet the needs of the armies, so the Val-de Grâce school accelerated the training of another 260 of them between July 1916 and October 1918.[60] Having returned to civil life, these 'neoradiologists' as they were called by Colonel Mignon, considerably swelled the ranks of the profession. Of course, radiology was developing, but mainly within the hospital framework,[61] as the increasing cost of the material was often an obstacle to its use in private practice. Inclusion as a radiotherapist in a cancer department could be a good launching pad to the establishment of a private practice for those who were convinced that the handling of radium did not pose major difficulties. Far removed from the concerns of the Curie Foundation, since they did not have as their aim the building of a discipline, that is, a basis for the scientific treatment of cancer, but rather more prosaically the search for a local position, these radiologists were hardly inclined to agree with those points of view held by Regaud. Hospital surgeons had no difficulty in including in the cancer centre's organisation plan a doctor, specifically retrained as a specialist in radiation treatment, and even more ready, because of this, to recognise the authority of the former to carry out treatment.

In itself detrimental in Regaud's eyes, the development of radiotherapy by practitioners not having the required competence became a phenomenon particularly alarming within the context of the times. In fact, between 1923 and 1925, the clinical research work carried out at the Curie Foundation was able to revolutionise curietherapy techniques, and current innovations allowed the prospect of transformations in depth, making a re-evaluation of state intervention necessary.

Radium puncture, without being totally abandoned, tended to become for certain locations such as the cervix only an extra treatment, supplementing the action of a new method, perfected and available from 1924 – distance curietherapy. In this technique, radium was no longer implanted into the tumour itself, but used in external irradiation carried out by 'bombs'. The intensity of the effect obtained varied directly according to the amount of the radiant product. They went rapidly from bombs containing 1 g (1924) to 3 g (1925) then 4 g (1926).[62] At the current price of radium, the cost of the equipment appeared out of proportion to the original forecasts of the Cancer Commission, which was based on the use of tubes or needles the content of which was of the order of one milligram. Therefore, the exceptional credit of 5 million, voted by Parliament in 1924, to assist the financing of radium centres, would hardly have sufficed for the manufacture of a single bomb. Further, the Curie Foundation was only able to invent this new method of treatment thanks to loans (5 g between 1923 and 1925) granted by the Haut-Katanga (Belgian Congo) Mines Company with the agreement of the Belgian government.[63] Regaud used this fact as an argument to invite the Commission to a global consideration of the cancer centres' future.

> When the first official centres were created, we wrongly believed that the problems of radiotherapy for cancer were nearer to a solution than they really were, and we greatly underestimated the difficulty of the task . . . The skills, the material means, the organisation which the cancer centres need are not matched by stability in our scientific

acquisitions . . . Three years ago, progress which appeared to be considerable had just been made in roentgentherapy instrumentation, and
curietherapy techniques led us to believe that *this progress had a
sufficiently definitive nature to allow several copies of the first department which
existed in Paris to be reproduced* . . . [Now] in X-ray and radioactive body
technology, there are great changes in the offing; they will lead to
greater effectiveness, they will not make treatment easier, but they will
make it more specialised; they will require enormous injections of
capital ... Will the State be able to keep up with the progress at all the
centres which it has created? Will we be able to put up with their being
some well equipped and other badly equipped centres? And what will
the main interested parties, the patients, say? I am just asking such
difficult questions . . . [my emphasis].[64]

In this way we clearly perceive how the actual number of centres was
crucial. Obtaining a strict *numerus clausus* allowed both a dangerous growth
to be halted and the future to be prepared. For want of being able to
concretely oppose the start of local anti-cancer structures and to prevent
heterogeneousness of practices regarding the treatment of cancers, Regaud
took the opportunity which Justin Godart gave him to suggest a global
redefinition for the organisation of the fight against cancer. While affirming
that radiotherapy was the *raison d'être* of the centres, he put forward the
idea of a division of territories. The regional centres would not have a
public monopoly over cancer, they would only be concerned with a minority
of patients, the majority returning to normal services (general and
specialised surgery departments). But, at that point, these centres would
have to be, as much as possible, placed under the direction of specialists
competent in radiation treatment. Now, by taking action to block the
process of state recognition, he created a situation which still allowed a
both satisfactory and strong relationship. In fact, amongst the centres
already labelled as 'regional' we find all those which were managed by a
radiotherapist (Bordeaux, Caen, Nantes, Rheims, Strasbourg and Toulouse),
and only five of the sixteen projects under the direction of a surgeon
(Lyons, Montpellier, Rennes, Marseilles and Lille). Aiming to preserve
'protected areas', Regaud's logic was hardly hindered by 'geographical
inconsistencies', especially as pressure from the surgeons became greater
and greater.[65]

By adopting the spokesman's conclusions, the Cancer Commission
instituted, in the proper meaning of the phrase, a distinction between
cancer practices which were under the responsibility of the state and those
which only involved the local authorities. The symbolic effects of this
distinction are considerable, since the weight of legitimacy which the
different structures could claim were not of the same order. In addition, the
Commission's decision created conditions for a concentration of state
financial resources around several care units, the consequences of which in

time, as Regaud anticipated, would prove very serious. Before dealing with these, I would like to close this chapter by trying to reply to a question which we have the right to ask: why did the Cancer Commission, where the members of the medico-surgical elite were largely in the majority, side with the opinion of the Curie Foundation manager? The absence of archived documents relating to the debates only allows hypotheses. The very composition of the Commission provided a suggestion for the reply. The 'provincials' were very few, less than twenty (out of eighty), and what is more, nearly all were in towns where a cancer centre had already been officially created.[66] Now, we have seen that the early directors of the regional centres were unanimous in asking, from 1923, that the number of centres should not be increased. Not all felt the same way as Regaud. (Professor L. Bérard, director of the centre in Lyons, was himself deeply convinced that the management of the centre should go to a surgeon.) On the other hand, they said that they shared the concern for not seeing the state dissipate its financial aid. The opinions which came from the provinces were therefore mostly in favour of the spokesman's position, and as the 'excluded' towns only had, all in all, two representatives present (including the deputy Emile Vincent who was to bring the controversy before the Chamber), they were to carry little weight in the debates. By this time avoiding conflict regarding the conduct of the treatment and by proposing a division of territories which comprised, for the surgeons who were already centre managers, a satisfactory compromise, Regaud finally encountered only limited opposition, and little of it in a position to make its point of view felt.

7 The rise of 'big medicine'

When Regaud was wondering about the state's capability of financing a coherent policy regarding the equipping of cancer centres, only a few people, at the time, like him, perceived the problem in all its dimensions. Anticipating the social and economic consequences of the distance curietherapy that his team was perfecting, he sensed the unexpected arrival of imbalances and pointed out the possibility of a risk which the promoters of the fight against cancer had not foreseen: that of seeing patients not able to benefit from equal opportunities for treatment depending on the centre to which they had access. The future confirmed the appropriateness of his forecast. On the eve of the Second World War, the disparity between organisations looking after cancer patients was considerable. A handful of model institutions offered their patients the most modern treatment technologies, while the great majority continued to use the same treatment as at the beginning of the 1920s. And the line of division between these two 'cancerologies' went right through the state cancer centres network. This differentiation was the result of a two-stage process. The first stage corresponded to the setting up of official and 'free' institutions. The inequalities of development were obvious, but the effect on treatment was limited to quantity. 'Rich' and 'poor' centres differed essentially in the number of patients which they could claim to treat annually. The second stage was marked by the introduction of new technologies in treatment which only a few centres were to be capable of acquiring. Hence a hierarchy of institutions arose based on the quality of treatment which they offered.

Cancerology was the sector where the first form of 'big medicine' grew up and, more than any other medical field, it proved sensitive to financial fluctuations. The turning point came at the time when France in her turn entered the great recession of the 1930s. This resulted in a chaotic situation producing paradoxes, which revealed the limits of adaptability of a health system inherited from the nineteenth century. Let us try to look at things in order, follow their sequence and capture the dynamics of their development.

Provincial differences . . .

Paul Strauss's cancer policy took from the hygienists their vision of the role of the state. The intervention of the authorities was necessary for every project of national scope, it became essential the moment the aim was to motivate the creation of a specialised network on a national scale. But the 'healing factory' must be managed by competent staff; hence, the limits regarding choices of sites and therefore their number; hence, also, because each centre would have to be responsible for patients at a regional level, it was deemed necessary to have the requisite radiotherapy and radium equipment. Overall, it was a question of putting in the hands of the few competent specialists the greatest number of 'curable' patients. From this point of view, the state was not the only participant, it acted as master of works, encouraged initiatives from local authorities and was expected to ensure the relative harmonisation of the growth of the organisations.

If the cost of treatment impressed minds little used to taking this aspect into account, the size of the necessary investments caused problems, particularly with regard to the overall cost of equipment for the country. The purchase of the first deep radiotherapy equipment producing 200,000 volts was within the scope of a council or département authority or private enterprises, as long as they were motivated. The technique of curietherapy by radium puncture, because it used only a fractional portion of radium – from 1 to 10 mg per tube or needle – lent itself to a strategy of progressive accumulation; each new quantity acquired, however small, allowed the treatment capability of the care unit to be increased. Moreover, it was these material conditions which made it possible for both the almost immediate inauguration of the majority of regional centres, and the multiplication of projects requiring their official recognition. They also contributed to the explanation as to why the drastic limitation of the number of state centres was a relatively ineffective measure: it did not prevent local political, administrative and charitable authorities from continuing to focus on 'their' cancer department. Of course, as treatment techniques had not been codified, differences in methods of dealing with the same cancer types existed. In one place radiotherapy alone was preferred; in another, surgery; elsewhere the two techniques were combined, in an order and in accordance with arrangements which were themselves subject to variation. The important point is that these differences did not concern equipment, but arose from decisions taken by medico-surgical teams, and that these decisions might all have the air of legitimacy and claim for themselves a referring authority. In addition, the idea of sending the poor to be cared for in a regional centre, far from their place of residence, went down very badly when there existed locally or nearby the possibility of apparently identical treatments. The active survival of these departments diverted the aid of many of the local committees of the League from the official centres, emphasising in several places their difficulties in getting started. A look at the cancer equipment at the end of the 1920s reveals strong disparities (see Table 7.1). On the whole, the contribution of radium is what differentiated the state centres and municipal centres the most. All the state centres with two exceptions, Caen and Rheims, had at least one gram of radioactive material, while the municipal centres had only been able to accumulate a few dozen milligrams, or, at the most, a few hundred milligrams. The result was that the former were able to treat between five and ten times more patients by curietherapy. On the other hand, for deep radiotherapy equipment, the line of division passed through the centre of the regional centres: Toulouse (five machines), Bordeaux, Nancy, Nantes and Lyons (four machines) were outstanding, taking all types together.

The causes of these inequalities in development were due to several relatively independent factors and the way in which, in a given region, they were combined. State aid, in principle the most regular, was far from being uniform, because there were two distinct sources of finance, the ministry's cancer budget and the funds originating from the tax on gambling. It was only in 1931 that a 'Commission for the consideration of requests for financial aid from the regional centres for their fight against cancer' would be set up to harmonise the distribution of funds.[1] Contributions originating from local authorities – civil hospices, municipal councils, département council – themselves differed considerably, more or less reflecting the 'wealth' of the town where they were situated and the economic activity of the region. Finally, and this last element was not without repercussions on the commitment of the local authorities, the existence, or not, of an active movement against cancer attracting private funds towards the regional centre was important in the progressive accumulation of wealth.

The centres became 'rich' when all these factors operated in a positive fashion. Let us take the case of Bordeaux. The state particularly felt that it should support Professor Bergonié's institution. He was the spokesman for the project before the Cancer Commission; Paul Strauss was his personal friend. But he was also and above all a great 'heroic' medical figure who sacrificed everything to his duty. Everything was done so that he might see a model healing factory, in his lifetime. In a few months, the accumulated contribution of contributions from the Tote (300,000 francs, then 700,000 francs), from the municipality (200,000 francs), from the départements (100,000 francs), from the Anti-Cancer Association of the South-West (160,000 francs) allowed the centre to have, from the time of its inauguration, four radiotherapy machines and several hundred milligrams of radium.[2] In addition, the state undertook to finance the construction of new premises, using the opportunity provided by the laying of the foundation stone to honour Bergonié (who was raised to the rank of Grand Officer of the Legion of Honour by Marshal Pétain in person).[3]

We find at Toulouse and Lyons a set of favourable circumstances which, with just a few small differences, were of the same order. Here state aid was as important but took longer, and local dynamism was very strong. The civil hospices, the faculty of medicine, the municipality, the département council, delegates of the chambers of commerce and associations for the fight against cancer were all directly involved in the provisional board of management of the two cancer centres. The financial aid received to carry out their setting up soon exceeded one and a half million francs.[4] In Nancy, the absence of a League committee was compensated for by the philanthropic activity of local employers, the association of textile industries and the Solvay company who contributed 1.2 million to the start-up costs.[5] Nantes was provided with four radiotherapy machines thanks to the efforts of the municipality and the département of Loire-Inférieure.[6] Strasbourg was in a completely different situation. The hospital had already been equipped with roentgentherapy by the German administration. The three départements of Moselle, Haut-Rhin and Bas-Rhin had inherited a health system installed by Bismarck, which was preserved after their return to the French fold. There was, on the one hand, a smooth running social insurance system, the funds of which paid for the cost of treatment and hospitalisation of those who were entitled. On the other hand, treating 'paying patients' had become accepted: it largely contributed to ensuring a centre's budgetary income, which allowed it to partially equip itself (a 1930 statistic showed that more than half of the centre patients were 'paying');[7] finally, as a secondary benefit, it attracted private contributions from grateful families.

When, on the other hand, all these different factors were negative, the almost caricatural situation of the Caen centre existed.

A short time before the official establishment of the project, a journalist from the *Bonhomme Normand*, boasting of the merits and efficiency of the Calvados council, was overcome by enthusiasm and declared: 'We will have at least 10 centigrams of radium'.[8] The wretch did not know how far he was from the truth. After five years of practice, Professor Osmont, director and radiotherapist of the establishment, had only 122 mg of radium, a single deep radiotherapy machine, and he had had no financial support from the Tote.[9] Forgotten by the authorities, the centre existed only on the funds allowed it by the département (50,000 francs annually), and Norman charity took no notice of it, including the Association for the Fight against Cancer of Seine-Inférieure, which seemed more preoccupied with support-ing the Rouen and Le Havre hospitals.[10]

In Rheims, a few meagre grants from the Ministry attenuated the gloom of the picture. Deciding to open in spite of the fact that the establishment was well below the standards recommended by the Bergonié report, the director, Dr Techoueyres, little by little increased his stock of radium by using his operational budget.[11] No better off, but more enterprising, Dr Papin, from Angers, managed to double his allocation (and to reach one gram of radium) by borrowing from Radium Belge.[12]

The presence in neighbouring départements of organisations affiliated to the Anti-Cancer League did not prove to be of more help. The Ardennes

Committee was not concerned about the Rheims centre:[13] the Loir-et-Cher League turned to Paris, and, ignoring the centre of Angers, tried to direct 'its patients' towards institutions in the capital.[14]

Caen, Rheims and Angers were faced with the handicap of being 'medium-sized' towns, which was not the case with larger regional metropolitan centres such as Marseilles, Montpellier or Rennes, whose luck was only slightly more to be envied. The state made its contribution of radium, but it was not – or only slightly – assisted by the local authorities. The Alpes-Maritimes League concentrated its efforts on the hospital in Nice, the Committees of the West and of Hérault were short of money, collections brought in very little, hardly compensating for the meagreness of the municipal and departmental grants which ensured a minimum annual funding, but neglected to assist with their setting up.[15]

These inequalities of supplies had effects on the levels of activity in the centres, which might vary in giving treatment by a factor of two or three.

... and Parisian complexities

With its fourteen deep radiotherapy machines and its thirteen grams of radium (1928 balance), 'Parisian cancerology' did not suffer completely from a lack of finance. However, it was confronted with serious organisational problems. Originating before the Cancer Commission had defined its programme, the capital's cancer institutions had difficulty in integrating with a common structure under a single management. The Curie Foundation, the small centre of the Paul Brousse hospice and each of the six curietherapy departments of the *Assistance Publique* hospitals were set up as so many relatively independent entities under the authority of a single 'head'. In addition, these eight units had three different administrative statuses. The specific nature of the Curie Foundation, a private law association, meant that its case had to be dealt with separately. It was recognised as a regional centre for the fight against cancer in 1926.[16] The project to form an association of all the other departments – having taken into account that they belonged to the public sector – once drafted, rapidly proved an unsatisfactory solution. The connection with two different administrations – the departmental commission of the Seine hospices and the *Assistance Publique* – was not an insurmountable obstacle, but the group set up in 1925 revealed its limits. Brought together at the prefect's instigation, the municipal council of Paris and the Seine département council managed to agree on the principle of a 'Paris regional cancer centre' to which the specialised wards of the *Assistance Publique* and of the Paul Brousse hospices 'were to contribute'.[17] However, this result could only be obtained by making adjustments to institutional realities. The impossibility of compromising with the *Assistance Publique* regulations (in force since 1849) led to two of the most original provisions granted to the state centres being discarded. With respect to the separation of technical and administrative responsibilities, the power of the head doctors was limited to medical aspects alone. It was no more a question of the *Assistance Publique* relinquishing its 'legal entity' for the benefit of one of its dependencies, it was the only one to have the right to receive and manage donations and bequests destined for the fight against cancer.[18] In order to achieve standardisation, the Paul Brousse cancer ward was subject to the same restrictions.[19] But what contributed even more to make this 'Paris regional centre' an institutional oddity, was that its organisation did not wish to affect the 'sovereignty' of the heads. The unity which the name implied was only an empty phrase covering seven cancer departments perfectly independent of each other. The various sources of public finance (state, town, département) and private gifts were therefore divided more or less equitably, in such a way as to avoid the allocation of credits becoming a bone of contention. A many-headed structure, the cancer centre of the Paris region seemed badly organised to face the competition from the Curie Foundation. The reputation which this had already acquired internationally eclipsed that of each department. Had it not just been chosen by the league of Nations Cancer Commission to represent French cancerology in a multi-centre study which was evaluating the radiotherapy techniques used in cancer of the cervix and the womb?[20] The fact that a marginal institution in the Paris hospital universe, having no links with the university medical elite, had the foremost reputation in an area whose importance was ever increasing was a paradox which was not very pleasant for the authorities of the faculty of medicine. The need to reorganise was necessary, but which ones? How was one to build a centre of activity capable of rivalling the Curie Foundation's prestige?

The solution was not easy. It was difficult to choose between the six surgeons at the head of a cancer department. What criteria were to be used to single out one of them? Neither the Faculty Board nor the *Assistance Publique* Hospitals Board could risk involving them in what would, in fact, be a hierarchical structure.

The horizon cleared when, in 1925, Pierre Marie succeeded Déjerine as the head of the Nervous Diseases Clinic and left the chair of pathological anatomy.[21] His pupil, Gustave Roussy, was able then to succeed him. The transformation from 'almost nothing' into 'almost everything' which affected him (to use Regaud's formula), enhanced the prestige of the place where he worked; at the same time, the removed and subordinate nature of his position as head doctor of a suburban hospice became for him a major trump, a credible alternative compared with the *Assistance Publique* cancer division. Roussy seized the opportunity to give substance to the ambitions which up to then had only been a plan. He suggested transforming the Paul Brousse cancer department into 'An institute for the research and treatment of cancer', linked to the chair of pathological anatomy. His idea was to bring together on one site a set of research laboratories and a hospital area to deal with a common subject: cancer. Unlike 'ordinary' cancer centres which made use of the services of one or two university or hospital laboratories for the purposes dictated by the clinic (pathological anatomy diagnosis, monitoring of intercurrent infections, etc.), and very secondarily for research, the Cancer Institute intended to be the leader in treatment, clinical research and the progress of fundamental knowledge in relation to the aetiopathogeny of the disease. The idea was clearly to construct a 'model' institution for cancerology, which would serve as a counterpoint to the Curie Foundation. Supported by the Faculty of Medicine, the project was put to a study commission by the Seine département council on the same day as it ratified the decrees organising the Paris region Cancer Centre, which then were to become very quickly obsolete.[22] In December 1925, the principle of the creation of the institute was adopted and its first operational credits agreed. The département conceded by long lease, at the price of one franc, a piece of land adjoining the Paul Brousse hospice and committed provisional funds for the construction of *ad hoc* premises. The expression of a political will to go beyond circumstantial formulas in the interest of research and the establishment of the objective was the outcome of debates before the département council. The first condition was to open up the Villejuif unit belonging to the Paris regional centre. The Seine département council declared the hospice's cancer service independent by a decree of 1 October 1926. Roussy, while keeping his duties of head doctor at Paul Brousse, was appointed director of what became the 'Paris suburban cancer centre', a temporary name while awaiting the opening of the Cancer Institute. The same decree undid what the adjustment of the *Assistance Publique* articles had set in motion. The director regained the prerogatives of his provincial counterparts, that is twofold technical and administrative responsibility.[23] The second requirement was to ensure conditions for the relative financial independence of the future Institute. A private foundation was immediately set up; chaired by Paul Strauss, it brought together in its board of management the dean of the faculty of medicine and several département councillors including Jean Varennes, the usual spokesman on health questions, a member of the Cancer Commission, Léopold Bellan, the founder of a private hospital, who provided beds for incurable cancer sufferers, and Henri Sellier, the future health minister of the Popular Front.[24]

Setting an example, the 'département' released a credit of 1 million for the building of premises (December 1926); on its part, the Paris municipal council made a grant of 500,000 francs;[25] but it appeared, at least in the eyes of the local authorities, that their contribution would not be enough. Jean Varennes severely criticised the state's lack of interest regarding research and painted a dark picture of the under-provision of laboratories in France, compared with what was happening abroad. In 1928, a new effort was made by the département (1 million) and the City of Paris (1 million); this time the Ministry of Public Education and the Ministry of Health helped with a grant of 1.5 million.[26] The entry into the picture of the authorities accelerated things and on 18 March 1930 the Cancer Institute was officially inaugurated, creating, according to Gustave Roussy's words, 'a new trend which is trying, both in the field of medicine and in that of biology, to group under one management all disciplines and all orientations which may contribute to clarify a scientific problem'.[27] Alongside the hospital cancer departments were the research laboratories, each with a department head and an assistant; Leroux, appointed under-director of the scientific section, occupied himself with pathological anatomy, Dr Verne, the histology *agrégé*, with experimental cytology, Dr Oberling, the pathological anatomy *agrégé*, with experimental medicine, the *agrégé* Grandclaude with bacteriology and serology, and finally Prof. Sannié simultaneously managed the physiological chemistry and biological chemistry laboratories.[28]

After the fleeting interlude of the 'Paris Regional Cancer Centre', Parisian cancerology regained its original tri-partite approach, but the relationship between the different structures had been modified. Social influence had precipitated the faculty of medicine's decision to centre its efforts on Villejuif. Caught in a development system which tended to become more and more selective, the *Assistance Publique* Cancer Centre remained incapable of resolving the problem of its break-up into six independent units. It was condemned, at the beginning of the 1930s, to play a secondary role to the Curie Foundation and the Cancer Institute and to miss the turning point of 'big medicine'.

'State-of-the-art' institutions and ordinary centres

The years 1929 and 1930 were the culminating years of the prosperity of the inter-war years. Optimism was in fashion, the government was convinced that France was immune to the crisis which had hit other countries. The coalition of the right in power, having several billions of francs in budgetary excess, was involved in a policy of social reform, and financed the establishment of National Insurance voted in 1928, started free secondary education and retirement for combatants.[29] It also began to modernise the national capital equipment; a draft law submitted to the Chamber of Deputies in February 1931 was passed in December and became effective the following year. Of 3,476 million employed, 409 were in the health and social security sector, including 180 to renovate hospital stock, and 170 to create, enlarge and equip establishments for combating social diseases.[30] The text of the draft law, anticipated contributing 20 million to the cancer centres. In the discussion which followed, a certain number of deputies and senators anxious to start it up were heard. It was a notable event: supporters for a large funding for cancer were found over the whole range of parties, on the right (Paul Strauss, François De Wendel), on the centre left (Justin Godart, Henri Gout), in the French Socialist Party (SFIO) (Alexandre Rauzy) and in the Communist Party (Jules Fraissex).

Their arguments emphasised the meagreness of the ordinary budgetary funds, the debt contracted with Radium Belge, the age of the premises used for the majority of the centres and the need for re-equipment. But the divergence was at its greatest regarding the number of centres. Camille Blaisot, the Minister of Health, wished to use a fraction of the 20 million to open a few extra regional centres. Henri Gout challenged him by using, on his own account, the ideas adopted by the Cancer Commission and asked for a reduction in their number. He advanced the technological development which began with curietherapy ('When the use of radiation began . . . radium masses were of the order of a few centigrams; today, they are a hundred times larger, we estimate that a minimum of five grams is necessary to achieve useful treatment. The Curie Institute is the only establishment I know which has a radium mass of more than five grams . . .'),[31] and the one which was starting up in roentgentherapy with the perfecting of new machines capable of yielding a much higher voltage than the classic equipment of 200,000 volts, but of which the cost of manufacture was increasing in proportion.

The combination of these pressures at various levels made the minister partly relent and he agreed to increase support for the provision of cancer equipment, by granting it 70 million.[32] A sign of the times, cancer received more than 40 per cent of the total amount destined for social diseases and, for the first time, took the largest part. We can certainly get the size of the amount in proportion when we compare it with the 30 million granted just for the modernisation of the thermal establishment of Aix-les-Bains,[33] but, as regards what the state had invested in combating cancer since 1922, the amount was considerable. The centres were to receive, at one and the same time, more money than they had had in nine years.

How would this financial manna be distributed? Camille Blaisot had not abandoned the idea of opening several extra establishments and wanted to have new premises built at Rheims and Montpellier, but he had only budgeted for two priorities: the setting up of a new hospital for the Curie Foundation on a piece of land adjoining the Radium Institute (12.5 million) and the completion of the work at the Cancer Institute (11.5 million). The decision came at the right time for Gustave Roussy. The Foundation for the development of the Institute had made it clear that the costs of construction at the end of December 1930 (9.5 million) exceeded the available resources by 3 million and that it was necessary in addition to equip the laboratories. Due to lack of material, they had not been able to start work.[34]

In February 1932, the Senate overturned the Laval government (which had wanted to introduce a reform in the method of balloting), causing new elections which the Union of the Left won. The radicals returned to government and the right was excluded from the ministerial cabinets which were to follow. Camille Blaisot gave way to Justin Godart, and once again the president of the League was the Minister of Public Health; it was he who, in fact, was appointed to direct the cancer policy, boosting the selective system (no new centres), while accentuating its effects. Even if, very incidentally, the radium contribution for the poorest centres was brought back to standard (Caen eventually acquired one extra gram)[35] and if Godart did not change his mind concerning the refurbishing of the Rheims centre (which received 2 million for this purpose) and of the Montpellier centre, he also added Lyons (of which the mayor, Herriot, was the president of the Council) and Strasbourg. The essential part of the public funds was concentrated on the modernisation of a few institutions, where the local authorities could best carry out his purpose.

The Cancer Institute should have been a 'model cancer establishment' and for research and for radiotherapy it was. In 1934, the laboratory section was equipped. The result cannot be compared with anything that existed at that time in France for biomedical research. Charles Oberling, in his speech inaugurating the laboratories, even felt the need for justification:

> Several people might have been astonished to see these admirable research departments and laboratories whilst thinking about those makeshift, or rather wretched laboratories of Pasteur, Claude Bernard or Curie. They might have wondered if modern science has become so exacting and whether the creation of these research centres is essential to the progress of our knowledge. To that question the answer is yes . . . All those who are even slightly familiar with the complexity of the questions raised by the study of cancer know that to deal with them effectively, we can no longer be satisfied with a microscope and a few test tubes. The branches of scientific activity dealing with cancer are always increasing and it is impossible to know from where decisive progress will come.[36]

In parallel, the therapy section received five extra grams of radium, converted into a bomb for distance curietherapy. Funds were also released so that the Institute might acquire a so-called 'ultrapenetrating' radiotherapy apparatus. The system, which had just been perfected in France after having been invented in the United States,[37] linked a very high voltage electricity generator to a giant tube capable of releasing 600,000 volts. That of the Cancer Institute weighed two tonnes and to use it a special lift allowing it to be raised or lowered was required.[38] Completed in 1934, the Cancer Institute operation was to have cost 34 million, 25 supplied by the state, the rest by the département, the City of Paris and private gifts (which did not exceed a million).[39]

State aid to the Curie Foundation was accompanied by a most substantial private contribution. The time when Marie Curie had to undertake a 'tour' in the United States to collect money for a gram of radium was past. In fifteen years, the Institute was to have received more than 15 million francs in grants and bequests made by 'benefactors' (Elie Lazard gave 3 million to the Foundation in 1932),[40] and by 'grateful sufferers', without including the seven grams of radium provided free of charge by Belgium.

In 1936, the centre had fourteen grams of radium, including eleven for distance curietherapy (three bombs worked); ten X-ray generators of 200,000 volts completed the equipment. The introduction of ultra-penetrating radiotherapy tubes was suspended while the works at the new hospital were finished.[41]

In the provinces, only four centres were in a position to adapt to the revolution in treatment technology. Lyons and Bordeaux were able to accumulate enough radium to each build a 'bomb';[42] Lille, the opening of which was delayed until Autumn 1931,[43] benefited from left-over amounts from the Comity for Relief in Belgium (an organisation financing compensation for war damages), and principally from an anonymous donation of four grams of radium,[44] which allowed it to be equipped for distance curietherapy. But the only establishment capable of rivalling these two Paris model institutions was that of Strasbourg. The funds granted for the improvement of the national apparatus for the equipping of new premises acted as an incentive to local dynamism. A centre whose patients were recruited from all classes of society, including the middle classes of the area, it could be supported by the combination, unique in France, of public aid, support from the social security funds and financing by patients, to which were added gifts and bequests. The turning point of 'big medicine' started in 1932. The radium contribution increased from two grams (1931) to ten grams (1936), the pool of deep radiotherapy equipment from three to eight.[45] The construction of new premises was put to good use for the installation of 'two giant ultrapenetrating tubes' in a special building.

> The high voltage generators are on the ground floor and the user stations were on the first floor. The 600,000 volt tube, being extremely heavy, is not as mobile as the ordinary tubes. It must therefore to be limited to a rotatory movement about an axis . . . A mobile floor, driven by an electric motor, moves the patient closer or further away. A second station is installed differently. The outlet tube is placed under the floor and its radiation passes through a hole in the floor directly under a radiation table on which the patient is lying.[46]

The contrast between these sometimes spectacular creations and the situation of the other cancer centres was even greater when the latter, deprived of exceptional funds, saw their 'standard of living' go down during the same period. The financial recession and the measures taken to avoid a budgetary deficit directly affected the amount of annual funds allocated to cancer, which from 1931 regularly decreased, reaching its lowest point in 1935 before returning to its 1928 level (see Table 7.2), when the franc had lost two-thirds of its value.[47] The money allocated to Rheims and Montpellier was only just enough for the construction of new buildings which were to shelter 'old equipment'. Because of the crisis, gifts became rarer, collections resulted in only very small donations. The director of the Nancy centre was disconsolate because charity in Lorraine had dried up[48] (it must be said that the production of the textile and iron and steel industries had negative rates of annual increase from 1929, a situation which was not very propitious for the expression of 'generosity'). One of the real consequences was that even the process of progressive accumulation of radium stock ceased. In 1939, the large majority of 'ordinary' cancer establishments, the state centres and, even more so, the others, had the same equipment as ten years before, and the methods of treatment which they used could not evolve. Proving Regaud's pessimistic forecasts right, the state could not modernise the network of regional centres and was constrained to favour certain areas. The 'rich centres'/'poor centres' opposition took on a 'qualitative' dimension, and the greater part of the country was deprived of the 'leading' treatments. However, it was not regional inequalities which caused the most indignant recriminations, but rather more a paradox, the appearance of which surprised everybody: the first 'victims' of the cancer policy were the 'rich' who, because they could pay for their treatment, did not have access to public sector institutions. As they could see that this was an unfair and absurd aberration, the officials of the Anti-Cancer League, who were looking for ways to put it right, were obliged to reconsider the organisation of the whole health system.[49]

Privilege of the unfortunate, misfortune of the privileged

The dividing line between the private sector and public medicine prescribed the hierarchical organisation of the social world in the organisation of the health system according to an opposing system of medical care for the 'rich' and medical care for the 'poor'. The society elite and the poor could receive the same medical treatment, be cared for by the same doctors, the differences were in the mode of the patient's social treatment. The distance which separated the Berghof from *The Magic Mountain* of any working-class sanatorium, however large, hardly affected treatment, in return, they were notable for the hotel comfort, the doctor–patient relationship and the disciplinary rules of the establishments.[50]

The care of cancer patients was also related to this dichotomy. Even if there were no private cancer profit-making centres, certain surgical clinics equipped for deep radiotherapy and curietherapy offered their patients identical treatments to those which took place in the public centres. However, the very high cost of the treatments created a problem for certain categories of patients who, because of their income level, did not qualify as poor. Certain directors of regional centres, considering that the limitation of the patients to poor people was too restrictive in the strict sense of the word, decided to open up their institutions to those they called 'small payers'.

> By a special decision of the board of the Toulouse cancer centre, it has been agreed that we will cater for 'small payers'. These 'small payers' belong to the category of patients who, not being registered as poor, do not, however, have the means to pay for radium treatment in a private clinic. They are received in the centre at the same rate of hospitalisation costs as poor people, and have to make a payment for the costs of radium which does not exceed 600 francs, whatever the dose used. The payments made by the patients are used to pay off our debts and improve our laboratories.[51]

This type of initiative was very badly perceived by those who had made themselves the vigilant guardians of liberal orthodoxy. They saw in it an attempt to acquire paying patients, which was unfair in principle and contrary to ethics. These 'ultra-liberals' were gaining influence everywhere in the medical association movement which had been taking place since the end of the war,[52] and, where they predominated, they took up the controversy with the centre management. The Practitioners' Society of Lyons sent a protest to Professor Léon Bérard, which was immediately supported by the Union of Doctors of the Rhone, who were indignant that the cancer department of the General Hospital used tariffs for 'small payers' which amounted to less than four-fifths of the specialists' tariffs.[53]

The conflict was even more acute in Alsace, because of the existence of the social security fund. The low tariffs of the Strasbourg cancer centre were denounced as insupportable competition to the fund. Professor Gunsett was accused

> of touching on one of the most sensitive issues of the sickness funds, that is their unhealthy concern for economy, by offering prices defying all competition, ridiculously lower than, certainly, the same funds could wish for. . . . By this knowingly voluntary degradation of the tariffs . . ., material harm has been caused to a fair number of very well thought of and very competent radiotherapy colleagues, in the region. These colleagues, provided with radium and modern equipment obtained largely at their own expense, gain not inconsiderable income from the treatment of the patients paid for by the fund. At present, these colleagues . . . are obliged, because of the provisions made, to treat all the deep cancers of most of the population of Alsace for a derisory amount.[54]

The situation was peculiar to Alsace, but, when discussions started on the question of welfare insurance, it appeared to the union managers that it threatened the future of private medicine.

There was no shortage of pressure on the city doctors since the centres needed their co-operation to recruit their patients. In addition, in certain places, the associations were able to bring direct pressure on the cancer centre by making use of *ex officio* representatives on its board of management. These representatives succeeded in imposing strict regulations on the conditions of admission for the 'small payers'. The compromise reached in Toulouse was given as an example: no 'small payer' was admitted who was not first passed by the family doctor.

> There is no doubt that the admission of this type of patients to a regional centre is a very delicate matter, as the label of 'small payer' may open the door to every abuse and we could be made to treat at a reduced cost for patients whose means would perfectly well allow them to pay for the costs of treatment in town. . . . The 'small payers' *will only be received and cared for at the centre on the express request of their attending physician.* The attending physician is usually aware of the financial means of his customers, and he can perfectly well judge whether a particular patient, who although not poor, deserves to be treated at the centre. There cannot be the slightest misunderstanding, on the one hand, between the publicity and treatment organisations which are the responsibility of the National Assistance and, on the other hand, practitioners and specialists who treat cancer.[55]

But even these understandings were not really desirable in the eyes of the most 'liberal' doctors; in Nancy and Rennes, the surgeons managing the centres, professors Hoche and Marquis, active supporters of the 'hard' line, undertook that access to these establishments should be strictly limited to the poor.

However, until the beginning of the 1930s, the 'small payers' were a subject of secondary importance for those responsible in the fight against cancer. The role of this type of patient was marginal, and when the League review talked about them, it was to give information devoid of comment relating to such and such a cancer centre. But the development of the socio-economic situation of the country created the conditions for the problem to acquire a completely different intensity. The rapid impoverishment of part of the middle classes affected by the crisis emphasised the relative inadequacy of the health system and its difficulty in adapting to the new situation. An American philanthropist resident in France, also a League member, began to create a hospital project for the 'middle classes', which he was partly to finance the 'Foch Foundation' in Suresnes.[56] For the first time, on 28 April 1931, at the campaigners' meeting, the secretary general of the League mentioned the drama with which the intellectual and liberal professions and more generally the 'average Frenchmen', were confronted when they had to face, with the danger of ruining themselves, the costs of a long and costly illness:

> The *Assistance* hospital was not built nor the treatment centre designed for him [the average Frenchman], in the same way the hospital on

which he depends has provided nothing for the poor. Is this not an anomaly? We create centres, we provide them with the best equipment, we entrust them to the most competent masters and, instead of being widely used, these model clinics are not organised to receive patients requiring a certain amount of comfort.[57]

For quite a time, the League held the view that a real problem existed, without making any progress in getting to the root of it. It recognised the need to change the hospital organisation, particularly that of the cancer centres, but denied that it wished to 'introduce competition between the public and private sectors'.[58] The progression towards the idea of the 'modern hospital' for a socially diverse public, offering different services, was presented as a 'natural' process, in time unavoidable, the idea of which 'could only progress with the approval of the medical body which has professional rights which it is not appropriate [for us] to discuss'.[59] The contrast between the content of the analyses, which each time showed up the defects of the health system, and the conclusions extolling the wait-and-see policy bore witness to the strength of the consensus of opinion which still dominated the medical field. The dichotomy of the market between the hospital and the liberal sector was perpetuated without meeting too many obstacles, because the hospital doctors who comprised the elite of the profession were also doctors practising privately; paid symbolically for their hospital activities, they lived (very well) from the patients they treated privately. But the need to introduce reforms making this method of organisation more flexible began to be felt. Certain specialists were confronted with the fact that they could not have equipment in their private clinics to match that which they were using in the hospitals. It was incontestably for cancer treatment that the gap seemed the greatest; no private clinic was able to pay for the heavy technical equipment which the 'model' cancer centres had, and amongst these only the Curie Foundation and the Strasbourg Centre admitted patients of all social categories. Another party favourable to the adjustment of the system was the hospital administration. It saw in the introduction of pay beds a source of budgetary compensation for the constant increase in the cost of equipment. In Paris and in the provinces this type of initiative tended to develop little by little, favoured by the setting up of social security funds, giving some credit to the obsessions of the medical unions. The latter, in order to thwart the beginning of this programme, launched a campaign denouncing the scandal of 'hospital queue-jumpers'. They hoped to attain their goal indirectly by using as an argument the fraud by which certain tight-fisted 'rich people', disguised their situation in order to be admitted to hospital and in this way benefit from treatment at the hands of the greatest masters at the lowest tariffs.[60] Raoul Brandon brought the matter to the attention of the prefect in a council meeting on 30 December 1933. The director of the *Assistance Publique*, present at the meeting, averred that 'no legal text has forbidden rich patients from receiving care in public hospitals' and that if the latter were charitable towards the poor, the opening of wards to paying patients was a perfectly legitimate right.[61] Commenting on the arguments exchanged, Robert Le Bret still refused to take up a global position and kept to the question of the fight against cancer:

> Can we, on the pretext that hospitals have been provided for the poor, deprive rich people of the benefit of this treatment, especially when it is a question of radiotherapy, a treatment which is only effective when the applications are sufficient and correct? The cancer centres are a completely new creation and have to adapt to present conditions. Is it not necessary for them to be organised so that they can receive all patients at prices which range from free of charge to full price?[62]

The dynamism of the game exacerbated the antagonism between the different points of view. The Director of the *Assistance Publique*'s reply, by appealing to the legal void relating to the organisation of relationships between private sector and public hospital, emphasised the absence of a legal basis for the consensus, which, until then, had prevailed and had made for a new challenge. The reaction of the medical unions was not long in coming, their partisans in Parliament supported a draft law published by Raoul Brandon, which aimed at forbidding everyone not included in the category of permanent or temporary poor access to hospital. Tabled on 28 July 1936, the draft specified in its first article:

> The hospital, with the exception of the special cases listed below, is exclusively reserved for poor people and for persons temporarily deprived of resources. The status of being a poor person will be given to any person without resources, admitted to the benefit of free medical support or assistance from the welfare office. By a person temporarily deprived of resources is meant any person who is in a condition of relative financial embarrassment, or even a person who would have to undergo a long and costly treatment, outside his resources.[63]

The cases of people who are not poor who may exceptionally be the subject of an admission are limited to victims of accidents or illness on the public highway (it being understood that they must leave hospital for a private clinic as soon as their condition allows it) and certain patients infected by or suspected of being infected by serious contagious diseases needing isolation.

The level of reply chosen by the ultra-liberals obliged those who might be satisfied by the current development to take part. By wanting to transform into law what was only a tacit understanding founded on a consensus, the Brandon draft directly threatened the partial adjustments made in order to relax the conditions of admission to the cancer centres, to the great displeasure of the League officers. Relying on the paradoxical situation which was developing in the cancer sector, the League secretary denounced the stupidity of a point of view which deprived rich cancer sufferers of the benefit of new therapeutic techniques.

> A strange question arises: telecurietherapy, which requires several grams of radium, that is to a value of several million, for one bomb, can now be practised in a few cancer centres: it cannot be practised elsewhere. Will a certain group of patients be deprived of telecurietherapy treatment, precisely a group which can pay for it? It is hardly believable that this question can arise! And yet it has, following a set of circumstances which we are trying to resolve . . .
> The medical unions, who have the task of defending doctors' professional interests, have vehemently protested against the admission, to public hospitals, of patients who are able to pay the costs of a private clinic and the justified doctors' and surgeons' fees. The argument has reached such a pitch that a draft law has been tabled to the Chamber to forbid hospitals from admitting well-to-do patients . . . In reality, there are only a few abuses, but a principle has been raised which needs to be considered: should a public hospital refuse entry to a patient because he is rich?[64]

The League secretary, replying to his question, submitted a principle basing the reputation of medical liberalism on a historical relativity. Yes, the hospitals originated because of the charitable wishes of benefactors who thought about the poor, but there is nothing to make us think that they wanted to bar one category of patient. Because they were carrying out a philanthropic duty, doctors and surgeons refused to be paid for treatment, unless it was a token payment. For a long time, the question of the admission of a patient from the well-to-do classes had not arisen, none of them would have wanted to go to the hospital to be treated. But all this was now largely over, hospitals had evolved, the best doctors practised in them, nursing staff were trained with the greatest care. The buildings had been considerably modernised, the equipment was of the very first quality. And then another development took place, this time social, which created a category of persons who deserved to be helped and who should have been able to receive good hospital treatment, at an acceptable price.

> Choosing between a poor man who has a privileged right to the hospital and the rich man who has no right threatens to become difficult. I am leaving it up to others to find a solution for hospitals in general, but I will return to the cancer centres. . . . The idea of refusing this perfected treatment given to the poor, to a category of patients who can pay makes no sense![66]

Convinced by his polemic, Le Bret did not hesitate to rewrite history by affirming that the cancer centres were not conceived just for charity patients, but 'as model organisations for fighting an illness which strikes rich and poor alike'.[66]

The discussion of the Brandon project was postponed, new elections resulted in the left holding a majority in the chamber, which resulted in the Popular Front government. The question was taken up again at the general meeting of the League which took place on 4 May 1937, before Parliament discussed the project. The head of the health minister's office, Dr Hazemann, was present, the context of the acute social and political crisis weighed heavily on everyone, the atmosphere was tense. The League secretary gave his longest report, tackling all the questions of importance, including obviously the one mentioned above. For the first time, he particularly criticised the position of a centre director, Professor Marquis, criticising him for having anticipated the adoption of the draft law by introducing a regulation explicitly closing the Rennes office to those who were not officially registered as patients and who had the right to free medical assistance. The medical unions were denounced for 'their inadmissible pretension' and accused of wanting to hamper the freedom of the hospitals by themselves regulating the conditions for the recruitment of patients. Refusing to humour the ideology still largely dominant among doctors, Le Bret played on the fantasies of nationalisation which obsessed their minds in order to better plead the need for a reform of the system safeguarding private medicine, since the conservatism of those who refused any development risked making way for collectivist temptations.[67] This reform proposed to organise the competition between the private sector and the 'modern hospital' by introducing within the latter, in so far as it was acquiring a vocation to receive patients of all social classes, several categories of 'pay beds', the price range of which covered different types of hotel service. As a counterpart of this competition, doctors would receive fees according to their performance. Thus transformed, the public hospital sector could make its management profitable: 'By compensating for losses incurred with small payers and the poor by making a profit from paying patients, it will create a rational and fair balance and . . . will weigh less heavily on council budgets and all taxpayers.'[68]

Established because of a controversy, the League's spokesman's reformist ideas gained strength and embraced the questions posed by 'covering' users' health costs and took its place in the social security debate. Here, too, Le Bret challenged the critics of the factions of the medical body who were the most hostile to the 1928 law,[69] but, arguing for it to be limited to employees whose income did not exceed a certain ceiling, he was advocating the additional development of private sickness insurance. Taking advantage of the relationship which it had since the start with certain insurance companies,[70] the Association for the Fight against Cancer was keen on convincing them to organise this until then too-neglected branch of activity, and to make supplementary provisions concerning the adoption of radio-therapy costs.[71]

These opinions directly referred to challenges which, in addition to the framework of the 'fight against cancer', concerned medicine and the health system as a whole. In so far as it was conceived in part as a response to problems posed by the growth of the cancer centres and by the care of patients, this political vision was linked to the development of cancerology, but it drew its coherence from a representation of the social world as being developed from the point of view of an all-embracing class which was worried about the balance of the strong relationships between the various social groups. This explained the recurrence of the theme of the 'misery of the middle classes' in the arguments for the proposed reforms; this eminently political subject, during a period of extreme social tensions, was used at one and the same time to impose the image of a defective health system, to justify the proposed measures and to invalidate the relevance of the representations favouring a dualistic method of division of society. The 'sociological' archaism of the rich–poor division, which was conveyed by the Brandon project, and the ideologies of the class struggle were impartially dismissed, in the name of the attention to be paid to this new class 'which grew up with modest resources', comprising 'the most solid framework of France' and which the crisis 'has seriously affected in its everyday life'.[72]

We cannot completely understand the strategy of an association which recruited its members from the ruling classes whilst misjudging this dimension of the politico-ideological fight or by awarding it a minor status. The idea of the hospital becoming the place of practice of 'leading' medicine, open to all social classes but respecting their hierarchy by including it in the 'categories of different pay beds', as the concept of a triple method of social protection (free medical assistance, social security, private insurance) expressed the point of view of a group engaged in debates which pervaded the field of power. Within this reformist project, the need to provide answers to new requirements proper to the introduction of 'big medical technologies' was inseparably related to a political objective: to ward off the existing risks that the 'middle classes' could no longer play their role as a stabilising influence within the balance of the strong relationships.

8   Between science and charity
The question of incurables

The day came when the last wounded soldier had left, the last song been sung, the ward contained only cancer patients. Charge nurses and nurses felt somewhat at a loss; they missed their wounded men and found the ward bleak.

But very quickly, they had all recovered; a new transformation had taken place in them and a little later, I heard the charge nurse say: 'Well, I prefer these patients to the wounded, they're so grateful for what you do for them, they need us so much!'
'They need us so much!'
I can remember these words, because they show us women where our duty lies.[1]

(Mme Hartmann)

A subject for experimentation

When he suggested that poor incurable cancer sufferers were of no social worth, Alban Bergonié was only crudely expressing a point of view largely shared by the medical elite of his time. The use of categories taken from economics to classify and locate sick persons gave rise to medical opinions devoid of all humanistic references. The effacement of the suffering individual originated with the clinic. The social conditions presiding over the practice of hospital medicine – where, in exchange for free care, the 'poor person' lent his body to learned investigation – were such that the idea of taking an objective view of the patient proper to a clinical anatomy approach could play its full part. The patient tended to be considered as a receptacle of the illness, the subjectivity of which would be incidental. As soon as the illness was considered incurable, the terms of the exchange were altered, the patient came under palliative care, no longer needing the intervention of a doctor and becoming a long-stay patient of relatively no further medical interest everything predisposed the clinician to see him as a being of no social value. Hence this trend to relegate him to other organisations where the cost of his care was reduced to a minimum and which the Paris *Assistance Publique* described by using the evocative description 'depot'. It might, however, be shown that the ideology of social utility could find in the incurable a source of interest for the community, as a subject of experiment contributing to medical progress. But that, under certain conditions, was a matter for professional ethics, not scientific relevance. It was thus laid down that an experiment useful for the advance of knowledge but unethical should not be practised. The meeting on 23 June 1891 of the Academy of Medicine was relevant to one of these. The hypothesis of the inoculability of cancer came up again since several works had mentioned the possibility of grafting cancer cells from one affected animal to another of the same species.[2] But the paper presented that day by Professor Cornil concerned two observations made on a human being. The surgeon who was the originator, whose name was not to be divulged, contacted the academic (Cornil was the holder of the chair of pathological anatomy) for the first time so that the latter could analyse fragments of tissue from breast cancers, one primary, the other secondary, following an attempted graft. While he was carrying out the removal of a 'large breast cancer' the surgeon 'cut off a small portion of it and inserted it under the skin of the other breast which was perfectly normal. The operation had been performed while the patient was under the influence of chloroform, taking the most rigorous antiseptic measures.'[3] Two months later, a nodule 'of the size of an almond', which had developed on the 'grafted breast', was removed by the same surgeon. The histological examination made by Cornil on the fragments of the two tumours revealed that 'the tissues of the first and second showed an identical structure'.[4] The patient died a little later of an 'acute intercurrent illness'. A second experiment, repeating the preceding one and under the same conditions, on another patient, should have been, according to Cornil 'less demonstrative and less complete' since 'the patient did not want to have the operation to remove the graft which had become a small tumour. She left the hospital and was not followed up'.[5]

After having discussed the results, Cornil came to the conclusion that the 'hypothesis of grafting . . . takes body [*sic*] and becomes reality'. The paper provoked a general outcry, Léon Le Fort protested on behalf of French surgery, Moutard-Martin talked of an essentially criminal act, Cornil acquiesced and the Academy unanimously condemned the experiment. However, in spite of the fierce denunciation, the position of the medical authorities was not free of ambiguity; in the first place Cornil declared: 'I would not undertake . . . to justify the experiment, in all ways to be condemned', before adding: 'These remarks would never have been published if they had not seemed to be of great scientific interest.'[6] Was he not also led, in spite of his moral reticence, to collaborate in the observation by analysing the tissue fragments? The attitude of the holder of the pathological anatomy chair explained the connection which, if looked at solely from the scientific point of interest, placed the surgeon's research within the field of legitimate experiments. This academic legitimacy was granted as much by the decision to present the work as by its publication in the Academy's bulletin. We see here that ethical indignation existed alongside a morality based on utilitarianism. Morality to which Cornil subscribed when he disapproved of the action, yet he participated in the research and also supported the Academy when it denounced the outrage to the profession, without including in its reprimand those members who had taken part. In other words, the highest medico-scientific authority stood by its principles, which required that once the evil had been done, there should be no opposition to gaining knowledge from it. Because of this, the graft carried out by the unknown surgeon, because of being a rare action (although not isolated, as experiments of the same type were publicly discussed in Germany),[7] was nonetheless not a phenomenon without social significance, in so far as it marked a limiting point to this logic. The surgeon would no doubt have argued that the evil had already been done, since the illness was bound to lead to certain death, and why should it not be used in this way for the progress of knowledge? The reason why the Academy rejected this point of view, in considering the surgeon's act, was clearly because it seemed harmful to the patient's interest, however useful the element of new knowledge he was bringing to society, and contravened the principle of *Primum non nocere* [first do no harm]. But it is remarkable that, in this affair, the Academy, whilst posing as the guardian of professional ethics, limited itself to verbal condemnation and did not depart from respecting 'professional confidentiality' and so did not nominally denounce the offender, leaving him his anonymity.

If the fact of taking the patient's interest into account is what imposed a moral limit on human experimentation, no restriction was imposed when the experiment claimed to be treatment and appeared to coincide with the interests of the individual, science and society. Under these conditions, the poor cancer sufferer was put in the position of a subject for experiment, a position which, in hospital, corresponded to a situation which we may describe as waiving a principle. Indeed, as we have already seen regarding tests of treatment by radiation, the incurable could find himself entrusted to a physician with no clinical responsibility, and this same doctor might arouse the hostility of his colleagues if the idea took him to try to treat a patient affected by a curable illness. The creation of cancer centres, by recognising radiotherapy as a completely clinical 'discipline', modified this situation. Treatment by radiation, placed on an equal par with surgery, changed its base, and it was moved from the laboratory to be used in hospital. Similarly, the idea that the method of application of radiation had passed the experimental stage was established. But by being codified, radiotherapy changed its aim and became a part of the treatment arsenal for 'curable' illnesses. Hence Bergonié's change of opinion: the poor incurables who, until that point, had been used to establish radiotherapy were to be excluded from the centres. If, at the time when it started to be institutionalised, cancerology never intended to take on incurables, the movement in the struggle against cancer, on the other hand, which supported its development, immediately made of the 'bad luck which struck the incurables' a privileged subject for operation. In addition, very quickly, the codification of radiotherapy was reopened for discussion by those who, like Regaud, did their best to develop a scientific medicine of cancer founded on constant innovation in treatment. We will see how, with the union of this double dynamism, the question of incurables was considerably developed, until it challenged the redefinition of hospital medicine.

A new sensitivity

By taking a direct part in the process of caring for incurables, the League campaigners put the charitable ideas of the association into practice. Less than twenty in 1918, then forty in 1922 and more than one hundred in 1930, the ladies of the 'support section' divided themselves between visiting hospital patients and following them up at home, with Paris and its suburbs as their area of action.

The 'League ladies' threw themselves into an area of activity ignored by hospital staff and general medicine '[visiting] patients regularly and bringing to the most neglected little comforts which made their abandonment and suffering less painful'.[8] Those who visited the hospitals assisted with consultations, drew up a medical file for each patient recognised as affected by cancer, listing in seven files the various examinations and treatments which he had had, opened a social file and occupied themselves with his recall. Home visitors took over as soon as the patient left the hospital, 'monitoring him and encouraging him – if appropriate – to return to the department where he had been treated, helping his convalescence, return to work, etc., while completing [the] welfare form with details concerning accommodation or lifestyle, which were impossible to collect at the hospital bed'.[9] The charitable approach authorised the 'epidemiological' investigation and its scientific aim. 'By allowing us to care for the unfortunate, we share in their gratitude and it even allows us to collect some information which, one day perhaps, will have a place in the history of cancer.'[10] During the period between the wars, 36,000 individual files were in this way to be stored at the head office of the association.[11] The activities of the visiting ladies were in keeping with the voluntary nursing work which had motivated thousands of women during the war,[12] the cancerous poor replaced the wounded soldier. 'It is no longer a case of First World War soldiers arriving from the battle with their youth, their flesh healthy and vibrant, their vitality active . . . it is the sufferer who carries within him the deadly seed.'[13]

These society ladies also discovered a world of which they had been almost entirely ignorant. The experience of war medicine had confronted them with men from working-class backgrounds in the institutional framework of the hospital, visits to home put them in direct contact with the reality of certain misery, the sordidness of daily life and the family crises caused by the illness. All this was apparent from the social files which they drew up and the letters they sent each other.

> A particular patient was living with a married daughter, a mother of three children aged fifteen, thirteen and eleven. With the son-in-law, there were six people sleeping in the same room, and three in one bed, including the sufferer. A kitchen completed the accommodation ... I myself visited the family which had been referred to me. The father is a navvy, the mother and the fifteen-year-old daughter work in a stationer's shop. It is the youngest boy who stays at home to look after his grandmother ...[14]

> I have been to see your poor cancer patient and I have just had a telephone call from Saint-Michel telling me that they are hoping to admit her ... I met an unfortunate woman, completely dispirited, whom it was a pity to see, she had gradually sold all she had. She is alone night and day, except for an hour in the morning when a cleaning lady comes to help her wash, make her bed and light her fire, then at noon and at seven o'clock the doorman himself brings her some soup and stays five minutes ... She would want to die if she wasn't leaving a son of ten who is staying with a level-crossing keeper, her nurse, who has been looking after him and keeping him free of charge for years [but who] is herself very ill, and the unfortunate woman is wondering what will become of her son if both women die ...[15]

The psychological and social motives for charitable action are clearly very complex, and this work does not attempt to make an exhaustive analysis of it. The interest of the ruling classes in attenuating the most extreme consequences of the violence of social relations, by giving urgent help and by activities putting interpersonal relationships into play, is not nearly enough to explain the individual commitment of the visitors. Those journeys to the suburbs, those staircases climbed to the 'servants' quarters' (which they jokingly emphasised), this feeling of bringing some comfort, these smiles to each other, the smile that they wore to gain trust and the one that they received as a mark of gratitude, certainly contributed to bring to a mundane life an 'enrichment of the soul'. In any case, the poor sufferer who had been helped brought meaning to the existence of the society woman.

> Can I say that this activity and this enthusiasm cause feeling of a contentment which surprises even us? Should I tell you that the flame which enlivens us burns so brightly that it inspires charming and unexpected words, such as the ones which you will allow me to repeat.

Just lately, we wished to lighten the load of one of the visiting ladies, a task which never seemed heavy enough for her joyous activity: 'Do not take me away from this work' she implored, 'cancer is the sunshine of my life'.[16]

The 'charming words' pierce the superficiality of the message and give us a glimpse of the ambiguous relationships which grew up between horror, misfortune, need and pleasure. Of course, the driving force of charitable investment was not just one thing, it was in a sense research and a source and mode of pleasure and a need for reparation combined. Mme. Hartmann, describing her colleagues, sketched out a type.

> They come to us, some because goodness, in all its manifestations, is for them just as urgent a need as the air we breathe, others because during the Great War, they became used to leaning over a bed of suffering . . . others are women who have suffered, before whom we bow lower, . . . they have come, those who, in their deep pain, were seeking the sorrow which goes hand in hand with their own; by forgetting themselves, they have learned to live again and close to our sufferers, they have found that they still know how to smile.[17]

This 'support' – Mme Hartmann said the word is not enough 'to express what our hearts contain of pity and compassion for the unfortunate victims of the scourge'[18] – found its choice of subject in the patients that the institutions rejected. The question of 'incurables' emerged at once as a subject for major anxiety. 'Our great worry, a problem ceaselessly renewed, is the placing of our incurables.'[19] This suggestion from the chairwoman of the 'support section' echoed the indignation expressed by Robert Le Bret at the time of the General meeting of 1922. 'By what incredible injustice have they become true pariahs? They are turned away by the hospitals or admitted so late, with such difficulties, that they have almost reached the end of their suffering when they are finally admitted.'[20] The League was to lead a campaign for them to be no longer 'left on the hands of the hospital', and confirmed its principles:

> The cancer sufferer, whether he is inoperable or curable, is a being who suffers; *he has the right to be cared for* [my emphasis].[21]

> Let us see what happens to cancer sufferers: official doctors declare themselves at a loss with regard to most of them. They proclaim them 'incurable', they refuse them at the clinics. The hospitals and even the cancer centres reject them.[22]

Seventeen years separate these two quotations, demonstrating that at least official medicine remained reluctant regarding a 'right to be cared for', in spite of the pleas of a permanent campaign inciting the authorities and the medical body to end this scandal.

Contrary to what a certain medical sociology, prone to ascribe to the 'medical profession' a spontaneous tendency to extend its field of intervention, would have expected, the first initiative in bringing medical care to patients suffering from incurable cancer appeared in the form of a claim made by a movement which included hardly any doctors. The attitudes defended by the spokespersons of the League demonstrated above all the expression of a new 'sensitivity', which existed in individuals, essentially women who in the course of their work were faced with the suffering, anguish and confusion of patients.

> I have been caring for some time for an unfortunate woman whose awful distress is breaking my heart! This poor woman is suffering from a very advanced cancer . . . on which, I feel, it is difficult to operate due to the great weakness of the patient. This martyr is enduring it in her distressing hovel in the outskirts. She is absolutely alone (she has lost all her children), in an indescribable material and moral destitution, but she shows the most magnificent and radiant Christian resignation.
>
> At a certain hospital, which shall remain nameless, to which she went, she was treated very harshly and is very apprehensive about this hospital.
>
> At Saint-Joseph, they do not admit incurables.
>
> At the Calvaire, only external cancers are admitted. I do not know which way to turn![23]

Such 'contact' with social reality was a crucial experience for all those who experienced it. Robert Le Bret himself was deeply affected by it, hence his relentlessness in defending 'everyone's right to be cared for', and what could be noticed as 'projections' in the talks held and in the arguments put forward.

> The very strange chances of life have sent me on a mission for which I was not prepared. At the end of the general meeting at which the Anti-Cancer League was set up in 1918, without my being consulted or even forewarned, I was appointed as secretary-general . . . I was thus suddenly plunged into a circle of hell, without even having, like Dante, an informed guide to lead me. And I have seen long and sorrowful processions of patients in pain and suffering. Those who were suitable for surgery were admitted to hospitals for the period of the operation but were sent away as soon as possible afterwards, finding themselves among the incurables; and all these incurables wandered like outcasts and died, some in their own homes caring for themselves, others in indescribably awful conditions of hygiene and some in special annexes from which doctors averted their eyes.[24]

The primary objective of the League was to consist firstly in favouring the development of an institutional point of view which allowed the alternative mentioned by Le Bret to be avoided: 'home' or 'annex'. If both of these situations were considered equally shameful, the first allowed free rein to descriptions strongly coloured by 'expressionism'. Here was evoked 'the agony of cancer sufferers, the miseries which accompany it and the nauseous odours', 'the haemorrhagic purulent and finally putrid flows' which turn the patient into 'an insupportable burden', an 'object of hate', of 'disgust', of 'repulsion' in these 'hovels without water and conveniences', where 'poor families are packed together in minimal accommodation'. These images of 'the horror' of 'overcrowding' sustained opinions stressing the need for preventive action similar to that which launched the fight against tuberculosis, but for different reasons.

> Tuberculosis sufferers are looked after because they are considered as presenting risks of contagion ... Contact with a cancer sufferer is intolerable; is this not a reason to get him out of his family or his neighbours' surroundings, where overcrowding cannot be avoided?[25]

Rejection of the 'special annexes' was made more discreetly. These large wards (36 beds for men at Bicêtre, 55 beds for women at La Salpêtrière),[26] 'where never the hope of a cure could glimmer' for the patients who were crowded in there, deserted by the medical establishment, were criticised for their therapeutic 'nihilism'.[27] To these leftovers from the medical world of the Ancien Régime, Robert Le Bret opposed an institutional concept, inspired by the operation of the 'Saint-Michel Hospital'. This private general surgery hospital, built for charitable purposes and managed by Dr Récamier, for a long time personal doctor to the Duke of Orleans, was annexed from 1899 as a refuge for incurable cancer sufferers of both sexes.

The hospital–asylum combination fulfilled three functions. It made it possible that 'patients arriving for consultation when they could no longer receive the appropriate care at home should no longer be sent away', that incurable and 'recovering' convalescent patients could be mixed together in the same ward, thus keeping up the spirits of those who were doomed; finally, it created suitable conditions for a search for better treatment, for 'progress towards cure or at least towards the relief of suffering'.[28]

Because of gifts of radium and thanks to the income from a subscription opened free of charge in its columns by *Le Figaro*,[29] the League helped to provide the radiotherapy equipment for 'Saint-Michel'. It dealt in the same way with the Paris Oeuvre du Calvaire, giving it several radioactive needles, so that in 1923, operations of a therapeutic nature could be performed for the first time.[30] But the impact of these initiatives for private establishments hardly affected the social extent of the problem. Given the conditions under which diagnosis of cancer was made, the great majority of the patients were 'screened' at a very advanced stage of the development of their illness and fell into the category of 'incurables'. The few existing charitable institutions were very quickly overworked by the number of patients and, in spite of their activism, the ladies of the 'support section' could not manage to 'place' all their 'cases'. And the opening of the cancer centres contributed to increasing their work still more. 'The question of the hospitalisation of incurables is still worrying', explained Alice Le Bret, 'as with all hospitals organised to care for cancer sufferers, as soon as nothing more can be done for a patient, we are asked to admit him to a department for incurables.'[31] If, initially, the League did not fundamentally oppose the philosophy which presided over the operation of the 'healing factory', it still pleaded vigorously for a solution allowing responsibility to be taken for those who made up the majority of cancer sufferers: the addition of a general medical department to those concerned with treatment and research. 'When a patient can no longer be treated by the lancet or by X-rays, he must free his place which is so precious to those who are waiting, and by doing so be returned to the care of the doctor who, if he cannot defeat the illness, must at least try to alleviate its ravages.'[32]

> We still have a duty to first admit the man who is still strong and the mother of a family and lose no time before looking after them! But what a pity to see these poor wretches alone and abandoned. . . Since the other cancer centres are increasing in number, it is to be hoped that each will agree to have a small ward which would have a tenth of the beds and which would be called 'Pity'.[33]

Such an addition would allow, without harming the profitability of the centre, human problems to be resolved, protecting the people around the patient and serving the progress of science. 'Would it not be possible to benefit from this group of cancer sufferers by making scientific attempts at research? At the same time there might be a ray of hope [*sic*].'[34]

But the League directors had to accept the evidence; their campaign found little response from the civil hospice administrations and the directors of the cancer centres. Certainly, the *Assistance Publique* decided to equip the special annex in the Brévannes hospice by attaching to it several clearing beds for convalescents arriving from the six cancer centres of the Paris hospitals, but its reluctance regarding the problem of hospitalisation of incurable cancer sufferers was hardly tackled. Its great construction project for a new 'modern' hospice of a thousand beds, at Garches, explicitly excluded such sufferers, using the argument that since they were affected by a rapidly developing illness, they could not be placed in the same category as chronic patients.[35] In the provinces, the situation was even worse. Except for the few existing houses of the Calvaire (Lyons, Marseilles, Rouen and Saint-Etienne) which, apart from Lyons, were reserved for women, and those with 'open sores', there was generally an absence of *ad hoc* structures. There is no choice but to accept that this hardly seemed to worry the doctors in the cancer centres even though everyone, unanimously, deplored the fact that most of the patients arrived too late to be treated and that, under these conditions, only Professor Marie, the director of the Toulouse Cancer Centre, tried to overcome the institutional shortcomings that prevented the care of incurables. Certain centres, faced with a relative surge of patients, operated on a selection procedure at the time of the consultation, and only agreed to treat those cases which were most likely to be healed.[37] In Rheims, private doctors were asked by letter to make this choice themselves.

> It is useless to send us patients whose general condition is serious or whose wounds are too extensive for any attempt at surgical removal, or even sufficiently effective total irradiation. I would therefore be obliged if you would not commit yourselves regarding patients to whom the absence of treatment would cause injury which it is best to avoid.[38]

Questioning the notion of incurability

It was necessary to wait until the beginning of the 1930s to hear a few of the public hospital doctors mingle their voices with those of the League campaigners (male and female) and claim the right to hospitalisation for incurable cancer sufferers. Bringing an academic legitimacy to the claims of the charitable association, their support influenced the argument which until then had been developed in a more radical way. In a 1930 text published in the League's *Bulletin*, Dr Renaud, head doctor of the Brévannes hospice, contested the manner in which the question of incurable cancers was normally voiced, by first emphasising its non-specific nature:

> The idea of incurability does involve cancer alone. So, saying that a cancer is incurable does not mean that it is a question of an illness of a particular type, but means very simply that it is an illness whose lesions will not regress.[39]

This explanation was aimed at the negative effects of an administrative classification which awarded a particular status to incurable cancer sufferers, whilst medical knowledge did not ontologically establish incurability. Such a state of affairs was due to a simplistic concept by clinicians who were disinterested in what they could not heal and granted in practice, if not in theory, a false specific nature to cancer. The Brévannes doctor suggested another approach, which could take into account both the variable and unforeseeable nature of the development of the illness – which made it impossible to prejudge life expectancy – and the banality of the problems observed, common to many other illnesses. 'This,' he concluded, 'leads us to think that the so-called incurable cancer sufferer is an individual affected by a progressive and undefined disease, whose life expectancy will be very variable but sometimes very long, *and that it is a matter for general surgery.* [my emphasis].[40]

This dismissed of the idea of incurable, by which it was felt, with a turn of phrase widely adopted later (cancer sufferers, known as incurables), that it was only a matter of 'common sense' was without doubt familiar to the institutions. The introduction in Brévannes of therapeutic practices (the department was provided with a small amount of radium and one radiotherapy machine), which were, moreover, relatively sophisticated within a hospice, had indeed contributed to transform the 'cancer depot' into a 'medical' department. The belief that patients who were treated there 'were suitable for general medicine', a noble form *par excellence* of hospital medicine, was definitely part of the strategy of the re-evaluation of the hospice, in that it tended to abolish the distance separating the practices which were used there from those in use at the hospital. But, beyond the interest which underlay it, such a point of view had a 'normalising' effect aimed at modifying the image of these patients. Following his retirement in 1929, Professor Marie, who was committed to the establishment of a 'cancer sanatorium', which he financed in part from his own funds, explained this idea of 'normalisation' even more clearly. After having reviewed the different methods of treatment which could be used when faced with complications linked to the development of the illness, he wrote:

> There is therefore no further need to put the so-called incurable cancer patient in a class apart from other patients ... Our knowledge of the condition of *cancer sufferers at an advanced stage of the illness* is considerably detailed and it has become *inhumane* to consider them as outcasts who must be left to their wretched fate. On the contrary, *it has been demonstrated that they are sick like other people*, who can be comforted and whose life-span can be extended [emphasised in the original].[41]

Doctors who, like Maurice Renaud or Théodore Marie, took part in the political action of the League remained very isolated in France, as in other countries concerned in the fight against cancer. At least these are the conclusions which Robert Le Bret reached in his report regarding medico-social support for incurables, which he presented at the congress organised by the International Cancer Association in Brussels, in September 1936.

> We have tried to take a look at what is going on in various countries regarding the hospitalisation of incurable cancer sufferers. We have come up against an almost complete dearth of information. It seems that everywhere, the same prejudices exist. The incurable cancer patient is treated as undesirable and is only admitted to the establishment especially provided for him. There are no links between the surgery and radiotherapy departments which treat cancer sufferers and the annexes to which the incurables are banished. Doctors, even

those specialised in the care of cancer patients, ask 'charity' to rid them of an outcast who takes up their beds and services.[42]

Although, between the beginning and the end of the period between the First and Second World Wars, 'ethical' indignation was always foremost in the messages of the League, the argument had, notably, developed. The 'preventive' advantage of the hospitalisation of incurables was put second and the questioning of the erroneous nature of incurability occupied a central position, justifying the need to rethink totally the duties of medicine towards sufferers.

It is firstly the notion of incurable which we must get rid of. Whether the illness is or is not incurable, the doctor owes it care. We can say that life itself is an incurable illness, because it inevitably ends in death. There are always fatal diseases. Should a doctor abandon a patient when he knows that he cannot save his life? Why should it be different in the case of cancer?

For cancer sufferers, the doctor can always do something. There are dressings, there is care which relieves misery, there are above all remedies against pain. There is also moral reassurance. Modern treatment methods, by radiation, offer new possibilities. How many patients may be comforted and their life extended! It is no longer possible to make a distinction between curable, improvable and hopeless cancer sufferers.

The question of the hospitalisation of incurables will be resolved on the day when, in addition to charitable works like the Calvaires, the public hospitals consider it their duty to admit cancer sufferers who are from their region, whatever the degree of their illness, and when the cancer centres welcome those who appear at their surgeries needing care which cannot be carried out there, and also those who have relapsed after a first treatment.[43]

Within a period of a few years, charitable preoccupations affirming the right of incurables to be cared for had sketched out a reform of hospital medicine challenging the essentially 'curative' purpose of the institution. If there was clearly a divergence of opinion on the question of incurables between the League and the majority of the medical world, the opposition did not so much achieve a confrontation between two opposed speculative concepts of incurability as a mismatch of the points of view on the problem.

'Scientific medicine' for cancer largely contributed to demolishing, in practice, the notion of incurability as it was still used by Bergonié, that is as the prior classification of the illness. But it did not speculate on the social and institutional consequences. The line of thought supporting the initial programme of the organisation for the struggle against cancer, which was in accordance with the idea of a surgical empiricism (operable cancer/ inoperable cancer), became null and void with the advances in treatment made by the radiation clinic. The categories:

localised cancer	—	generalised cancer
curable cancer	—	incurable cancer
treatment centre	—	charitable work

tended to become more and more inoperative from the time when, for certain cancers, the effectiveness of radiotherapy, always tending to develop in accordance with the latest innovations, was no longer bound by previous limitations. In 1925, Regaud redefined the type of patients who were suitable for cancer centres, but made no mention of the criteria of incurability – this was because, in the Curie Foundation, such criteria very quickly stopped being a factor for the selection of a particular group of patients.

> The present reasons for which a certain number of patients . . . are not considered as suitable for treatment by radiation fall into three categories: a) contra-indication of a clinical nature; b) radiotherapy . . . already under way in another establishment; c) shortage of available places. *Contra-indications of a clinical nature are difficult to specify here, as it is a question of individual conditions rather than general rules*: ideas on the subject have always varied; the increase of the power of treatment methods and the use of new technical procedures have allowed us to extend radiotherapy to categories of illnesses which . . . would have been considered hopeless a few years ago [my emphasis].[44]

The contra-indications mentioned depended on assessments made of particular cases (general condition of the patient, cachexia, certain meta-stases), and recurrences or the existence of metastases were no longer enough to exclude the use of the treatment.

Similarly, the fact that radiotherapy allowed a temporary remission of certain inoperable cancers and sometimes a 'cure', led doctors to perfect a system of classification of 'stages of development' of the tumour when the simple opposition of localised cancer and generalised cancer was no longer appropriate. Therefore, for cancer of the cervix, the need to evaluate the effectiveness of treatment methods led to the empirical classification of 'four stages of development'. The evaluation showed that for any given treatment, the various rates of survival were according to the stages of the disease, and that the conditions were met for a curable/incurable opposition to co-exist alongside a complex vision of the 'probability of a cure'.[45] From the moment when 'incurability' stopped being – in certain cancer centres – a practical category which allowed a section of the population to be defined and excluded, it became a notion applicable to 'individual situations', characterising the final phase of the development of a treatment process, in which all the curative treatments had failed and the patient was now only a subject for palliative care. It was concerning the status of patients for institutional admittance who had reached this stage that points of view diverged. The doctors, in particular those at the Curie Foundation, asserted that attending the dying was not appropriate to their specialised competence and that institutions of a religious nature were much more likely to be able to deal with the problem.

> Poor people, who are exclusively patients of these special hospices, have not received the refined philosophical education which is alone capable of supplementing defective religious beliefs, when a painful and inexorable illness marks a near end to life, the exact outcome of which is still unknown. The unbelieving stoic may, it is true, suffer and see the approach of death without searching to voluntarily escape an insufferable life; but stoicism has always been the prerogative of elites and it is not widespread. For most humans, the consolations of religion are necessary, to help them bear a very long agony.[46]

The commonplace 'opium of the people', where the agnostic republican elite is found, was here used to justify the disinterest in practices which were not therapeutic. In this sense, 'specialists' saw in the incurable only the final stage of cancer which was beyond their field of operation, while the directors of the League saw a social problem to be resolved.

Robert Le Bret challenged a method of operation and organisation in the hospital which, by excessively favouring the healing dimension, neglected taking medico-social responsibility for patients and even excluded it when it involved – as in the case of cancer – complex procedures and not simple care. Such a system dissociated science and charity and engendered soulless premises which could well overcome the illness, postpone the arrival of death and blur the margins between the curable and the incurable, but in the end it treated someone who would not get better as 'debris' to be thrown out and rescued by women who were devoted but deficient in the necessary technical competence.

Speculating on both the negation of the idea of incurability held by scientific medicine and the limits of charitable action, the League general secretary eulogised a concept of the duties of medicine to the patient, which assigned to the hospital the complete role of taking responsibility, in such a way that the scientific ideal and the Christian ideal could finally combine.

9 Publicity, education, supervision

As soon as Europeans had rounded the Cape of Good Hope, Publicity took pride in subjugating the neighbouring peoples and converting them.

(Voltaire)

A miracle of publicity and public education against cancer! This so terrible word, which still sounds in the ears as an irrevocable death sentence, is starting to be uttered... What has therefore happened? How can one explain such a transformation in the public mind? Yesterday, the conspiracy of silence, false pride and great dread still existed! And today, there is free speech and trust!

(The Publicity Commission
of the National Health Office)

When the authorities decided to get involved in the fight against cancer, the role and the aims of the private associations which until then had occupied the essential part of that area were redefined. Although the state – through the ministry responsible for health problems and its Cancer Commission – intended to supervise the process of the building of cancer centres, at first it left to the League the task of ensuring the organisation of publicity.

In a 1923 text, Claudius Regaud wrote:

Indisputably, the first and the most important duty of any anti-cancer organisation is still to favour early diagnosis and treatment: on the one hand by means of a tireless publicity with the public; on the other by perfecting the means of instruction and information to be used by doctors.[1]

During the whole of the period between the First and Second World Wars, the 'public' and the 'non-specialist doctors' were to be the target of an incessant symbolic manipulation aimed at converting them to the ideas held by the promoters of the fight against cancer and to modifying their practices in a 'suitable' way as a result. But the educational action undertaken was accompanied by an indispensable consequence: the denunciation of 'quackery'. 'Beneficial publicity' had to be part of the struggle, because it defined its enemies: all those who, by becoming purveyors of 'false beliefs', played on the credulity of sufferers, sought to divert them from the correct path in order to satisfy their commercial instincts and, by this, condemned them to certain death. Because these heretics, murderers in effect, were sometimes unscrupulous doctors, public education and training of general practitioners went hand in hand with a willingness to reinforce the supervision of treatments, and gave rise to an appeal for 'Order'.

The paradoxes of early diagnosis

The decision to create centres endowed with equipment allowing treatment of cancer by modern methods caused a new optimism. Belief in the healing effectiveness of new methods which the specialised establishments were to provide was expressed almost without restraint. 'We can say that an accessible cancer, diagnosed very early, is a disease which medicine is certainly able to cure,' wrote Regaud in a booklet aimed at general practitioners.[2] However, being aware of the difficulties which it was necessary to resolve in order to create good conditions for early diagnosis was at once to temper enthusiasm a little. In fact, things were far from simple. Since the causal agent was unknown, it could not be identified in the body, which, on the whole would not be too damaged if one could, by a test, recognise the manifestations or defence reactions showing its existence, or if one knew how to isolate, in the blood, the stools or urine, specific biochemical components showing its presence. Unfortunately, all attempts to perfect a simple method of biological diagnosis were doomed to failure. The 'discovery of a cancer' had always been the outcome of complex clinical investigation and needed to be established with certainty, to have passed through a clinical anatomy examination, often carried out at the first therapeutic intervention.

Faced with the practical impossibility of a simple method of examination of the type used for mass screening of tuberculosis or syphilis, there was no alternative but to try to involve family doctors as well as the patients themselves.

If the role of generalists could not be ignored, all the 'cancerologists' were faced with this negative fact: their training had not prepared them for the discovery of the clinical signs heralding the onset of cancer.

'The student learns the general history of the various cancers, no-one draws his attention to the most important early signs of which we must be well aware if we wish to increase cures,' said Henri Hartmann in an issue of *Paris Médical* in 1923.[3] Regaud was even more explicit in his criticism. Because he had not been appropriately educated regarding the signs of cancer 'the general medical practitioner unfortunately must accept a large part of the responsibility for the delay in the diagnosis of cancer'.[4] It was necessary to fill in the gaps, so the League issued, from 1922, a very brief booklet which was sent to all the practitioners in France. There was a disillusioned comment from Hartmann: 'Most will certainly have thrown it into the waste paper basket without reading it.'[5] As a supplementary initiative, the Association for the Fight against Cancer persuaded the magazine *La Presse médicale* to publish in its columns short and concise articles on the early signs of cancer, produced by the most obvious 'authorities' in the area.[6]

The content of courses on cancer, designed for the mass of medical students, gradually became more 'up to date', with the 'older' generations of professors being replaced by clinicians directly concerned with cancer treatment and therefore interested in the question of early diagnosis.

But however important it might be, the training of general practitioners was not enough to resolve the problem; it was still necessary for patients to attend a consultation while there was still time. As Robert Le Bret explained, one was faced, 'with this paradoxical situation that the public is the first essential agent for its own safety and [that] *it must be taught to be anxious about signs which are not painful, or characteristic, or even worrying*' [my emphasis].[7]

Trying to resolve the problems highlighted by this paradox is an extremely ambitious aim: it involves attempting, through publicity, to encourage 'each' person to seriously modify the way in which he perceives his body, to acquire the capacity to distinguish as 'signs' symptoms up to now considered as harmless, and to be capable of interpreting them as indicators of a potential danger. In fact, it was under such conditions, and only under such conditions, that patients were to be persuaded to take the step which would get them to a doctor.

The League officials were aware of the difficulty of the task confronting them, but they had no choice but to tackle it, since 'publicity for early diagnosis' was not only a key part of the scientific and social fight against cancer, it was also an element vital to the very existence of their institution.

In fact, if it was taken for granted that an association like the League could not avoid talking about cancer, having to hold a public discussion on this disease made it absolutely necessary, in the context of the 1920s, to make early diagnosis a central theme of the discussion. In the words of the main officials, talking about cancer was in itself a decisive political action which determined all possibility of later publicity.

'It was necessary to attack on all fronts at the same time and we resolutely entered into action. First, we openly pronounced the word 'cancer'. An enemy which we dare not name cannot be defeated.'[8] To publicly name 'the enemy', was to start to have power over it, and make it lose the aura of terrifying strangeness which was part of its strength because it contributed to the inhibition of every vague desire for defence.

Above all, in this crusade which we were undertaking, the first thing to do was to familiarise ourselves with the word cancer, the terrible evil whose name we dare not utter. It was our duty to shake ourselves out of this lethargy, and to create a movement of public opinion, in all milieus, and we have undertaken to achieve it.[9]

Throughout the years to come, the League spokesmen would constantly insist on the validity of their progress, on the audacity which was theirs and on the merit accruing to them because of it. 'The creation of the League marked the beginning of a new era; we decided to utter the word CANCER, to display it, to address ourselves to the public,' declared Robert Le Bret at the General Meeting in 1937; '[it] has had sufficient strength and authority to set such a revolution in motion.'[10] Was this a circumstantial suggestion? A display of vanity from a secretary-general who desired self-satisfaction? Such a judgement would be harsh and particularly hasty. Le Bret's words showed even more the deep contentment of those who, having wagered their institutional existence on a difficult throw, felt that they had won their bet. By addressing the public to 'familiarise' it with the word 'cancer' and attempting to mobilise them, the League openly supported the argument that cancer could be conquered. It was an affirmation which was at least risky in a context where the effectiveness of medicine was not yet socially perceptible, since cases of cures remained fortunate exceptions and the great majority of sufferers were considered incurable.

The League might well assure the public that fatalism was no longer appropriate and guarantee it, and it was also necessary for it to appear credible in spite of the shortage of tangible proofs supporting its argument. It was because it knew that it was risking both its authority and legitimacy that we can understand why the question of early diagnosis occupied a central position in its discussion. It lent a coherence and strength of conviction to its campaign; the silence which surrounded cancer was harmful, it could only encourage the mistaken idea of its incurability. Contrary to appearances, medicine knew how to cure cancer, but only if it was treated within the required period. The problem was that the patients consulted the doctor too late, and it was because of this that it was necessary for them both to put up with the consequences. When the excuses and the falsely reassuring events were over, it was necessary to face the danger, to watch out for oneself and one's family, to act resolutely and not hesitate to entrust one's fate to the expert hands of specialists.

'Any work is fruitless if it is not understood and sustained by public opinion' said Robert Le Bret; the age of the League, its development and the influence of its operations demonstrated that its 'message' would have been received if not by the 'public' at least by those who counted as 'public opinion'. The nuance was not subtle. In fact, several recent surveys had shown that the association of cancer with inevitable death remained an idea which was firmly held by the people and significantly more so as one went down the 'social scale'. The League's success was to have persuaded the 'elite' to support its argument, the 'elite' which it had first targeted in its strategy of mobilisation against cancer. To win them over, was to 'shake up governments, legislative assemblies, département and town councils and administrations; to ensure the attention of philanthropists, voluntary subscriptions, spontaneous aid';[12] and also to obtain publicity from the press and radio, allowing the broadcasting of the message. It was finally to 'convert' those sections of the population whose manners, lifestyle and behaviour were held as a model of reference and then more or less in the long term to influence the behaviour of the middle classes, then the lower classes.[13] By writing that the success of the League lay in having been able win over the 'elite' to its argument, I also intend to emphasise – in terms of practical effectiveness – the limits of its campaign for early diagnosis. Nothing in the information at my disposal suggests that on the eve of the Second World War, patients affected by cancer would be detected earlier.

Several indications lead to this belief. The rate of mortality of cancer between 1917 and 1943 apparently never ceased to increase. Moine, when calculating this rate from the declared mortality rate, obtained the following results: 1917: 74/100,000; 1927: 95/100,000; 1936: 105/100,000.[14] Another statistic, established by the National Health Institute for the 1936–43 period, which gave the rates of mortality and now took into account undetermined causes of death, also showed, an increase: from 140/100,000 in 1936, the rate went to 158/100,000 in 1941 and to 161/100,000 in 1943.[15] If the interpretation of these figures requires much care (it was a question of presumed causes of death, and the conditions under which they were recorded, as well as the quality of the census, varied greatly between départements), we can nevertheless progress on one point and say that the campaign for early detection had no direct measurable impact in terms of a reduction in mortality. This element allows us to give some credit to the claims of the directors of the cancer centres, when they complained of receiving too many 'incurable' patients,[16] or to the secretary-general's words when he, pleading for the admission of incurables, declared in 1937 that the latter still represented 90 per cent of cancer patients.[17]

At last comes the final argument: it was due to the observation of the relative failure of the policy followed until then regarding early diagnosis that the decision was made, in the 1950s, to set up, at the cancer centres, 'detailed consultations responsible for improving detection'.[18]

The conversion of the 'elite'

We must allow the essential notion to reach everyone that suffering which is generally the safeguard of health because it warns of problems which threaten it here comes too late. This must be taught to the rich, who have too many mundane excuses for postponing an examination which troubles the pleasures of life; to businessmen, to intellectuals who are reluctant to drag themselves away from their occupation; to the not very wealthy public who dread costly operations, loss of wages and the risk of leaving a job.[19]

In principle aimed at the whole population, the 'League's message' was addressed, at least during the first few years, almost exclusively to 'society'. The Ladies of the publicity section at first wanted to gain more influence in the social environment which was theirs, by increasing the initiatives capable of gaining its understanding: charity fêtes, collections in grand restaurants, artistic galas, theatrical soirées. Baroness Mathilde de Rothschild's position, savoir-faire and sophistication worked miracles. The charity sale which she organised in 1924 in her Chateau de la Muette was one of the great occasions of that first period, which merited an account in *Le Gaulois*:

It was in the superb setting of Baron Henri de Rothschild's mansion and park that there took place on Tuesday the great charity sale for the benefit of the cancer struggle, that terrible scourge which claims so many victims, and for which a Ladies' committee, whose enthusiasm never fails, worked with ceaseless devotion [*sic*]. In the great hall of honour, in the village hall, there were varied counters attended by personages from Parisian high society and groups of foreigners. There was dancing in one of the salons, and another was occupied by bridge and mah-jong players. In the grandiose dining-room the buffet was set up, very well frequented by the buyers and sellers. And on the lawns, under the fine shades and around the marvellous flower beds, crowded an elegant throng, full of admiration for this residence, one of the most beautiful to have been built for many years . . .[20]

The journalist gave a list of the stalls and the names of a few 'devoted sellers', before concluding by expressing his sincere gratitude to the owners, to all those ladies and to 'Parisian businessmen, who, in a magnificent charitable gesture, had generously stocked the counters', and to the 'public who contributed so generously'.[21]

At the same time as they ensured an income for the association, these fêtes provided many opportunities 'to repeat [a] word of warning and slip in a few words of advice'[22] and also to 'familiarise' the audience with cancer. In a world of fine shades, flower-beds, bridge and mah-jong, where elegance rivalled charm and wealth, the scourge seemed less threatening, almost to the point of appearing tamed. By becoming a pretext for charitable trade, it entered the civilised world by the front door. A certain number of things were worthwhile to be put forward as arguments. The following in particular: that is that cancer is an 'egalitarian' social scourge which, unlike all others, affects rich and poor alike. The success of the League with the elite was also due to the fact that it was a charitable work unlike any other: it did not only propose to motivate society in favour of a single category of 'under-privileged', it also made it realise that its own interest lay there.

In this attempt to make the ruling classes aware, the campaign was more specifically directed towards the various female associations involved in this social work. The presence, in the Ladies' central committee, of officials belonging to several of these associations allowed close links to be established. Fourteen local committees of the Red Cross societies were members of the League. In 1924, the Union of Frenchwomen, by a decision of its national council, committed its campaigners to assist cancer sufferers and was associated with its educational publicity. The nursing schools dependent on its authority included the subject of 'cancer considered as a social disease' in their training programme.[23]

The visiting Ladies of the assistance committee (of which 'each is a convinced publicist') took advantage of their participation in the meetings of the 'Works Union' which took place regularly in each district in the capital to explain the League's aims to other charitable ladies present.[24] A particular effort to broadcast knowledge on cancer was aimed at the 'para-medical' world. Several meetings were held in the Musée Social [Social Museum] directed by Georges Risler,[25] and Mme. Le Bret was invited by the school of health visitors belonging to the Tuberculosis Defence Committee and by the social service practical school.[26] The doctor who put the most effort into these classes was unquestionably Dr Proust. The younger brother of Marcel, he was a surgeon, a director of the cancer centre of the Tenon hospital and a member of the League Scientific Council, and perhaps because he had inherited from his father a love of social medicine, he increased his involvement with the nursing school of the Frenchwomen's Union,[27] the factory social workers' school of the French Ladies' Association,[28] the parent house of the Saint Vincent de Paul Daughters of Charity,[29] the Marie-Thérèse clinic in Malakoff and, from 1928, when the League decided to organise, a regular training course (two annual sessions of seven lectures each) at the Charonne clinic open to nurses, social visitors and social workers, it was he, with his radiotherapy assistant, Dr de Nabias, who was to take on responsibility for the teaching.[30]

In the provinces, the subsidiaries of the League were not outdone and took on the task – in the same way and with the support of local medical notabilities – of a series of conferences essentially about early diagnosis. During the course of the years between the wars, 'the women's army' against cancer was increased and managed to find work in all of the medico-social institutional fabric. The League was to owe its perpetuation to it.

An education in health awareness

Until 1926, publicity aimed at the 'public at large' was almost non-existent, being limited to the dissemination of 'advice' in clear texts in the large Paris theatres[31] and to the production of a poster whose publication, a few thousand copies, remained secret. It was necessary for the Ministry of Health to intervene, in the form of a grant for 100,000 copies to be printed and sent to all the town halls.[32] The text of this poster, repeated in a leaflet, was produced by the Association for the Study of Cancer and was extremely concise, but it carried a message which one could see was not devoid of ambiguity (see Figure 9.1). The upper half of the poster was dedicated to a (re)presentation of the protagonists. The name of the association, in large characters, surmounted a sort of triptych, with, at its centre, the emblematic image of the struggle against cancer, a woman of proud bearing, clad in a Grecian tunic, holding out her arms as if to contain a monstrous crab whose erect claws framed the head of the character. On each side of the drawing, there was a slogan: on its right 'Cancer is one of the most feared scourges'; on its left: 'Cancer kills 40,000 persons per year in France'. The composition used the effect of symmetry to emphasise the contrast between threat and protection, but the drawing was not at all 'realistic' in effect and idealised the adversaries in an allegorical form (it could be called the scientific and social struggle protecting humanity from the scourge of cancer). The only trace of reality was the figure for annual deaths whose function was clear: to enforce the idea that cancer was a social plague which killed on a grand scale.

In this first manifestation of the many ways in which the League 'advertised' its existence, publicity for early diagnosis completely occupied the lower half of the design. A sentence in two lines, and underlined, justified the evocation of danger:

Cancer can be cured
if it is treated early

Below, was the warning 'Watch for its first signs', and the enumeration, line by line, of its main symptoms, grouped together opposite the word 'Beware' in large letters, then the invitation to consult a doctor ('See your doctor, have a thorough examination'); finally, at the very bottom, the final piece of advice emphasising the whole by this scarcely veiled threat 'Don't delay – it will be too late'.

The design of this second part of the poster relied on a construction which put into perspective and brought out the different sequences of the discussion. The wording, expressing either an act of faith (cancer can be cured) or advice regarding the action to be taken, framed the informative part, and, because of its design, clearly attracted the public's attention. On the other hand, understanding the various warning signs required active decoding. Correlatively, the language for the first half used 'simple' and easily intelligible formulas, while the informative wording largely sacrificed clarity to 'technical jargon' having recourse to academic words or expressions such as 'painless indurations', 'ulcerations', 'cutaneous tumours', 'persistent digestive problems'. On the face of it, the designers of the text took for

OFFICE NATIONAL D'HYGIÈNE SOCIALE

AFFICHE ÉDITÉE PAR LA

LIGUE
Franco-Anglo-Américaine

CONTRE LE CANCER

Reconnue d'utilité publique le 22 nov. 1920 sous le n° 464 — *Siège social :* 2, avenue Marceau, Paris

LE CANCER

est un des plus

redoutables

Fléaux

LE CANCER

tue en France

40.000 personnes

par an

LE CANCER PEUT ÊTRE GUÉRI

S'IL EST TRAITÉ A SON DÉBUT

SURVEILLEZ SES PREMIERS SIGNES

Méfiez-vous
- des indurations indolores du sein
- des ulcérations persistantes de la langue ou des lèvres
- des petites tumeurs cutanées qui augmentent et s'ulcèrent
- des troubles digestifs persistants, surtout quand ils s'accompagnent d'amaigrissement
- de l apparition après 40 ans, d'une paresse de l'intestin
- de toute perte anormale de sang

VOYEZ VOTRE MÉDECIN
SOUMETTEZ vous a un EXAMEN APPROFONDI

N'attendez pas -- Il sera trop tard

Figure 9.1 A poster produced by the Association for the Study of Cancer.

granted, without being aware of it, that the 'public' were much more familiar with medical language than they really were, and thereby failed in their educational aim. As long as the informational content remained unclear, it was only a poster carrying a more or less ambiguous representation of cancer (it was one of the most fatal scourges – it was an illness which could be cured), which urged the public to beware, to monitor themselves, to act quickly by consulting doctors, but without really clarifying what they should beware of. And the failures in educational communication were to be repeated throughout the whole inter-war period.

The entry on the scene, with effect from 1927, of the national Health Office which put its advertising department in touch with all the great charities (including the League) to encourage a preventive public health plan changed nothing.[33]

The new poster, prepared in 1930 (see Figure 9.2), only altered the factual list of suspect signs very slightly, but the representation of the struggle against cancer completely changed in tone. For discussion, a single concise and effective slogan was placed at the top of the poster:

> Kill cancer!
> before it kills you . . .

The message tried to overcome any effect of alienation from the potential reader. It was no longer addressed to the 'public at large', but tried to reach each one individually. It no longer talked about cancer on an apparently objective and explanatory tone (cancer was a scourge which killed many, but which, in certain conditions, could be cured), because all characterisation had become superfluous. Between the individual and cancer, it could only be a question of a fight to the death, the victor of which would be the one

Figure 9.2 A later poster using a more concise and effective slogan.

who killed first. The presentation of the informative part was in accordance with this warlike philosophy of 'watch . . . and destroy'; under the 'Beware' and its grouping of suspect signs there was a list of treatment centres.

The imagery occupied a larger space and put the struggle into its correct focus. This time, the crab was in the foreground, outlined sideways and extended by a projected shadow which increased the size of the claws, and a pointed sword between its eyes replaced the protective goddess. In 1930, the fight against cancer was in tune with the political propaganda of the age. It played, no doubt unconsciously, on the analogies of images and implicit parallels. Cancer had just become part of the range of the evils threatening society. In 1930, cancer publicity changed style, and scale. The League, in collaboration with the Social Health Office, intensified its campaign with the creation of a 'cancer week'. The new poster, produced for the occasion, was reproduced on postcards (250,000) and on blotters (200,000). Many newspapers printed in their columns articles dealing with cancer, written by the 'best specialists'. The fight against cancer made its voice heard in the daily radio chat shows. The whole thing was supplemented in the provinces by the organisation of touring lectures and the showing of a 'social health film for public instruction' by Jean Benoît-Lévy, soberly entitled *Cancer*, made under the scientific direction of Gustave Roussy and patronised by the League. In the credits, the film showed a real crab, this time inside a terrestrial globe.[34]

The tone of these 'campaigning' lectures was, following the example of the poster, deliberately warlike: 'Tuberculosis is now being surrounded . . . Syphilis is subject to fierce blows each day and is retreating. Let us attack cancer without delay, after unmasking it';[35] 'Early diagnosis . . . is the war cry which will be repeated and which will echo all the publicity organised by the League'.[36] And deliberately terrifying:

> Let us all relive our memories.
>
> Of course, we can all imagine a dear being, a beloved friend, gradually declining, deprived of his strength and his substance, smiling only with effort so painful is his body.
>
> And, however, with surprising passivity, our country has long allowed itself . . . to be the prey of the worst of physical degradations, to consider as an unavoidable fatality the long torture of the living flesh, which confirms the triumph of cancer.[37]

> It then gets nearer and nearer, it gets bigger, it gets deeper, it reaches the lymphatic system, it reaches the ganglions, it enters the circulation, it colonises, it invades, it causes suffering. It is then too late. . . .[38]

To the voices which were raised in concern about the effect that this type of message might have on the population, the Health Office publicity officer, Lucien Viborel, replied by condemning the 'dangerous pessimism' which the critics demonstrated. 'If we spread fear, it is a healthy fear . . . it has been proved that fear never killed anyone, whilst cancer itself has claimed innumerable victims, and it is only under the influence of emotion that any action is taken'.[39]

Although publicity did not produce a general panic, its consequences began to be felt in doctors' surgeries, to the point that, at the time of the 1932 cancer week, a radio talk was dedicated to 'cancerphobics'. Dr Jacques deplored the frailty of human understanding and its difficulty in showing wisdom.

> What can we say about the crowd of worried, anxious people, the obsessed who, dominated by fear of cancer, lay siege to the specialist's office at the smallest suspicious sign; then, insufficiently reassured by a favourable diagnosis, go from door to door in search of the dreaded confirmation of their doubts.[40]

Certainly, cancer is a disconcerting adversary. Its perfidy means it should be discovered at its first signs, but how does one get its victims to recognise it in time, without warning them of the insidious nature of its attacks and so risk instilling 'the germs of a morbid obsession which an inevitably incomplete knowledge of the signs . . . may put into badly prepared minds?'[41]

The Homo medicus

To better 'prepare minds', educational publicity was deployed in two directions. It further explained suspect signs by using newspapers and radio, and sought to train young minds to be alert and save themselves from cancer.

From the 'second cancer week', the chats became more precise and, thanks to the agreements reached with newspaper managers, were published in the main daily papers. Thus 'Breast cancer may be cured if it is treated early' by Professor Forgue was published in *L'ami du peuple*; 'The struggle against cancer of the womb' by Professor Faure in *Le temps*; 'The true and false cancers of the tongue' by Professor Sebilleau in *Le Journal*; 'The cancers of the skin, how they start, how to safeguard oneself against them' by Dr Darier in *Le Petit Parisien;* 'Bone tumours' by Professor Bérard in *Le Matin* and 'Stomach Cancer' by Professor Gunsett in *L'Intransigeant*.[42] Each year until the eve of the war, the same procedure was to be used, with new speakers and several variations in the types of cancer mentioned.

From 1937, in agreement with the Ministry of National Education, the League publicised in schools, colleges and grammar schools *Leçons pour la jeunesse* [lessons for youth] in the form of two small texts, one 'for children', the other for 'young people'.[43]

An analysis of these conferences easily reveals the limits of their educational effectiveness. It was as if these professors from the faculty of medicine were addressing an audience of students. The description of the early signs was presented in the style of a course textbook.

> When, without an appreciable reason in an already mature patient, preferably a man, a persistent difficulty [in swallowing] occurs over more than two or three weeks, which is fixed in one place although variable in intensity and even more so if you add to it reiterated expuitions [*sic*] of blood, it will be the most elementary prudence to call for an examination . . . [44]

> The first sign of cancer [of the womb] is a discharge of blood, outside regular menstruation. This discharge is rarely abundant, at least at the start of the illness, and that is very natural, as it comes from a slight ulceration. It is generally reduced to a few drops which appear from time to time, with the greatest irregularity. It is reduced by rest but increased on the other hand by walking, movements and the particular violence to which the cervix is normally exposed [*sic*].[45]

Apart from the use of language normally used by an expert, the doctors' message invited the potential patient to adopt an objective point of view towards his own body, as if he could be divided in two and be at one and the same time the examining doctor and the patient examined. Here is how Professor Forgue suggested teaching women to palpate their own breasts:

> You must know how to look for hard nodules, which show that a tumour is starting. Be careful, when palpating your breast, not to take it sideways between your fingers, otherwise you would be in danger of a false alarm, as this sideways pressure of a breast, even if normal, can give the disappointing [?!] feel of a false tumour. Palpate flatly, the ends of your joined fingers, applying the breast against the surface of the chest. If you sense a resistant, hard, grainy kernel, with badly outlined contours, causing a thin ridge on the skin when you try to move it, immediately ask for a doctor's examination.[46]

We could add to the examples and ramble on about the incompetence of the doctors of that time (but have things changed much?) in putting over knowledge in a lecture accessible to lay people, but the important thing is rather to try to understand the reasons for it. Awkwardness and a lack of savoir-faire certainly had a role to play in this lack of communication, but these aspects were only a part of it. More fundamentally, the problem was in the thinking which underlay educational progress. The idea that each human being must look after his own health was not new, but it had, however, long been limited to questions of lifestyle with an emphasis on the great importance on diet.[47] The involvement of the 'public' in the early diagnosis of cancer (and by extension, for patients treated, in monitoring signs of recurrence) implied a relationship with medicine other than that which originated from the simple observance of rules relating to a 'healthy lifestyle', or, more exactly, by making the potential patient an agent of the technical division of the medical work, it redefined a 'healthy lifestyle'.

> It is truly surprising to see how the modern woman, whose desire to look elegant so often causes her to look in the mirror for a 'touch up', a little rouge, or to arrange her hair, neglects to monitor her essential organs. The woman who is approaching fifty is preoccupied with the appearance of her breasts . . . How many are there who, occasionally, palpate their healthy consistency and who, without becoming obsessed with cancer, for a simple measure of precaution, check if anything abnormal appears?[48]

To convert the frivolous woman, according to Forgue, and convince her to overcome her modesty, according to Rechou,[49] were worries which resulted directly from the specialists' view of the process leading from discovery to treatment. Monitoring suspicious signs, making a diagnosis, its verification, the decision on treatment and starting it constituted from their point of view a succession of differentiated technical acts, as much because of the type of knowledge required (from the general to the specialised) as because of the agents summoned to realise it. Taking on the position of 'Master of works', the collective specialists of the cancer centres delegated to others the task of screening, diagnosis and referral to their institutions. It was a delegation which implied that these less qualified 'others' were technically capable of fulfilling these functions, but one that also, and we will return to this later, implied that they should not exceed their role. According to this way of thinking, the potential patient becomes a medical auxiliary. The first link in the chain, he is in a way the watchman who alerts the general practitioner. Hence the importance accorded to the 'training' of this 'patient watchman', with all that that assumes in the way of a 'trans-formation', so that the frivolous woman and the modest woman become a *Homo medicus*, that ideal subject of medicine capable of viewing his/her body as a clinical object. A coherent and rational project if we look at it from the specialist's point of view, but an illusory project condemning its originators to be ceaselessly astounded by the paradoxes of a human understanding which does not seem to comprehend the simplest things or which, when it does comprehend them, does not grasp their consequences. An illusory project, because the vision which inspires it is blind to the main point. Dividing medical practice into a succession of hierarchical tasks, it isolates one elementary task, the discovery of 'suspect symptoms' but forgets that the signs which the potential patient should recognise are the signs produced with regard to a 'medical body-object' constructed for him too. The signs are therefore identifiable and vehicles of sense only in the case of a global knowledge of this 'medical body-object' of which the patient is deprived, and that finally the perception of the signs which this 'medical body-object' implies suggests a position of exteriority (condition of objectivisation) with regard to the subjective body, impossible for the patient (even when the latter is a doctor).

But saying that a project rests on an illusion does not mean that, when put into practice, it is without effect. The anti-cancer publicity initiated a growth of the mind, which was to be accentuated during the second half of the century, because of the larger and larger place which these pre-occupations were to occupy relative to the 'chronic' degenerative diseases of mature age. Individuals were not going to manage to cast a 'medical eye' on themselves, but they were to progressively acquire, with clearly large variations according to social classes, the suitable capability of 'getting worried' because of suspect symptoms in their body and going to consult a doctor. 'Self-monitoring' and its corollary, the lowering of the 'sensitivity threshold' to symptoms suggesting a disorder, were to become characteristics of 'civilised behaviour'. In the short term, the anti-cancer publicity succeeded in making of cancer an illness of 'public interest', seriously competing with tuberculosis and syphilis. A crowning point of its success, the issue in 1938 of a cancer stamp, was the occasion for launching a financial appeal for the first time on a nation-wide scale.[50] But the dynamics of mobilisation had effects which the League's directors had every reason to consider 'pernicious'.

Parasite publicity

> Never in the past had this feared word appeared in newspapers. . . . Today, there are hundreds of newspaper articles, reports of conferences, and I shall add – which is the reason for our benevolent publicity – even dangerous and often fallacious advertisements for useless products and illusory discoveries.[51]

For a movement which had made the early referral of patients towards specialised treatment the essential plank of its policy, the charlatan was an enemy who had to be fought with the greatest determination. It diverted away from the only true path a 'naïve' willingly credulous public which 'allowed itself to be completely deluded', attracting it to 'old wives' remedies' and 'miraculous cures', which caused it to nurture the hope of an effortless and painless cure. Together with the start of the policy of struggle against cancer, 'it is indispensable' wrote Regaud in 1924, 'to start a vigorous campaign against all forms of quackery which are so harmful to cancer sufferers'.[52]

Justin Godart, at the time of his transfer in 1924 to the Ministry of Health in the government of the Coalition of the Left, made complaints against several establishments which 'assume pompously the name of institutes and do not mention any doctor's name'.[53] The increase of these shady dispensaries 'which promise to cure cancer without surgery or radiotherapy and extort often considerable sums of money from the "wretched sufferers" ', was evidence of the vitality of a parallel market of cancer treatment which neither official medicine nor the League seemed able to easily reduce. When reading the abundant literature dedicated to the problem, it seems that 'quackery' was a very polymorphous phenomenon in its manifestations which did not allow itself be entrammelled, except occasionally, by the tangled web of the law. The main charges which could be brought to counter the 'harmful practices' of these objective allied 'curers of cancer' were few, badly adjusted to the situation, and, because of this, easily circumvented. Therefore the law of 24 *germinal* year IX may well have forbidden the advertising and sale of secret remedies and only authorised the magistral remedy of a doctor's prescription or a medicinal remedy in accordance with the Codex or accepted by the Academy of Medicine. Nevertheless, it was enough to suggest a medicine conforming to these requirements and indicating the name and the dose of the substances which it contained for its sale to be legal. 'The law against secret remedies can hardly be applied' averred Robert Le Bret somewhat bitterly; 'for a cancer patient, the danger is also in the confidence which he places in an ineffective remedy, whether the remedy is secret or not, matters little.'[54]

The accusation of fraud necessitates, so as not to be made in vain, being able to prove that there has been deliberate deceit concerning the suggested remedy. But how can criteria be established which will allow a 'fraudulent pseudo-invention' to be distinguished from a true therapeutic innovation, without risking sacrificing this on the altar of the medical orthodoxy of the moment?

> It cannot be a question of codifying scientific truths, of establishing treatment guaranteed by the State and of instituting a medical infallibility. Science is continuously developing, therapy feels its way through often bold but never definitive tests. Chance and daring are often, with conscientious research and judgement, elements of progress. The best inventions have only triumphed after passionate struggles and discussions. However, the public must be protected from charlatans.[55]

To get round the problem, several deputies, Couteaux in 1924, Gratien and Caujole in 1930, tabled draft laws suggesting that all publicity in favour of treatments or pharmaceutical preparations by way of press or advertisement should be forbidden and that they should be confined to scientific and professional journals only. These initiatives, which in any case did not succeed, hardly raised any enthusiasm in the League. Of course, the 'lying advertisements' would in this way be deprived of a great part of their publicity, but such a measure would penalise at the same time 'useful, prolific and necessary' advertising. To prevent some was to prevent others, as 'discrimination between the two rested on good faith, the assessment of which is delicate'.[56] The idea of drying up the audience of charlatans by monitoring the nature of the advertisements was utopian to put into practice. Even if they accepted such a check in principle, the directors of the publications were unable to take action, and unqualified to do so.[57] Was it therefore necessary to involve the authorities?

> To monitor advertisements in newspapers, to read posters, to distinguish between those which are dangerous or tendentious, to notice offences made up of subtle components, to take the initiative in legal proceedings, to risk failure, the ministry has other more urgent, more important and less difficult business.[58]

While not being able to do otherwise than be a vehicle for the quackery of the press, the League visibly intended not to alienate a medium very useful to its own cause. 'There is in the newspapers here a nerve which it is prudent not to strike. We cannot ask them to deprive themselves of a large income, nor to check the truth of advertisements, it is the public whose gullibility we must overcome'.[59]

The third angle of attack possible on the legal level was indictment for the illegal practice of medicine. The 1892 law required a doctor to practise in his own name after obtaining certificates which proved his ability. But here too, the legal weapon, which was very imprecise, often failed to reach its target and when it did reach it, was in danger of producing the opposite result to that required. As Robert Le Bret wrote:

> If the absence of certificates allows proceedings to be taken against those who treat patients without being approved by the faculties, it is still necessary to reach an understanding on what is meant by treatment of patients, and many charlatans marginally remain within the limits of the definition given.[60]

The discriminatory power of the legislative body still had serious limitations on this point. The medical associations understood the situation and took it seriously. Anxious to condemn healers for the illegal practice of medicine, they found they were faced with magistrates divided on the legal definition of the medical act when the practices condemned were inspired by religion.

The Valenciennes court, in a sentence passed on 12 November 1930, considered that

> there is no offence in the illegal practice of medicine by a healer who does not diagnose and does not indicate any treatment to be followed or remedies to be taken, and limits himself to a laying on of hands and to an invocation to God. Such a method is not specifically medical and

is totally different from the usual procedures of doctors and surgeons, in the same way as it uses none of the contentious remedies contained in the Codex of pharmacy to heal the sick.[61]

The Toulouse court in a similar case gave an identical verdict; on the other hand, the Seine court condemned a healer who treated patients by prayer, laying on of hands and the drinking of water from the Paris Water Company blessed by himself. The argument was that, for an illegal practice of medicine to exist,

> it is necessary and it is enough for the healer to take part, habitually or in following a direction, in the treatment of the sick. Once the treatment is carried out, the use of magnetic passes and the laying on of hands, which comprise a healing procedure, are not important.[62]

Even if the healer was sentenced, the dissuasive effect of the punishment was, in the opinion of the League's secretary, less than certain. The applicant, if he was able to prove his ability, could benefit from the proceedings brought against him.

> He showed that he treated patients free of charge and emphasised on the contrary the exaggerated fees charged by doctors. He produced as witnesses a series of patients who claimed that they owed him their life and health. The result is an increase in his patients.[63]

In any case, in the illegal world which traded in illusory remedies,

> these healers, these bonesetters, are not very often the most harmful. The danger lies mainly with those who have a certificate and abuse it to ensnare the patient by patter which deceives, or fleece them by taking undeserved fees for feigned care . . . We constantly read advertisements for treatment or remedies curing cancer without operations or radiotherapy, even going so far as to malign surgery which supposedly mutilates and radiation which burns the patient without saving him. There is always a doctor's signature.[64]

The law was ill-equipped against these 'sharks', the 'grasping doctors', the 'quacks' who were – excuse this awful pun – the black sheep [translator's note – the play on words is between the literal translation of the expression used for 'quacks' of 'brown doctors', and 'black sheep'] of the profession. Not only did it not allow proceedings to be taken against them, but it imposed caution on those who wished to denounce them.

> Read the law and jurisprudence and you will judge . . . Any allegation or imputation of an act of nature to attack the honour or the liability of

a person, any insulting expression, term of disdain or invective may be subject to corrective proceedings and may be the subject of damages. *Proof of defamation is not allowed.* . . . We are therefore constrained to accept philosophically the accusation of pusillanimity, weakness and imprecision. We do not have the right to prove that an affirmation which the Faculty proclaims as false is really false. And if we were authorised, how would we do it? How could we prove that a particular patient, whom a particular doctor affirms that he has cured of cancer, did not really have cancer?[65]

Well aware of the limits of legal action against the problem, the directors of the League were conscious that the struggle against quackery included all the aspects of the intervention of the anti-cancer policy. Publicity had to make the effort to save the public from pernicious influences, by recalling at every opportunity that treatments by surgery and radiation were the only ones capable of 'killing cancer' and by taking precautions against the peddlers of illusions.[66] By pressurising the authorities, the Association for the Fight against Cancer persuaded the ministry to despatch a circular to the prefects advising them to ensure that 'scientific' quality was respected at conferences on cancer taking place on the premises of public institutions.[67] The denunciation of quacks, however important it might be, was not enough to reduce a phenomenon whose success was fed by the failures of medical science, and also by the illogicalities of the organisation of the health system. How could one insist that official medicine should have the monopoly of therapeutic interventions if it was not interested in the fate of the majority of cancer patients? The subject of the fight against quackery here came to aid the reformist aims of the League, making the hospital accessible to all classes of society and taking responsibility for incurables by using the general medical services.

I emphasise the duty of the cancer centres to open their doors wide because I can hear doctors complaining about quackery. Where do you expect cancer patients to go, if the centres only accept the poor, and even then only the small proportion which is those who are curable, if the hospitals refuse the inoperables and if the established doctors persist in associating the idea of incurability with cancer? The cancer patient turned away in this way by the official establishments and discouraged by the pessimism of his own doctor goes back to the quack who tells him: 'Come to me, I will cure you without an operation and without radiation.' The patient will not be saved, but he will have been welcomed and given a little hope.[68]

These profound changes in medicine could not in any case be purely effective unless they were supplemented by a third section which dealt with the problem of the legitimacy and methods for monitoring the practices of the professional group. On this point too, the League had an opinion. It resolutely sided with those who asked for the creation of an 'Order of doctors'.

The call for an Order: a necessary solution, but a partial response

By tabling, at the extraordinary meeting of the Parliament of 28 November 1928, a draft bill relating to the institution of an order of doctors, Xavier Vallat, Edouard Barthe, Braise, Bertrand d'Aramon and Colonel Calais intended to make the idea prevail which had for a long time been preoccupying the medical world and the authorities. After the law of 19 *ventôse* year XI had ended several years of 'free practice in the art of healing' by re-establishing the monopoly of certified doctors, projects linked with the organisation of the profession regularly saw partisans and adversaries who were opposed to a medical policy which controlled the activities of its members.

Until then, repeated attempts to set up a disciplinary authority had not been successful. Already in 1812, a commission chaired by Cuvier and Dupuytren pronounced on the setting up of 'disciplinary boards' composed of experienced doctors and put under the responsibility of the Ministry of the Interior. It had to go into reverse gear when faced with the fanatical hostility of liberals who denounced the return in strength of the nepotism of the Ancien Régime. The idea was taken up again by Salvandy, Louis-Philippe's Minister of Education, but the law which was put before Parliament could not be passed as, at the same time, the February 1848 Revolution broke out, sweeping the regime away. It resurfaced in another form, thirteen years after the Third Republic was set up. Two local officials of the General Association of the Doctors of France, Doctors Surmay and Mougeot, tabled a 'Doctors' Order' motion aiming at curbing what seemed to be at the time excessive competition, in the first rank of which was the 'poaching of customers' by unscrupulous colleagues. But the majority of local sections voted against it, rejecting 'press-ganging', and the modifications towards flexibility suggested by Dr Lassale in 1897 did not change anything, as the fear of being controlled was too significant.[69] If an Order could not be imposed on the heart of the profession, the reasons which regularly encouraged certain people to renew the proposal remained topical. During the 1920s, the combination of several scandals involving doctors in the traffic of clients and the prospect of the application of laws on social security relaunched the project. The main official to suggest the law, Xavier Vallat, was a deputy from the extreme right close to Action Française [the nationalist and royalist party], whose influence was growing on medical unionism. The explanation of the reasons showed the need to allow the medical profession, which was for the most part extremely honest, 'to take the law into its own hands regarding the black sheep who risked bringing discredit to the whole profession.'[70] It emphasised the need for a respectability and professional conscience which were indispensable to gain the patient's trust and for the considerable social role which the doctor needed to fulfil because of all the relief laws. Finally, because medicine was not an 'exact science' and that 'very dissimilar ideas can exist regarding treatment', the monitoring of practices could not be a matter for common jurisdiction, but for authorities originating from the 'organised medical profession'.

What with assessment, discussions, toing and froing between the Chamber of Deputies and the Senate and postponements while awaiting multiple changes of ministries, Parliament was to be occupied by the matter until the definitive adoption of the text of a law in 1940. Even if the initiative depended on a deputy from the extreme right, taking up positions for or against did not encompass the usual political divisions, as there were partisans and detractors in both parties. The defenders of the project used the crisis which shook medicine to justify their positions.[71] In their opinion, quackery was gaining ground within the profession, because of the combination of two factors. The first, the 'plethora of doctors', was a rehash of the topic of medical congestion, recurring throughout the nineteenth century. The growth in the number of doctors was larger than that of the population and tended to accelerate as never before. The spokesman to the Senate emphasised that between 1914 and 1932, the number of qualified doctors increased from 23,000 to 26,500 and that, in the same period, the number of students registered in the faculty doubled, increasing from 1,572 in 1913 to 3,125 in 1932.[72] The second factor was concerned with the 'revolution' in the type of clients and the rewards following the increase in social laws. Therefore, explained Robert Le Bret, at the same time as the congestion in the profession generated a 'race for clients', competition from specialists and the reduction of fees fixed by decrees incited the practitioner to put up with 'abuses from patients demanding unnecessary visits, incorrect certificates and exaggerated prescriptions', and it became inevitable in this obnoxious environment that 'certain consciences wavered' and finally 'lacked the principles and values of the ethical code of one of the finest human professions'.[73]

So the League's general secretary was to find an occasion to rejoice, during his final report to the campaigners' meeting of 1 June 1941, in the adoption of a law creating this order of doctors.[74] However, could the requirements to improve the ethics of the profession be limited to stigmatising the degradation of those who practised medicine 'under normal commercial conditions'? The anxious questions of certain cancer specialists faced with the therapeutic practices of some of their colleagues suggested that the opposition between, on the one hand, honest and virtuous doctors and, on the other hand, unscrupulous sharks only imperfectly accounted for the problems. The deceitful publicity used by the quack in order to obtain gullible patients was only the expression, in a manifestly reprehensible way, of a more general phenomenon linked to the development of medicine and particularly perceptible regarding the treatment of cancer. To advance the argument of the complexity of techniques connected with scientific advances in order to limit the building of cancer centres in towns likely to have competent people and in order to extol the need for multi-disciplinary teams to develop treatment strategies, was to affirm at the same time that the 'freedom to practise the art of healing ' legally granted to any holder of a doctor's qualification was in fact relatively null and void. The existence of specialised competences escaping the mastery of the non-specialist should dissuade the latter from making use in certain cases of the rights which the law granted him. The Cancer Commission did not affirm anything else when it re-adopted at its own expense the 'General principles deduced from the present state of therapy', drawn up at its request by Regaud in 1923. We can, therefore, read the following recommendations in this compilation of seventeen simple proposals which were to be used as a guide for non-specialist doctors:

- Proposal seven: There are particular rules in cancer removal surgery which, without in any way constituting a specialist surgery, require a certain pathological knowledge from the operator and certain operating procedures.
    No-one has the moral right to operate on a cancer unless he is in a position to satisfy its requirement from his own knowledge and ability.
- Proposal eight: Radiotherapy of cancer may only be carried out by doctors, surgeons or radiologists who have had special training in radio-therapy methods.
- Proposal nine: Cancer curietherapy, when indicated, requires the use of radioactive centres, the number and content of which must not exceed maximum and minimum levels – in any case very different according to the circumstances.
    The possession of a few needles or one or two tubes of radium does not make it legitimate for treatment of cancer to be carried out. There is no omnibus radium tube. In spite of the simplicity and the manageability of its material, in spite of the deceiving ease of its operating manual, curietherapy itself is difficult – firstly because of the physical, biological and pathological knowledge it requires, and secondly because of the incomplete development of its fundamental rules and its techniques.
- Proposal ten: Roentgentherapy . . . requires the use of equipment which must be very different from that needed for radiodiagnosis.[75]

The fact that it was necessary to write and publish such recommendations suggests that they were not thought to be obvious by non-specialists. The need to have to repeat these principles regularly, the request made to the authorities not to favour the use of radiotherapy methods outside qualified centres, showed that there was a persistent problem. In a memorandum for the radiotherapy sub-commission to the League of Nations Cancer Commission, Regaud harked back to these 'savage' practices.

> The difficulty in treating cancers of the womb surgically hardly needs demonstrating. . . . It is true that the difficulty of the operations, no less than the fear of immediate or imminent accidents, normally tempers the ardour of surgeons who have been insufficiently trained. But this restraint does not exist in the use of radium and X-rays. The handling of curietherapy and roentgentherapy seems so simple for persons who do not consider *the amount of knowledge and experience which go into gestures which appear easy, and which many people are tempted to add to their own practice, without giving themselves the necessary preparation* [my emphasis].[76]

According to one supporter of scientific cancer medicine, the situation which developed seemed dangerously uncontrolled. Not only were general practitioners, because of a lack of appropriate training, bad diagnostician-advisers, but some of them, as well as a number of 'ordinary' surgeons, gynaecologists and radiologists working in isolation or in small clinics, all motivated by the concern to keep their patients, proclaimed themselves radiotherapists. And they could do this all the more easily in that they were not breaking the law and did not risk too much discredit.

> The practice of medicine is free (under the guarantee of general diplomas) and it is secret (except in public hospitals); cancer abandoned to its spontaneous development is notoriously always fatal. Under these circumstances, therapy finds easy absolution for the errors and mistakes which are committed in its name.[77]

For someone like Regaud, who thought of radiotherapy as a scientific discipline and a meeting point between fundamental research and the clinic, the practice of which was to require full-time doctors dividing their time between the laboratory and hospital service,[78] the margin which separated these ill-timed practices of established quackery was narrow. But the director of the Curie Foundation was aware that any proposal tending to restrict the freedom of treatment which the doctors enjoyed would be seen as an intolerable attack endangering the private nature of medicine. 'Advising that in one way or another the right of doctors to freely practise cancer radiotherapy should be limited would be taking a path full of pitfalls.'[79] One could, therefore, only appeal to the conscience of the non-specialist to prevent him from treating his patients when he did not have the required competence, and, on subjects taken as mastered by the best specialists, to 'recommend' or 'advise against'. Therefore 'it is necessary to warn the doctors and the public against the insufficiency of quantities of radium with which it is notorious that doctors and small clinics try to treat their patients'.[80]

The power of these provisions depended on the authority of those who proclaimed them being recognised. It assumed also that doctors shared the same vision and agreed on a principle of hierarchising abilities based on the level of specialisation. If the authority of the surgeon directors of cancer centres was very strong, that of the radiotherapists was less so. Their discipline was not yet recognised as a speciality entirely apart and its teaching was still part of the radiologists' training course.[81] As regards the superiority of specialised abilities when compared with general abilities, the principle was still far from being uppermost in people's minds. The prestige of the general clinical chairs was great on the eve of the Second World War, and the influence of biomedical sciences still very weak. In these conditions, when nothing prepared them to discern 'the amount of knowledge and experience' hidden behind the 'gestures of simple appearance', how could doctors classify themselves as incompetent when dealing with radiation treatment?

In order to make up for their relative lack of influence in the university, the 'cancer specialists' were to find support in the League which was to echo their recommendations to the doctors, and also to the public. The speech in support of publicity for early diagnosis thus limited the generalist's role to the strict functions of screening and counselling. It dramatised the stakes – the urgency of diagnosis, the urgency of treatment, the risk of death allied to insufficient treatment and malpractice – to justify the place of each. The representation of cancer as a cunning, perfidious and fearsome enemy which knew how to take advantage of the smallest weakness or the smallest imperfection in treatment to extend its ravages and sacrifice its victim to death, directly supported a strategy of trying to impose a legitimacy in the medical field, which aimed at dispossessing the generalists of part of their social authority by subordinating them to that of the hospital specialists.[82]

10 A modern illness

The institutionalisation of cancerology and the first developments of the policy of the fight against cancer were closely connected to changes in the social field. If the emergence of a new view of an old illness was a preliminary to their inauguration, this contributed in return to the image of the scourge of cancer of modern times, which is today part of our common experience. But this change which saw cancer take on a more and more significant role, to the point where it became the main preoccupation regarding illness, did not happen independently of more global changes: it was the whole system which evolved and, with this, the world vision which changed. The appearance of the very idea of the 'cancer peril' was part of this process.

Genesis of a new representation: preliminary conditions

For a pathology which preferred to attack 'mature' adults and the elderly to acquire the features of an illness threatening the stability of society, it was necessary for the population as a whole to show certain characteristics in terms of their relative importance to the various age groups, which differed from what they were, for example, at the end of the Ancien Régime or even during the course of the first half of the nineteenth century,[1] and that the growth of this demography should be perceived (and therefore assessed) as such, at least by the ruling classes. In other words, the notion of the danger of cancer could only take substance within an aged society which had internalised the idea of its ageing. This assumed an increased average life span, a low birth rate and statistical census methods which allowed the phenomena to be objectivised, leading to a certain level of 'socio-economic development' and the existence of a 'modern state'. However, these necessary conditions were, for all that, not enough and several other elements had to be considered, in themselves very necessary too. This was the case with the curability of cancer. Obtaining the first successes in treatment was a preliminary to its recognition as a scourge, for two reasons.

On the one hand, these first successes modified the challenges which cancer presented in the medical field. Interests were focused on it which were no longer only found in the area of clinical or biological knowledge. The treatment of cancer was entirely part of the modernisation of surgical practices connected to the 'revolution' of antisepsis and asepsis. In addition, it became the cornerstone supporting the construction of a 'radiation clinic'. All this at the beginning of a period in which medicine was trying to achieve a much greater curative effectiveness than before.

On the other hand, as it was an illness which could not be curbed by preventive measures, these first successes were essential for political action, which saw cancer as a threat, because political action could not bring about a change in public opinion unless the threat in question was presented as one which could potentially be overcome.

But, and this was the case in France, the fact that it was possible to begin to cure cancer in a society where the ageing of the population was a common, exhausted theme,[2] did not automatically provoke a change in the social image of cancer. A few individuals might well have advocated, before the First World War, the organisation of a fight against cancer, but the lack of response which they had received showed that in this matter, forceful ideas were not enough. It was also necessary for health, as an ideology and in practice, to have sufficient impact on social education. In effect, the idea of the 'cancer peril' was only real if:

- the state was allocated a major role in the protection of public health, a role which was expressed above all by the commitment of the authorities to the fight against the great infectious pathologies;
- infantile mortality and, more generally, mortality because of infection had begun to decrease in an obvious manner, so that they stopped being the focus of total concern for public health;
- clinical doctors, and, in particular, those who were the most directly concerned with the treatment of cancer took into account the epidemiological dimension of the illness.

Future scourge and modern medicine

The combination of all these conditions was a preliminary stage necessary for constructing the image of the scourge of cancer, which was completed with the appearance of the anti-cancer movements. These movements were not institutionalised in the same way everywhere according to whether they were attached or not to learned societies or centres of research and treatment, or were organised in a single association or in several structures. Originating during the war, when it was a priority to make up the ground lost in the fight against diseases, the French League was founded as an independent institutional, unique and centralised model. It succeeded in becoming the meeting point for different types of interests in cancer. It brought together clinicians, scientists, hygienists and philanthropists, each having his own view of cancer according to his field of action. The League was a social meeting point for these different views, that is to say:

- a 'modern' clinical concept which set successes in treatment within a new natural history of the disease which formalised the basis for development in two successive stages, localised cancer and generalised cancer, of which only the first was accessible to treatment;
- a biological concept of cancer as a pathology of the function and reproduction of cells;
- a concept of cancer as a social disease affecting a large part of the population, particularly adults in their prime;
- a record of 'lay' perceptions, where numerous images borrowed from animal mythology were combined with the idea of an illness whose spontaneous progress led the patient inexorably towards suffering and death.

By virtue of its position, the League actively contributed to an image of cancer which combined various attributes proper to these visions. The picture which it was building up represented a logic in tune with the nature of the stakes of which the image of cancer was the subject, stakes which were themselves determined by the dynamism of the social game which the League was playing and which, because of this, grew in due course. The initial aim of the association was to win over the state to the setting up of an anti-cancer policy, and to establish a new image of cancer aimed, as the very principle of its construction, at imposing the recognition of the illness as a scourge. Hence a discourse which was at one and the same time about the topic of 'the evidence' (it was 'the evidence of the cancer peril which brought about the creation of leagues in several countries'),[3] and which tirelessly put on show the 'ravages' caused by cancer. Statistical arguments which 'show that the number of cancer sufferers is much greater than we thought and that this number is increasing' were used to convince the population.[4] This was based on a dramatic presentation of the information, with axioms of the type: 'In Paris, one cancer sufferer is dying every two hours.'[5] The slogan 'Cancer kills 40,000 people a year in France' was systematically taken up in all the publicity material (posters, leaflets, ink blotters), with an insistence which was not to flag for many years, and which makes one think that the 'evidence of the danger' took some time to become a commonplace notion.[6]

But, however necessary it might be, the argument of the effect of cancer on mortality would not be enough for it to be considered a social problem. According to this one factor, the 'cancer peril' would appear secondary in comparison to other diseases. It was especially so in a historical context where authorities and private charity were already committed to the fight against tuberculosis and syphilis, whilst cancer was an outsider in a market where the sources of finance were limited. The competition between the various anti-disease movements led them to consider themselves in relation to each other. The National Committee against Respiratory Diseases and Tuberculosis's poster was an indirect response to the League's slogan 'Cancer is a scourge as fearsome as tuberculosis', with the former gaining supremacy in a macabre horse race. Tuberculosis (150,000 deaths per year) won by a short head from syphilis (140,000 deaths), both leaving cancer well behind with its 40,000 deaths.

As it could not compete either in numbers or by appealing to morality, the 'struggle against cancer' was forced to represent its scourge by using a system of distinguishing features which presented its most specific and most susceptible properties in a bid to give it substance:

- the regular increase in its incidence, which contrasted with the decrease of the main causes of mortality. Already the principal cause of mortality in the large metropolises of those countries which had best been able to control tuberculosis, it was a future scourge;
- the peculiarities of its distribution which took no account of social differences, while infectious pathologies feed on poverty. Threatening rich and poor alike, it was a scourge which concerned all society;
- the terrible moral dilemmas which its appearance caused in families and which contrasted with the 'romantic mawkish behaviour' inspired by tuberculosis: with this, human beings were faced with suicide and euthanasia,[7] it was a tragic scourge;
- the bodily deterioration and suffering which it brought and which made it at all times a source of terror: a taboo illness the name of which was carefully kept quiet, it was like the crab which appeared in its coat-of-arms, a mythical scourge;
- the extent of the living species which it affected: it was the only one of all diseases to affect plants and animals as well as humans. Throughout human history, spreading its threat over the future and attaching itself to all forms of organised life, it was, under its different names, a universal scourge.

This dimension of universality resulted in the fundamental challenge which cancer posed to science. A disturbance of 'the cellular order' and of its reproduction, the aetiology of which did not seem to resemble any of the known pathological mechanisms, cancer was a challenge to the advance of knowledge of all biological disciplines. As Robert Le Bret wrote: 'it would take a more expert hand than mine, even to sketch an outline of the work which should be undertaken, to discover the mechanism and the cause of these morbid cancer phenomena, to get to the heart of the development of the normal cell, to define the laws which govern it, to discover under what influence this vital development becomes fatal. The person whose ideas will go so far as to penetrate this mystery . . . will open to science, like Pasteur, new dimensions of an immense range.'[8]

In this way, the combination of conditions which made possible the emergence of the image of the scourge of cancer corresponded to a time when its place in the life sciences appeared so central that solving its enigma could coincide with solving that of the great problems of ageing,[9] so that, by a dialectical reversal, the 'monstrous' universal scourge could become the bringer of the scientific utopia *par excellence*, that which envisaged human control of the development of life and the pushing back of the frontiers of death. This image, by making cancer the 'key' subject of a 'post-Pasteur' modern biology, which could give access to knowledge of the vital processes, placed its social importance beyond the single question of its incidence on mortality. Correlatively, the murderous scourge/scientific progress combination supported the strategy of those who, knowing of France's 'late arrival' in the field of experimental biology, pleaded for the state to be provided with the means of a coherent research policy (the Cancer Institute was to be the first substantial public creation in this matter).

Within the dynamics of the social game which it was playing, the representation of cancer, while emphasising its great number of characteristics, tended more and more to be defined in comparison with that of its great rival epidemics, according to an opposition between the present-past illness and medicine and the present-future illness and medicine: on the one hand lay what was regressing and no longer posed any further future problems for science, on the other, what was expanding and bringing radical changes to knowledge. And the same opposition was being replayed with clinical practices.

Tuberculosis and syphilis were subject to interventions which did not require an effective treatment to reduce their morbidity, whilst the control of cancer was obligatorily going through the stages of improvement in the quality of treatment. The fact that, in one case, the healing dimension was only of a secondary interest in comparison to preventive measures, while in the other, it was one of the main concerns, went hand in hand with another phenomenon. During the period between the wars, the treatments used against tuberculosis and syphilis had little impact on hospital medicine. At the most, a certain advance was noted in the surgery of the respiratory system with the removal of cavernous lesions and the use of the artificial pneumothorax.[10] On the other hand, the treatment of cancer was becoming an increasing challenge for surgery, at a time when the latter tended to be divided into specialities of organs and equipment. But above all, this scourge which could only be overcome by healing was the illness which brought medical practice into the 'industrial age'. It was a vehicle for innovations and the spreading of knowledge unparalleled at the time. The main meeting point for clinical medicine and the 'revolutionary' discoveries of physics, the therapy of radiation was connected to the development of 'the big science', to which it contributed through its introduction into the medical field. With cancerology, a new form of medicine was broached, more and more dependent on progress in technology, requiring the alliance of specialised qualifications of all types, and offering a market for the leading industries. It was a new form of treatment whose development demanded the perfecting of different financing mechanisms and which brought into question the public–private division of the medical market as it had been organised until then.

The scourge of cancer therefore directly relates to modern medicine in the course of its construction. And fascination was evident for 'these marvels of technical genius' which were the spectacular ultrapenetrating radiotherapy installations and the 'radium bombs', as well as for these 'temples of progress' which the few model cancer centres became, with 'what they represent of science, work, meticulous care and construction and planning of similar treatment factories . . . combined the work of doctors, engineers, physicists and architects'.[11] The first 'up-to-date services', in the contemporary meaning of the phrase, the cancer centres were a turning point in the development of the hospital, which really marked the end of the 'clinical' age. If, at the time of their creation, the spirit of the 'tacit contract between poverty and wealth' still seemed to prevail, its 'old fashioned' nature soon revealed itself. The hospital – as a place where clinical knowledge was developed thanks to the bodies of the poor – did not solve the problems posed by this new scourge of cancer. 'The healing factory' implied its transformation, and a transformation which, as a result, led to the global reorganisation of the health system. The industrial metaphor needed to be taken seriously as it emphasised two major elements of change: the primary purpose of the institution became 'the production of healing'; and the healing factory was a production line that was the opposite of the private medicine establishments, in the same way as the large company is the opposite of the small independent producer's workshop. It presupposed investments in machines, i.e. in fixed capital, on a completely different scale to those investments which brought private practitioners up to the level of private clinics, at least in France under the conditions at that time. And because of this, only the authorities were able to finance heavy radiotherapy equipment.

If making a priority of the healing objective was not in itself contradictory to the organisation of the health system set up in the first half of the nineteenth century, it tended to become so when its accomplishment depended more and more on state financial intervention. Only public establishments took advantage of the most perfected technical methods. This inequality of access to care, paradoxical in its inversion of social inequalities by making the poor the privileged, could not fail to need correction, all the more so since it was a question of treating a disease affecting the people in a much more 'egalitarian' manner than the great infectious pathologies.

The opinion of the League drew its strength from its anticipation of the inevitable: an adjustment of the health system to the new technical and socio-economic techniques of the practice of medicine, which took account of the structure of society. It was this adjustment, which began under the Vichy regime, that came into operation immediately after the Second World War, and which ended in what we know today as a hospital sector open to all social classes, classified in accordance with the degree of technical sophistication of services and in which the inequalities of access to care are simply a reflection of social inequalities.[12]

But the 'modernity' of the cancer scourge/fight against cancer combination was not reduced to just this technico-organisational anticipation. It also resulted in the complementary constituent of the setting up of cancer centres, i.e. the policy of early screening. Here, too, the comparison between the other scourges foretold the 'future' dimension of cancer.

The 'fight against cancer' and the 'civilisation of manners'

Tuberculosis and syphilis were at the time the privileged subjects of social medicine. The perfecting of diagnostic tests to be applied on a mass scale made their screening routine, and it was carried out largely outside hospital structures and private practice. To this taking of collective responsibility, which was administratively regulated and which passively involved individuals, was opposed, in the case of cancer, a strategy of development of early diagnosis, based in part on the active participation of potential patients. Without going back over what was described in the previous chapter, I will state here that the image of the scourge of cancer as a 'sly' insidious and perverted evil legitimised an opinion which called for the 'active' 'medicalisation' of the people. Since its dangerousness was disguised, cancer involved another 'look' at normal symptomatology, that is the medical education of each person, which would bring him to view his body in a different way. The dramatisation of bodily manifestations, until then considered harmless, which become possible signals of the illness, was part of a dynamic to strengthen the power of medical knowledge over the individual. And not only because it led to an appeal to go and consult a practioner, which was only here a secondary consequence. More basically, this dramatisation, which aimed at making of each person a 'watchman patient' tended to favour the internalisation of a new type of restriction on the body and under this heading took part in the long march of the process of civilisation analysed by N. Elias.[13] The aim was to transform the 'easy-going' behaviour brought about by a false perception of the signs of organic disturbance, too exclusively (and in the case of cancer, deceitfully) resting on painful symptoms, into 'responsible' behaviour, i.e. seeking medical advice, itself resulting from a (medically) educated perception of symptoms. This new type of anticipated behaviour was closely connected to the phenomenon of the increasing division of medical work and to the extension of the chain of people involved in the development of specialist skills related to their different functions. Here, too, the logic of this process of technical division tended to reduce to the maximum the gap which separated the professionals and the layman, by making the latter the assistants of the former. The strategy of implementing diagnosis was well able to target the 'population', as did the screening practices used in the fight against tuberculosis and venereal diseases, but underlying it was a different view of the people. The 'mass screening' population, as the term indicates, consisted of an anonymous group, whilst those who took part in the early diagnosis programme formed a whole composed of individuals. The effectiveness of mass screening depended on the quality of the medico-administrative arrangements and implied an attitude of respect and obedience by the people towards the instructions coming from the authorities (go and get yourself screened). The effectiveness of 'early diagnosis' itself depended on the quality of the information provided, but also, and above all, on the behaviour of each 'participant', as long as he regarded himself as involved in the medical activities production process and therefore, under this heading, 'responsible' for his own health (the publicity message left him to understand that he could well pay with his life for his lack of responsibility). Hence, relating to the individualisation of the 'target' of the message was a personalisation of cancer which, as a collective threat ('A scourge which kills 40,000 people a year'), also became the intimate enemy of the person to whom the message was addressed ('Kill cancer before it kills you!').

Even if the difference in the representation of the 'population' which underpinned the strategies of the mass screening and early diagnosis had something to do with the fact that the technical conditions, in one situation or another, differed, the relationship was not automatic. It was still necessary for certain sociological conditions to exist so that the absence of a simple test, and therefore the need to pass through a complex medical diagnosis procedure, might determine the idea of a strategy based on the training and motivation of the 'potential patient'. The 'public' involved in the fight against cancer supposed a society where the perception of oneself as a relatively independent person, free in one's actions (within the limits imposed by social constraints), and therefore a participant responsible for one's own life, was the method of relating to the ruling class, at least in certain strata of society. This leads me to make two observations:

1   This condition should be related to the fact that the League's publicity was addressed, at the beginning, as a priority, to the 'educated public', to be extended later to a wider population. However, during the inter-war period, the required aim was more to motivate intermediary groups in contact with the working classes than to 'educate' the latter directly. In other words, the differences in image of what made up the 'population', which underlay the two strategies, also corresponded to

sociologically differentiated 'targets', in so far as mass 'screening' itself concerned the whole of society, but mainly the working classes;

2   The development, within a social structure, of 'self-awareness' as an independent person was part of a process of development of Western society, the dynamics of which stemmed from the combined action of three interdependent phenomena: the more and more marked differentiation of social positions, connected with the increasing division of work; the relative loss of the protective function of the family group, linked to the previous item and to the great extension of the average life span; and the displacement of the protective function of the family towards the state,[14] including those questions related to health. Another aspect of these three phenomena were also to be taken into account when shaping the construction of the image of the cancer scourge/fight against cancer. Without an advanced process of technical division between specialisms, the cancerology of the cancer centres is unthinkable. Without the ageing of the population, the impact of a mature age illness cannot become a 'social threat'. Without a protective role in the health area assured by the authorities, no anti-cancer policy is possible.

These two observations invite us to look more deeply at the question of the 'modernity' of the fight against cancer with regard to the development of the process of civilisation.

The fight against infectious diseases which followed the 'Pasteur revolution' was a good time to extend the protective function of the state in health matters. It was involved in a programme establishing rules for personal hygiene, taught by the schools, which aimed at regulating the most diverse daily activities (washing one's hands, temperance, using protection in sexual relations outside marriage, sterilising babies' feeding bottles, not spitting on the ground, not blowing one's nose with one's fingers, etc.).[15] The general aim was to put the working classes (the 'savage' classes, as certain people called them at the time) in tune with types of behaviour already largely entrenched in the ruling classes. In fact, most of these precepts, if they appeared in the form of rules obeying medical standards, were found to correspond to the standards of 'good behaviour' which were part of the 'civilised' attitude of the aristocratic and middle class milieus (their internalisation, the product of several centuries of development, took place independently to any reference to health).[16] This 'connection' owed much to the fact that the process of internalisation of varied behavioural controls on what we would call today all forms of conviviality, contributed to place relationships between individuals in a physico-social space made of corporeal distancing (distancing the body and all the 'natural' products of the body, saliva, breath, nasal mucus, urine, faeces, etc.). Apart from certain particular moments (hugging and kissing rituals or moments relating to what we will specifically call 'intimacy'), contacts were limited to a minimum in order to preserve each person's 'personal space', what Goffman called the concept of 'the territory of the self'.[17] We understand, therefore, why the health initiative, as soon as it was applied to the corpus of knowledge of bacteriology, developed into a model fight against contagion, the expression of which in terms of individual behaviour tied in, apart from a few exceptions, with the already existing type of behaviour, the 'civilised' behaviour of the ruling classes. The 'advice to tuberculosis sufferers', the teaching of the staff doing the caring in the working-class sanatoriums were intended to produce a type of behavioural self-control, the purpose of which was to reduce contacts as much as possible (because of the risk of contagion) between the patient's body (and its possible projections) and those of the persons with whom he lived.[18] In fact the observance of these restrictions and the apprenticeship of the 'games of handkerchief and spittoon' contributed, as I. Grellet and C. Kruse wrote, 'to drawing an imaginary circle around him'.[19] With this 'medical' aspect of 'personal space', efforts to reduce 'the promiscuity of the poor' (who, apart from being a source of vices and defects, had become a source of contagion) found specific ways of action. Hence this idea, the ambition of which was to complement the theoretical view which developed during the process of civilisation,[20] that the extension of the protective role of the state in 'public health' was a decisive element in the social pressure which was exercised – via health politics and the strength of medical knowledge – on the working classes to change their 'habits' in order to become more 'civilised'. This idea led logically to envisaging, from the same viewpoint, the 'civilising' dimension underlying the politics of the fight against cancer. On the evidence, the latter was on another level. On the one hand, the education of the 'public' in looking for early signs of cancer was addressed to an 'already civilised' public, to an assembly of 'independent', 'free' and 'responsible' individuals in whom 'self-awareness' found an expression in appropriating and safeguarding a personal space and in its counterpart, the respecting of another's personal space. On the other hand, this education was not in the least associated with preventive measures at most, tobacco was beginning to be suspected as a risk, but, particularly in France, very few doctors took any notice.

What should a 'responsible person' be advised to do, when asked to behave as a medical auxiliary? To be very aware of what his body told him, not by monitoring its unusual signs, but by knowing how to interpret and so how to understand the signals it issued, thanks to a programme of inter-pretation which enabled them to be classified as signals either warning of possible danger or in fact harmless. If the ability to step back from oneself and consider oneself as an object was a specific characteristic of human nature, the attention to the body required here necessitated a scientific objectivisation of self. It assumed an 'educated' awareness of oneself using symbolic tools allowing one to view one's body and to interpret it like a doctor. It was as if the development of civilisation, after having consigned the manifestations of the body to an area of intimacy, was this time encouraging self-checking to be applied to the interior of the body, in such a way that the body would be deprived of all its subjectivity and appear under its own scrutiny as a 'body' of knowledge. If the protection of people against the 'scourge of cancer' involved arrangements for suitable treatment, it would also be subject to a 'development of manners'. The fulfilment of each of these two conditions did not happen at the same time. In fact, the building of the 'healing factories' advanced more quickly than the expected changes in mental habits, and this interval was very soon perceived as an obstacle to the effectiveness of the cancer policy. In addition, this interval of time was not sociologically uniform, in that social pressure for the adoption of new rules for the body was exercised primarily on individuals from the ruling classes. One institution had a main role: the Anti-Cancer League. In fact, the latter could expect to fulfil this educational role because it was a social area which structured relationships between the medical elite and the various components of these ruling classes.

Simultaneously involved in support for the construction of cancer centres and in public education, the League was predisposed, because of its position, to perceive the contradictions which undermined the policy defined by the authorities. For if the necessary 'development of manners' only began by involving the 'educated' classes of the population, the most 'modern' accomplishments regarding specialised centres were themselves aimed at 'working-class' patients. The anti-cancer network, the early aim of which was to ensure that poor curable cancer patients received equivalent conditions of treatment to those offered by private medicine, exceeded its objective and the private sector was unable to 'keep up' with technological development. Hence the feeling of an increasing incoherence which led the League to resolutely adopt a reformist view, questioning the principles of the division of the market between public and private.

In the same way, the tendency to view the public as a set of 'individuals', which lay behind any educational action taken by the League, also explained why its campaigners, as soon as they were committed to 'personalised' social work with the poor who were affected by cancer, became indignant at the luck which had befallen 'incurable individuals' and regarded the addition of these numerous cases as a 'painful' social problem.

An analysis of the institutions of this type is very important in order to understand the development of the protective function of the state in the field of health practices and its corollary, the strengthening of the hold of medical knowledge as a symbolic instrument regulating actions. We can see in fact how this development, which was part of a long historical process, gave rise to, at a given moment, the creation of structures the main property of which was that they were areas of mediation between the different sociological components of the field of power, which by uniting them tended to change them. In this sense, the League was a pressure group, but from a standpoint which went beyond the functions habitually attributed to a lobby. Its consequent defence of the interests of the 'fight against cancer' led it to commit itself to instructing the social classes of which it was the mouthpiece (by starting with its own campaigners and non-specialised doctors). At the same time, it fostered the awareness of the specialists in this work and contributed to turning them into 'teachers'. And what went for the League also seemed to go for all the associations who met in 1934 to establish the International Cancer Association.

In the light of the preceding developments, we can conclude that the social pressure for the development of 'mentalities' orchestrated by the movement of the struggle against cancer fundamentally responded to the need to put into new terms the question of the relationships between the medical world and the population – as an assembly of potential patients. The particularities of early diagnosis of cancer were such that the effectiveness of medicine came directly to depend on the behaviour of 'responsible' individuals, whilst the patient perceived as an 'active' individual found no place in the world of medical discourse (which also explains the term 'patient'). As N.D. Jewson stated,[21] the disappearance of the 'sick man' of medical 'cosmologies' was linked to the logic of objectivisation on which clinical knowledge, as it was carried out in the hospital, was based. As long as doctors remained employees in the service of the great houses of the aristocracy or of the families of the rich middle class, the latter monitored and used the product of medical knowledge for their advantage. Hence a knowledge which granted a central position to the 'sick man' and presented the disease as a state of global, 'psychosomatic' disturbance of the individual. It was necessary for the hospital to become the privileged place for the exercise of medicine, where 'knowledge' was developed, so that the 'art of healing' could change into a science of observation and new concepts could be born. Why? Because inside the 'modern' hospital the poor patient had no influence over the medical process, the supervision of which was entirely in the hands of the department head. The lowered social status of the sick person was one of the conditions which allowed the disease to be construed as a relationship between symptoms and an organic lesion having a body for its 'abode'. If the patient provided necessary access to the illness, his subjectivity and the way in which he perceived his body were obstacles which it was necessary to overcome to gain access to the reality of the symptoms.

In the approach proper to laboratory medicine, the trend towards reductionism was even more accentuated. The patient, as a clinical case, was replaced by an approach to the body which dealt with it as a complex cellular apparatus, ruled by biochemical processes the changes of which it was necessary to prove, by relying on results from monitored experimentation (animal experimentation). The patient, 'the best laboratory animal' as the endocrinologist Fuller Albright frankly said,[22] was excluded by this medicine as a person, to become merely a source from which samples were taken (of blood, urine, organs, etc.) for examination.

The disappearance of the 'sick man' presented no problems when it was a question of establishing a diagnosis (as an end in itself), classifying, analysing and explaining, i.e. while the main objective of medicine was not 'healing' the illness, but the gathering of scientific knowledge on the illness. It did not cause any extra problems when the efficacy required of it touched on the perfecting of preventive measures for the improvement of the 'environment' or the isolation of infectious sufferers, which might be regulated by the authority for administrative decisions. On the other hand, it was a drawback when the success of medical operations was subordinated to the behaviour of the 'public'. So medical discourse had to include as a condition of its practical effectiveness a new factor, the patient (or the potential patient) as a protagonist. In other words, when cancer became a public matter (and because it became a public matter) and the decision was taken to finance specialised centres, the need to invent a new mode of doctor–patient (and doctor–public) relationship was needed. This new method needed to simultaneously meet the target of social effectiveness which the fight against cancer set itself and to adjust to a medico-scientific way of thinking which recognised the doctor as the only actor. Hence the reintroduction of the 'sick man', not in the role which the 'sufferer' employing the doctor occupied, but in that of an agent participating in the process of medical advancement. The 'reappearance of the sick man' as a collaborator results from a symbolic blow which invented a fictitious individual. The new discourse was founded on a basic premise granting to human beings properties composed of the purest scientific ideology. *Homo medicus* was an individual whose aptitude of considering himself as an object was pushed to the limit, to the point where he had a split personality. The capacity which was attributed to him of being able to view his suffering body without any subjectivity made him into a being which was the embodiment of the doctor–patient relationship. It was because it could play on this presumed duality of the subject that the strategy of early diagnosis found its credibility: the 'publicity' was addressed to the potential medical collaborator existing in each person, aiming to train him by endowing him with the necessary rudiments of medical knowledge, while thwarting the pernicious influence which the dispensers of false knowledge and false beliefs might have on him. Resting on this symbolic blow necessary for political action, publicity led everyone, public and doctor, to the faith without which it would be unjustified.

Initially a response to the requirements of the anti-cancer movement, the invention of *Homo medicus* was to find more and more fields of application in the second half of the twentieth century, at the same time as medico-scientific and public health issues became concerned with the treatment of 'chronic illnesses' instead of 'acute illnesses'. *Homo medicus* was the indispensable 'collaborator' of 'leading' medicine, it was he who ensured the continuity of long-term treatment during the intervals between the stages of the 'heavy' treatment interventions carried out in the hospital.

A necessary illusion which all efforts of medical education tended to base on reality, *Homo medicus* nonetheless remained an illusion, an 'artefactual' individual who was not the sick person. But if the ignorance of the 'artefactual' nature of *Homo medicus* was a condition for action, it was also a source of perpetual disenchantment for doctors. They were therefore confronted daily with patients whom they thought sufficiently informed or trained who did not act as they, the doctors, had the right to expect. Hence an increasing questioning of these 'failures', an unease which was only placated with difficulty by the invocation of the frailty of human understanding and its tendency to the irrational, hence also the appeal to the social sciences and to psychology to try to better understand and control the reason for these types of behaviour.

The invention of *Homo medicus* led the patient in fact to occupy a double position, as if he was included as an agent in the process of medical production but it still did not prevent him from being included as a subject of practices. 'Collaborator' and 'patient', he was predisposed to experience the contradictions inherent in this double position, to question the conditions of his care and to criticise the double game of the doctor who did not always treat him as a collaborator.[23] Hence a rash of complaints, which, because of belief in the patient as a protagonist, used as an argument the lack of information given by the doctor and suspected its partiality, i.e. its influential function.

Within this crisis, which is today out in the open, the message regarding the 'necessity for public information' began to lose its credibility to a new message more in tune with the times, the key word of which was communication. Marked by the seal of the 'communication crisis', the vicissitudes of doctor–patient relationships opened wide the door to new specialists and to new paramedical professions. But there is every reason to believe that the contradiction which resulted from the co-existence of a relationship with the world constructed around self-awareness as a responsible person and on a medico-scientific logic granting no place to the 'sufferer' was not to be resolved by this new illusion that it was a problem in communication.

Order and anarchy

Self-awareness as a relatively independent, partly free and responsible person corresponded to a representation of the world outside oneself as the environment. This common idea underlay the epidemiological approach in its attempt to formally classify the many external factors capable of influencing health when it placed the individual in the centre of an assembly of varied environments (family, professional, social, physical, chemical, biological, etc.) which were supposed to have specific priorities. The analogy in the words used to characterise both 'natural' and 'social' levels of organisation revealed the strength of an outstanding idea of the social world, which considered human structures as 'things' endowed with a sort of life of their own, which, following the example set by the forces of nature, escaped the control of humans and imposed themselves on them. This tendency to naturalise the social world, the development of which accompanied the decline in religious beliefs, found its rationalised form of expression in a metaphorical characterisation of the social body as a biological organism the disturbances of which appeared in terms of pathological phenomena, as symptoms or diseases. In return, this concept of society as a biological unit tended to narrow the gap between political skill and medical skill (Auguste Comte),[24] and the health movement formalised the bridges over the gap by attempting to raise social medicine to the level of a government science. Like the inclusion of medicine in the art of government, the fight against the scourge diseases employed, in turn, a list of analogies to represent itself, which it borrowed from politico-social discourse.

We are therefore dealing with a metaphorical movement which operated in both directions, the illness or its agent being part of social disorders, the rhetoric of the combat itself characterising therapeutic activity and the social organisation of the 'fight' against illness.[25] The question therefore arises of a possible specificity of metaphors relating to the cancer scourge and the fight against cancer. As J. Schlanger rightly said, political 'nosology' is not systematic, because 'it is entirely subordinated to the immediate need for polemical reasoning'.[26] This can be seen clearly in the fact, for example, that cancer progressively replaced tuberculosis as the supreme category of anathema. Susan Sontag[27] had observed this in relation to the description of the 'Jewish peril' in Nazi propaganda speeches (from the 1930s, the 'Jewish cancer' tended to replace the 'Jewish tuberculosis'). As a 'polemical' category, cancer was not in the least specific, except that its use was extended as it took the lead in the contest with the other diseases. However, it appeared as a privileged metaphor representing the internal disturbances of the social body, when the latter were not imputed to a designated 'enemy', but presented as the consequence of the lifestyle of human structures which seemed to be out of all control. If syphilis took its place in the rhetoric of degeneration (of the race, of the French people),[28] if tuberculosis, the bacillus, the infected person and the refractory person represented as much a social danger (the threatening poor)[29] as the external enemy (the Hun),[30] cancer expressed more fundamentally a concept of chaos and came under this heading to signify and give meaning to the anarchy which seemed to reign in the world. A 'universal plague', cancer came to mean the anguish that the individual felt in relation to a social 'world' (in the proper meaning of the word) without order. It was in this way that it became the metaphorical disease *par excellence* of malfunctions of the economy (unemployment, inflation, over-production),[31] that is of the field of human activities mostly at supranational level, the regulation of which was perceived less and less as depending on the 'protective unit' comprised by the nation-state. The subordination felt by the nation-state at a higher level of social organisation blurred the view of this state as an 'organism'. The state only remained an independent 'organism' from a certain point of view, and it is enough to consider it from another point of view to see its 'nature' change and become an element (or organ) comprising a more complex whole. In other words, the growth of types of inter-dependence in human structures led to a 'crisis' of the rationalising role of the 'metaphor of the organism'. It is interesting to note that, precisely at the same time, the biological definition of the organism as a self-contained and independent unit endowed with fixed limits, was subject to a relativist questioning.[32]

The metaphor of the organism loses even more of its rationalising role when the 'higher organism', the supranational social world, is presented to individuals as a 'body' whose limits are difficult to appreciate, the directing centre (the head) difficult to identify and the methods of regulation other than ruled by anarchy, difficult to imagine. With regard to the First World War, the revolutionary crises which followed it, the increase in power of the dictatorial regimes, the great economic depression of the 1930s, the attempt to put in place, through the League of Nations, a structure of international regulation, might seem a very weak counterbalance. It was precisely in the field of this opposition that the French movement for the fight against cancer tried to set itself up. In a speech in 1934 to the League's general meeting, Robert Le Bret spoke about the similarities which existed between the world crisis and cancer in terms which went beyond simple metaphors. He saw cancer as a pathological phenomenon applicable 'as such' to social processes:

> Cancer is a universal plague, it is a great purveyor of death everywhere, in all races, and in all environments. It not only strikes humans but also animals and even plants, and we could call 'cancer' one of the generalised anarchies which have brought ruin to powerful civilisations and great empires and which threaten to destroy regimes who cannot quell the chaos in time.[33]

Cancer here is part of a vision of the world as a theatre where conflict between opposing forces is being acted out. In this agnostic view, purged of all supernatural force, cancer reminds one of the duality of the living being, the joint existence of order and chaos, a chaos born from life itself which changes it into a fatal excess of vitality. The affirmation that this duality was part of every level of the organisation of the vital phenomena, including those which concerned the social relationships of human beings, was clearly eminently to be criticised from the epistemological point of view and was a matter, sociologically speaking, of an 'abuse of language'. However, the idea that cancer could, more than a simple image, characterise the reality of the whole social world is worthy of attention, not merely because of all that it expressed about the 'malaise of civilisation'. For when the

League's general secretary characterised the world chaos as a pathology, it was to place the 'fight against cancer' in the first rank of the activities which could reduce it. In fact, the conditions which should be met to 'overcome' this universal plague led to an unprecedented effort of co-operation on an international scale:

> A union of scientists and practitioners – doctors, surgeons, radiologists – and charitable organisations under the supervision and with the support of governments, each playing his part in a common purpose, this is what common sense requires, this is the collaboration we must foster.[34]

Ardent publicists of the ideals of the League of Nations, Justin Godart and Robert Le Bret fully committed the French League to building an International Cancer Association, the first meeting of which was held in 1934 in Madrid. The aim for the International Cancer Association went well beyond the simple institutionalisation of scientific exchanges and the scientific and social fight against cancer wanted to oppose the ravages caused by this evil at all levels where the latter appeared.

> At a time when the general chaos caused by the devastation of the war, by the general collapse, by counterfeit money and by overproduction is creating rivalries and causing savage hostilities, interrupting inter-national trade and erecting insurmountable barriers, we are happy to find an opportunity to unite people in an area in which they all have the same interest and in which they can all fight against a common enemy. Cancer will bring at least one benefit if it shows human beings how race hatred, political dissension, and religious differences can be overcome, in order to try to find a remedy for it.[35]

The fight against cancer expressed, in Utopian language (the control of living and social processes), the development of the ideals of social medicine relative to the development of the interdependence of social structures and the changing of the scale of its political ambitions from the government of the nation-state to the government of the 'League of Nations'.

Reformist analyses and new ways of thinking

Included in the process of modernisation of French society, because of the very conditions which were in operation at its origin, the movement for the fight against cancer intended to work on this modernisation, by defining the outlines of reform: its aim was to adjust the medical practices, the organ-isation and operation of the health system to the growth in the social world. I have shown how, within the dynamics of implementing the anti-cancer policy, including, as highlights, the conflicts which the latter caused, this criticism was progressively constructed. Being actively involved in a strategy developing in relation to 'adverse' strategies, the League's message expressed a 'committed' point of view and therefore, under this heading, particular interests. But, because of the very fact that the League was an institution which structured a social space between the various components of the area of power, the particular point of view which it wanted to defend was that of the common good of its components, considered as being for 'the greater good of society'.

Within the operation of the collective 'intellect' which the directing authorities comprised, the personal role of the secretary was very important, as it was he who had the task of formalising – as 'spokesman' – the association's point of view. A cultured upper-middle class doctor of law, living on his private income, therefore able to detach himself from all professional ideas, and moreover, having the necessary time to commit himself fully to this activity, Robert Le Bret was predisposed to embody this function and to express both verbally and in writing 'the greater good of society'. The 'right man in the right place', he possessed the necessary aptitudes for shaping a more and more coherent message which took into account the the constraints relating to his position, i.e. without ever being seen as exceeding his position of spokesman. There was, however, an obvious paradox showing, as I said at the beginning of this work, that the different positions adopted by the League on subjects as various as the organisation of the health system, social protection, the question of incurables or the monitoring of medical practices, were progressively based on the dynamics of social practices which it did not control and which were in response to other positions, and also affirming that at the end of the period which we have covered, the League's message gained in intellectual coherence. This paradox ceases to be one when one considers that:

- The initial programme of the struggle against cancer was carried out very pragmatically as a compromise between what should be done, what was technically feasible and what all the restrictions which burdened the operation of the medical field allowed to be done. Its harmony was only rhetorical and did not hide its contradictions for long.
- The 'intellectual' role which the League filled precisely led it to theorise on the development of medicine and its adjustment to the more global development of society.

Having said this, the question remained: if there was any gain in coherence, how could it be seen in this theorisation?

The birth of a movement for the fight against cancer assumed certain advances in the progress of the technical division of medical work and contributed in its turn to its extension. It was in this way that the potential patient was called upon to take part in the production chain of learned activities, and that the tasks belonging to the various categories of professionals expected to get involved were specified and categorised. We have here a view of anti-cancer social organisation in which everyone took part and saw his role defined in accordance with his level of medical competence, including the 'non-doctor'. In other words, laymen and professionals were not in opposition to each other like two separate entities separated by a line marking the limit between no knowledge and medical knowledge, but tended to have a place in a hierarchical scale of competence: the medicalisation of the potential patient went together with the differentiation amongst the positions of the doctors. If the social barrier which the possession of a medical degree giving the right to practise continued to exist and really caused a division between the non-doctor and the doctor, it became inadequate as the only criterion for regulating practice. The debate on medical quackery was evidence of this. The repression of mercenary practices by a professional order which had the power to blacklist 'quacks' was only a partial solution to the problem. The development of specialisation, connected with the 'progress of science and techniques', made reality more complex, in particular in the area of cancer, and it caused situations which were not of professional jurisdiction, because nothing could prevent a general practitioner from treating cancer, except the internal feeling that he ought not allow himself to do so, unless he had the required competence.

Committed from its outset, both to the education of the public and to that of non-specialised doctors, the League theorised in its publicity programme a concept of the scientific and social fight against cancer, based on this classified differentiation of positions. At the same time, the League accepted, without questioning it, an opinion on the division of the patients, assigning the poor to the public cancer centres, and keeping the 'well-off' patients for the private sector, a point of view which corresponded to an idea that society was made up of two distinct classes according to their means. The putting into practice of the anti-cancer fight policy was very soon to come up against the problem of the 'small payers'. The differentiation between the poor and those who could pay, which had been in operation until then, stopped doing so from the moment when the cost of special treatment reached the level which the patients not meeting the administrative criterion of poverty could not afford . . . and the economic crisis intensified the situation.

The appearance, in the League's message, of the theme of 'poverty of the middle classes' marked a turning point. Apart from the need to affirm the existence of a category of the population insufficiently taken into account, it demonstrated a break with a certain vision of the social world and with the way of thinking which was appropriate to it. When a model made up of two opposite extremes is assumed to reflect social reality, the forming of a middle ground tends to be only an artefact not representing the reality of any group. To introduce into this model a third section in an intermediate position – i.e. a middle class – presupposes another representation of the divisions of society. The model here was not threefold – as for example that of the France of the Ancien Régime with its three estates (nobility, clergy, state) might have been – in the sense that it formed a continuity among the three poor-'middle'-rich categories and returned, in fact, to the idea of a whole made up of social positions structured according to a hierarchical scale. This representation is a prerequisite to the idea of the 'average Frenchman', an imaginary individual with whom a majority might identify. The fiction of the 'average Frenchman' also took on substance through many figures of social rank, at the same time different but sufficiently close, along the scale, to be grouped under this name. He might just as easily be 'the small landlord living off the rents of a house', the craftsman, the 'small trader', the employee or the 'small boss who often makes less profit than he pays in salary', as the teacher or the professional.

This vision of the social divisions was in tune with that of the organisation of the fight against cancer, as it took into account the increasing differentiation between social functions to make of them the principle of which society was structured. Of course, the categorisation was still rough – although sufficient to be used in a political polemical argument – because it was only supported by a spontaneous perception of these differentiations. A symbolic sophisticated instrument was not capable of grading category variations according to a precise hierarchical order. This tool was, however, not long in appearing, with the invention of the classification of the socioprofessional classes. The analogy between the above and the development of the League's message regarding incurability is clear. For the first time, while being outraged at the unfair luck of the incurables, the Association of the fight against cancer accepted the principle of an institutional division between services with a therapeutic purpose and structures for caring for incurables, except that it asked for the latter to be admitted to the cancer centres. Its divergence with the Cancer Commission's programme was only with respect to organisational methods. The purpose of the non-acceptance which its suggestion came up against caused it progressively to question the relevance of categories of classification which formed part of the medical way of thinking of the age. A questioning which, as we have seen, led to a stand on principles affirming that with the progress of treatment, it was no longer possible to establish a demarcation between curable, improvable or hopeless cancer sufferers. This position was based on the theory of deconstruction, operated by medical practice itself, of dualistic ways of thinking which structured the categorisation logic of the Cancer Commission: local cancer/general cancer; operable cancer/incurable cancer; treatment centre/charitable institution.

This time, we went from a vision of reality constructed on a twofold system of opposition to a 'complex' concept according a central place to intermediary situations. As soon as effective treatments were invented which caused surgery to lose its exclusiveness, curable and operable stopped being synonymous, cancers over which surgery had no power could be cured. In addition, the operable/inoperable distinction was complicated; certain inoperable cancers could become accessible to removal if the latter was combined with radiotherapy. There were new possibilities therefore for surgery which could improve its techniques. Finally, radiotherapy benefited from technological innovations which extended its field of action. As a consequence of this dynamism, the typology taking account of stages of development of cancer had in its turn to be refined. The local/general distinction had its limits and gave place to a more elaborate nomenclature which increased the number of pertinent 'stages' of treatments and prognosis. Within this context, not only was the notion of incurability no longer appropriate to define in principle a category of patients, but the curable/incurable opposition did not allow the reality of the many situations of temporary remission of greater or lesser in length, more or less possible to extend, or even later accessible to new therapeutic advances – to be taken into account. By advocating on this basis a redefinition of medical categories, the League historicised the notion of incurability, presented it as the survival of a bygone way of thinking, belonging to a 'pre-scientific' period of cancer medicine. But we can also see that this progress in treatment, which appeared to complicate the medical reality of cancer, was itself a result of the increasing complexity of the division of medical work. The discovery of the 'biological action' of radiation initiated new specialities and the development of oncological surgery became part of a process of surgical specialisation, and this tendency to specialisation also affected laboratory disciplines involved in the diagnosis and care of the sick.

Originating from the combined effects of evolution and demography, from the increasing division of work and the particular form that the latter took in the medical field and from biological research at a historical moment when the state was directly committed to a policy of fight against diseases, the movement of the fight against cancer became a vehicle for major changes in the medical field. These were changes which in the end involved a redefinition of the purpose of medicine, its organisation, its methods of control, its vocation to treat 'incurables', its 'educational' function, its relationship with the state, and, in short, its place in society. Furthermore these changes were involved in the regulation of relationships between states on the international level.

When creating their own institution, the promoters of the fight against cancer were unaware of the path to which they were committed. Their initial programme claimed to respect the main principles of medical orthodoxy of the time. They 'discovered' its implications as conflicts arose, conflicts which they analysed as so many 'symptoms' demonstrating the lack of adaptation not only of the system and its operation, but also of its way of thinking which assured its coherence. Against what it theorised as being the persistence of obsolete conceptions reflecting the reality of knowledge and social conditions belonging to a bygone age, the League had set up a project where medicine had to just as much adjust to the new reality of a 'complex' society as to the new reality of the illness which it was constructing. Another intellectual coherence was confirmed, where the logic of gradualist thought tended to replace dualistic logic. However, this was not totally excluded, it even reappeared in a central place, at the beginning of a global vision of a world threatened by cancer and having become the theatre of an epic conflict, the combat between the forces of order and the forces of chaos.

Appendices

Appendix to Chapter 3

Table 3.1   Holders of the chairs of medicine who are members of the AFEC

'Theoretical' chairs	*Professors*	*Teaching graduates*
Pathological anatomy	P. Marie	G. Roussy
Experimental and comparative pathology	Roger	
Medical pathology	F. Widal	
Pathology and general therapeutics	Bouchard – 1909 then Achard	
Surgical pathology	Le Jars	
Operations and equipment		Lecene
External pathology		Chevassu
Therapeutics	Gilbert – 1910	
Medical and biological chemistry	Gautier	
Physiology	Richet	
History of Medicine	Menetrier	
Hygiene	Chantemesse	Macaigne

'Clinical' chairs	*Professors*	*Teaching graduates*
Clinical medicine	Dieulafoy – 1910 then Gilbert Landouzy Debove Chauffard	
Clinical surgery	Le Dentu – 1910 then Reclus Delbet Quenu Hartmann	
Clinical therapy	Robin	
Ophthalmology	De la Personne	
Urinary tracts	Albarran – 1908 then Legueu	
Gynaecology	Pozzi	Faure

continued overleaf

Table 3.1   Continued

'Clinical' chairs	Professors	Teaching graduates
Obstetrics	Pinard	
Dermatology–syphiligraphy	Gaucher	

Chairs of which the holders were not AFEC members between 1908 and 1913.

I   'Theoretical' – internal pathology, parasitology, pharmacology, physical medicine, histology, forensic medicine.

II 'Clinical' – infant medicine, infant surgery, neurology, mental illnesses, otorhinolaryngology, obstetrics: TARNIER

Table 3.2   AFEC members who were 'Académie de médecine' members in 1908 and after

'Académie de Médecine' Sections	AFEC Committee of Honour	AFEC holders
Anatomy and physiology	Chauveau Dastre	Gley Richet
Medical pathology	Fournier	Bouchard – Chauffard Darier (1919) – Dieulafoy Gaucher (1910) – Landouzy Marie (1911) – Milian (1938) *G. Roussy (1929) *Masson (1935) *Ameuille (1944)
Surgical pathology		Chauvel – Delorme Faure (1924) Hartmann (1918) Labbe – Lannelongue – Monod – Pozzi – Quenu (1908) Schwartz (1909) Tuffier (1918) *Chevassu (1938) *De la Personne (1918) *Legueu (1924) *Lejars (1924) *Mocquot (1942)
Therapeutics and natural history		Debove Gilbert
Surgery	Duplay	Bazy (1913) – Berger Delbert (1921) – Guyon Le Dentu – Lucas Championnierre – Reclus Segond (1909) *Walther (1918)
Anatomopathology		Archard (1910) Lancereaux – Letulle (1908) Malassez – Menetrier (1914) Roger (1910) – *Brault (1911)

continued on page 205

Table 3.2   Continued

'Académie de Médecine' Sections	AFEC Committee of Honour	AFEC holders
Childbirth	Gueniot	Pinard
Public health and forensic medicine		Chantemesse Vincent – Widal
Veterinary medicine		Barrier – Petit (1919)
Physical and chemical medicine		Beclere – Gautier – Robin *Weinberg (Biological sciences in 1935) *Zimmern (Biological sciences in 1931)
Pharmacy	Guignart	
Free members		Roux

*Members who joined the AFEC between 1909 and 1914.

Table 3.3   The representation of the various disiplines within the AFEC

Discipline	Members 1908 N	Members 1908 %	Members 1910 – 1914 N	Members 1910 – 1914 %	Total 1908 – 1914 N	Total 1908 – 1914 %
Surgeons	26	43	10	30	36	39
Clinical doctors	20	33	11	33	31	33
Basic research scientists	8	13	5	15	13	14
Electroradio	2	3	7	21	9	10
Veterinary surgeons	2	3	0	0	2	2
Others	2	3	0	0	2	2
Total	60		33+7 unidentified		93+7 unidentified	

Table 3.4a   Generations and their propensity for communicating (in percentages)

	Group 1 [60 years and over in 1908]	Group 2 [51–60 years]	Group 3 [41–50 years]	Group 4 [40 and less]
0 com.	80	65	54	19
1 to 5 com.	20	29	31	56
more than 5 com.	–	6	15	25
Total	100	100	100	100

Source: AFEC Bulletin communications between 1908 and 1914

Table 3.4b   Date of joining and propensity for communicating (in percentages)

	1908 – 1909	*1910 – 1914*	*All*
0	67	31	54
1 and over	33	69	46
Total	100	100	100

Table 3.4c   Generations and propensity for intervening in discussions

	Group 1 *60 years and over*	*Group 2* *51–60 years*	*Group 3* *41–50 years*	*Group 4* *40 and less*	*All*
0	70	47	54	50	59
1 and 2	20	35	23	31	27
3 to 5	10	12	8	19	10
5 and +	–	6	15	–	4

Table 3.5   Subjects of communications

Subjects	*Communications* *(I)*	*Discussed* *communications (II)*	*Number of* *participants(III)*	*n(II)* *n (I)*	*n(III)* *n(II)*
Treatments	27% (n=48)	31% (n=17)	36% (n=44)	0.35	2.6
Anatomoclinical descriptions	30% (n=54)	39% (n=22)	37% (n=45)	0.41	2.0
Aetiology pathogenesis	16% (n=28)	23% (n=13)	22% (n=27)	0.46	2.0
Experimental cancer research	3% (n=6)	2% (n=1)	1% (n=1)	0.13	1.0

Anatomoclinical
   descriptions of
   animal cancers
	14% (n=25)	–	–	–	–

Biological diagnosis of animal cancers	7% (n=13)	9% (n=5)	5% (n=6)	0.38	1.2
Epidemiological research	2% (n=3)	–	–	–	–
Charlatanism and cancer	1% (n=1)	–	–	–	–
TOTAL	100% (n=178)	100% (n=56)	100% (n=123)		

Table 3.6a Communications relating to the various treatment methods

Treatments	Communications (I)		Discussed communications (II)		Number of participants (III)		$\frac{n(II)}{n(I)}$	$\frac{n(III)}{n(II)}$
Miscellaneous	1%	(n=2)	–		–		–	–
Radium	7%	(n=12)	9%	(n=5)	9%	(n=11)	0.42	2.2
Selenium	2%	(n=3)	4%	(n=2)	3%	(n=4)	0.66	2.0
X rays	0		–		–		–	–
Fulguration	14%	(n=25)	9%	(n=5)	5%	(n=6)	0.2	1.2
Surgery	3%	(n=5)	9%	(n=5)	19%	(n=23)	1.0	4.6
TOTAL	27%	(n=48)	30%	(n=17)	36%	(n=44)	–	–

Table 3.6b Communications relating to the aetiopathogenesis of cancer

Subjects	Communications (I)		Discussed communications (II)		Number of participants (III)		$\frac{n(II)}{n(I)}$	$\frac{n(III)}{n(II)}$
Pre-cancerous state	3.5%	(n=6)	9%	(n=5)	12%	(n=15)	0.83	3.0
Cancer and parasites	3.5%	(n=6)	7%	(n=4)	3%	(n=4)	0.66	1.0
Chemical and physical agents	3.5%	(n=6)	4%	(n=2)	2.5%	(n=3)	0.33	1.5
Heredity and cancer	1.5%	(n=3)	2%	(n=1)	3%	(n=4)	0.33	4.0
Miscellaneous	4%	(n=7)	2%	(n=1)	1%	(n=1)	0.14	1.0
TOTAL	16%	(n=28)	23%	(n=13)	22%	(n=27)		

Appendix to Chapter 7

Table 7.1 Provision of radium and deep radiotherapy equipment in official and unofficial anti-cancer centres – 1928

Official anti-cancer centres	Radium (in grams)	Deep radiotherapy (number of items of apparatus producing 200,000 volts)
Curie Foundation	7.2	3
Angers	0.99	1
Bordeaux	1.7	4
Caen	0.12	1
Lyon	1.45	4
Marseille	1.4	1
Montpellier	1.45	2
Nancy	1.25	4
Paris (public AC services)	3.45	9 *split amongst the six public hospitals
Reims	0.56	1
Rennes	0.99	2
Strasbourg	2.0	2
Toulouse	1.8	5
Villejuif	2	2

continued overleaf

Unofficial anti-cancer centres	Radium (in grams)	Deep radiotherapy (number of items of apparatus producing 200,000 volts)
Besançon	0.125	1
Dijon	0.152	
Le Havre	0.100	1
Montargis	?	1
Nice	0.100	1
Nîmes	0.300	2
Orléans	0.06	1
Rodez	?	1
Rouen	?	1
Tarbes	0.08	1

Table 7.2   Change in public credits allocated to fighting cancer

Year	Budget * for fighting cancer
1927	4,003,000
1928	4,703,000
1929	6,003,000
1930	8,203,000
1931	6,580,000
1932	4,835,000
1934	1,700,000
1935	900,000
1937	4,500,000
1938	4,500,000
1940	2,500,000

* This is the total of the credits allocated for expenditure by the anti-cancer centre organisations (ministry subsidy) and for the creation, fitting out or enlargement of the centres (circle tax subsidy).

Notes

Introduction

1 A. Berg, *Woyzeck*, Act II, scene 2,

2 Cf. M. Grmek, *Les maladies à l'aube de la civilisation occidentale*, Payot, Paris, 1983.

3 L.J. Rather, *The Genesis of Cancer*, Johns Hopkins University Press, Baltimore and London, 1978.

4 Ibid.

5 J. Le Brun, 'Représentations du cancer à l'époque moderne (XVIIᵉ-XVIIIᵉ siècles)', *Prévenir*, 1988, 16, 9–14.

6 A. Furetière, 'Cancer', in *Dictionnaire universel*, Vol. 1, Le Robert, Paris, 1978.

7 J. Le Brun, 'Représentations du cancer . . .', op. cit.

8 R.M. Bell, *Holy Anorexia*, University of Chicago Press, Chicago, 1985.

9 J. Le Brun, 'Cancer Serpit. Recherches sur la représentation du cancer dans les biographies féminines au XVIIIᵉ siècle', *Sciences sociales et santé*, 1984, 2, 2, pp. 9–31.

10 See R. Ledoux-Lebard, *La lutte contre le cancer*, Thèse de médecine, Masson, Paris, 1906, pp. 45–56.

11 J.T. Patterson, *The Dread Disease*, Harvard University Press, 1987, pp. 74–5.

12 Concerning the Deutsches Komitee für Krebsforschung, created in 1900, and the first German anti-cancer centres, see R. Ledoux-Lebard, *La lutte contre le cancer*, op. cit. concerning the Imperial Cancer Research Fund created in 1902, see J. Austoker, *An History of Imperial Cancer Research Fund, 1902–1980*, Oxford University Press, 1988. See also the following historical monographies about British anti-cancer hospitals: 'Middlesex Hospital', *Cancer bulletin*, 1959, 11, 53; 'The Christies Hospital and Holt Radium Institute', Manchester, *Cancer Bulletin*, 1961, 13, 11; 'The Royal Marsden Hospital', *Cancer Bulletin*, 1962, 14, 53; Concerning the American Association of Cancer Research, created in 1907, and the anti-cancer hospitals in the USA, see J.T. Patterson, *The Dread Disease*, op. cit; About the Japanese foundation for cancer research created in 1908, see N. Waro, 'A Pilgrim's Progress', *Cancer Research*, 1974, 34, pp. 1767–74; See also 'the Swedish society against cancer and the "Radiumhemmet" ', *Cancer Bulletin*, 1959, 11, 72; 'The Netherlands Cancer Institute', *Cancer Bulletin*, 1959, 11, 85.

13 'Conférence pour la fondation de l'Union internationale contre le cancer', *LCC*, 1934, 43, pp. 70–80.

14 N. Elias, *The Civilizing Process*, Oxford: Blackwell, 1994

15 P. Pinell, '*Cancer: Images, mythe et morale*', in Concertation nationale cancer, Synthèses thématiques, 1983.

16 P. Pinell, 'How do cancer patients express their points of view ?', *Sociology of Health and Illness*, 1987, 9, 1, pp. 25–44.

17 See, for example, J. Duvignaud and J.P. Corbeau, *Les tabous des Français*, Paris, Hachette, 1981; and L.V. Thomas, '*Mort redécouverte, mort escamotée*', in *La mort aujourd'hui*, Marseille, Rivages, 1982.
18 L.J. Rather, *The Genesis of Cancer*, op. cit.
19 Ibid., pp. 178–9.
20 See, for example, R.A. Rettig, *Cancer Crusade, The Story of the National Cancer Act of 1971*, Princeton, 1977; L. Breslow, *A History of Cancer Control in the United States, 1946–1971*, Bethesda, Department of Health, Education and Welfare, 1977.
21 J.T. Patterson, *The Dread Disease*, op. cit.
22 Ibid., 'Preface', p. vii.

1 A fatal and incurable disease

1 R. Ledoux-Lebard, *La lutte contre le cancer*, op. cit.
2 Dr Pol Gosset, 'L'hôpital pour cancérés', communication to Rheims Academy, February 1926, reproduced in *LCC*, 1926, 12, pp. 311–20.
3 Quoted by Pol Gosset, ibid., p. 313.
4 Quoted by Pol Gosset, ibid., p. 315.
5 Quoted by Pol Gosset, ibid., p. 314.
6 Ibid., p. 316.
7 Ibid., p. 318.
8 Letters of patent for the foundation of the first hospital for incurables (1637), quoted by J. Godart, 'La réhabilitation de l'incurable', *LCC*, 1946, 77, p. 130.
9 Ibid.
10 M. Foucault, *Naissance de la clinique*, Paris, PUF, 1963.
11 See E. Ackerknecht, *La médecine hospitalière à Paris (1794–1848)*, Paris, Payot, 1986.
12 E. Ackerknecht, 'Le cancer dans l'oeuvre de l'Ecole de Paris 1800–1850', *Clio medica*, 1986, 20, 10, pp. 125–33.
13 Ibid., p. 129.
14 E.L. Geoffroy, *Manuel de médecine pratique*, 1800, p. 331.
15 E. Ackerknecht, *La médecine hospitalière à Paris. . .*, op. cit., p. 188.
16 J.J. Cocheton, J. Guerre and H. Pequignot, *Histoire illustrée de l'hépato-gastro-entérologie*, Paris, Roger da Costa, 1987, p. 140.
17 E. Ackerknecht, 'Le cancer dans l'oeuvre de l'Ecole de Paris . . .', op. cit., p. 130.
18 E. Forgue, 'Lettre au Journal des Débats', in *LCC*, 1928, 21, 26.
19 E. Ackerknecht, 'Le cancer dans l'oeuvre de l'Ecole de Paris . . .', op. cit., p. 130.
20 F. Loste, 'Hôpital', in *Dictionnaire des sciences médicales, 1817–1821*, p. 490.
21 See J.P. Peter, 'Les mots et les objets de la maladie', *Revue d'histoire*, 1974, 246, 499, pp. 13–38.
22 See J. Léonard, *La médecine en France entre les pouvoirs et les savoirs*, Paris, Aubier, 1981.
23 See B. Lécuyer, '*L'hygiène avant Pasteur*', in C. Salomon-Bayet, *Pasteur et la révolution pasteurienne*, Paris, Payot, 1986, pp. 65–139.
24 R. Castel, *L'ordre psychiatrique*, Paris, Ed. de Minuit, 1976, p. 20.
25 P. Ariès, *L'enfant et la vie familiale sous l'Ancien Régime*, Paris, Le Seuil, 1973.
26 About this controversy, see E. Ackerknecht, 'Hygiene in France (1815–1848)', *Bulletin of History of Medicine*, 1948, 22, 562–93; B. Lécuyer, op. cit.; and F. Delaporte, *Le savoir sur la maladie*, Paris, PUF, 1991.
27 F. Delaporte, op. cit.
28 S. Borsa and C.R. Michel, *La vie quotidienne des hôpitaux en France au XIXᵉ siècle*, Paris, Hachette, 1985, pp. 23–7.
29 A. Vuilbeau, *Orthopédie et pédagogie*, Thèse de 3ème cycle, Paris VII, 1980.

30 E. Ackerknecht, *La médecine hospitalière à Paris . . .*, op. cit., pp. 277–88.
31 F. Legueu, 'Félix Guyon (1831–1920)', elegy given on the occasion of his centenary, *Bulletin de l'académie de médecine*, 1931, 39, pp. 561–88.
32 J. Guiart, 'Le cancer dans l'histoire de la médecine', *LCC*, 74, 1945, pp. 23–9.
33 Ibid.
34 See S. Borsa and C.R. Michel, op. cit., pp. 54–61.
35 A.J. Bengolea, 'Madame Garnier', *LCC*, 1936, 54, pp. 249–59.
36 Ibid., pp. 253–4.
37 'Calvaire (Dames du)', in *Encyclopédie du catholicisme, hier, aujourd'hui et demain*, Paris, Letouzey et Ane, vol. II, 1954, p. 400.
38 A.J. Bengolea, op. cit., p. 253.
39 F. Rocquain, 'L'Œuvre des Dames du Calvaire', communication to the Académie des sciences morales et politiques, December 1904, reproduced in *LCC*, 1924, 3, pp. 207–213.
40 Ibid.
41 See O. Arnold, *Le corps et l'âme : la vie des religieuses du XIXᵉ siècle*, Paris, Le Seuil, 1984.
42 Chanoine Chaffanjon, *Les veuves et la charité. Vie de Madame Garnier*, Paris, Vitte, 1922 (5th edition), p. 24.
43 F. Rocquain, op. cit., p. 213.
44 Ibid., p. 213.
45 A.J. Bengolea, op. cit., p. 254.
46 J. Le Brun, 'Cancer Serpit', op. cit.
47 F. Rocquain, op. cit., p. 212.
48 For sociohistorical studies of these associations, see L. Boltanski, *Prime éducation et morale de classe*, Paris, Mouton, 1971; F. Muel, 'L'école obligatoire et l'invention de l'enfance anormale', *Actes de la recherche en sciences sociales*, 1975, 1; see also 'Pour une histoire du service social', *Vie sociale*, 1987, 8/9.

2 The first successes in treatment

1 P. Reclus, 'Eloge de Paul Berger', *Bulletin de l'académie de médecine*, 1913, pp. 568–84, 577.
2 P. Mathieu, 'Eloge d'Edouard Quenu', *Bulletin de l'académie de médecine*, 1953, p. 654.
3 B. Cuneo, 'Notice nécrologique sur M. Edouard Quenu', Bulletin de l'académie de médecine, 1933, pp. 131–44
4 'E. Quenu', quoted by P. Mathieu, op. cit., pp. 653–4.
5 E. Ackerknecht, *A Short History of Medicine*, Johns Hopkins University Press, 1982, p. 191.
6 B. Cuneo, op. cit., p. 133.
7 R. Monod, 'Notice nécrologique sur le professeur Hartmann', *Bulletin de l'académie de médecine*, 1952, 11, pp. 14–17.
8 H. Hartmann, 'Bernard Cuneo', *Bulletin de l'académie de médecine*, 1945, pp. 53–55.
9 C. Mocquot, 'Jean-Louis Faure', *Bulletin de l'académie de médecine*, 1945, p. 69.
10 'Statistiques de l'hôpital Tenon', *Bulletin de l'AFEC*, 1908, I.
11 B. Pasveer, 'Knowledge of Shadows: the introduction of X-ray images in medicine', *Sociology of Health and Illness*, 1989, 11, 4, pp. 360–81.
12 A.P. Lachapelle, 'La radiothérapie en 1905', *Journal de radiologie et d'électrologie*, 1958, 39, 5–6, pp. 383–96.
13 J. Bergonié, 'Où en sont aujourd'hui les applications à la médecine et à la chirurgie de la découverte de Roentgen ? Nouveaux faits', *Journal de médecine de Bordeaux*, 1897, 27, 4, 37.

14 Ibid.
15 Ibid.
16 See B. Pasveer, op. cit.
17 A.M. Baudouin, 'Hommage à Antoine Béclère', *Bulletin de l'académie de médecine*, 1939, 121, pp. 351–6.
18 *L'enseignement médical à Paris, renseignements pratiques à l'usage des médecins, 1913–1914*, Paris, Masson et Cie, p. 172.
19 R. Ledoux-Lebard, *Assemblée générale du 4 avril 1922*, Paris, Ligue franco-anglo-américaine contre le cancer, 1922, p. 32.
20 J. Bergonié, op. cit.
21 Ibid., p. 37.
22 L. Bouchacourt, *De l'exploration des organes internes à l'aide de la lumière éclairante et non éclairante. Endoscopie par les rayons de Roentgen*, Thèse, Paris, 1898, p. 161.
23 Ibid., p. 163.
24 Ibid., p. 162.
25 J. Bergonié, op. cit., p. 37.
26 J. Belot, *Traité de radiothérapie*, Paris, G. Steinheil, 1905.
27 A.P. Lachapelle, op. cit.
28 L. Bouchacourt, op. cit., p. 160.
29 Ibid., p.162–3.
30 Ibid., p. 159.
31 Ibid., p. 165.
32 Ibid., p. 165.
33 Ibid., p. 166.
34 Ibid., p. 166
35 A.P. Lachapelle, op. cit.
36 Quoted by R. Huguenin, 'L'apport de la France dans l'étude du cancer', in *Ce que la France a apporté à la médecine depuis le début du XXe siècle*, Paris, Flammarion, 1946.
37 R. Rullière, *Abrégé d'histoire de la médecine*, Paris, Masson, 1981, p. 208.
38 'Extrait du compte moral et administratif de l'exercice 1923, Administration générale de l'Assistance publique', *LCC*, 1925, 9, 38–9.
39 J. Belot, op. cit.
40 J. Bergonié, 'Le radium au point de vue médical', *Archives d'électricité médicale*, 1904, 3, 175–87.
41 Ibid., p. 183.
42 J. Bergonié, 'Effets des rayons X dans le cancer du sein', *Journal de médecine de Bordeaux*, 1904, 13, p. 228.
43 J. Belot, op. cit.
44 J. Bergonié, 'Le radium au point de vue médical', op. cit.
45 J. Belot, op. cit., pp. 505–6.
46 Ibid., pp. 506–7.
47 Ibid., pp. 502–3.
48 Ibid., pp. 560–1.
49 Ibid., p. 503.
50 Ibid., p. 584.
51 A.P. Lachapelle, op. cit., p. 396.
52 Quoted by P. Douérin, *Essai biographique sur Monsieur le Professeur Bergonié*, Thèse en médecine, Bordeaux, 1978, p. 22.
53 Ibid., p. 22.
54 G. Meyniel, 'L. Tribondeau collaborateur de Bergonié', *Journal de radiologie et d'électrologie*, 1958, 404.
55 J. Bergonié, 'Le radium au point de vue médical', op. cit., p. 177.
56 J. Bergonié, 'Effets des rayons X dans le cancer du sein', op. cit., p. 228.

57 J. Bergonié, 'Le radium au point de vue médical', op. cit. p. 181.
58 M.L. Houllevigne, 'L'industrie du radium', *Le Temps*, 26 June 1927; article reproduced in *LCC*, 1927, 17, pp. 13–18.
59 Concerning Dominici's researches, see R. Huguenin, *'L'apport de la France...'*, op. cit., pp. 164–5; E. Forgue, 'Gesta Cancerologiae per Francos', *LCC*, 1936, 53, 178–9; H. Dominici, 'Du traitement des tumeurs malignes par le rayonnement ultra-pénétrant du radium', *Bulletin de l'AFEC*, 1908, I, 124–55.
60 C. Regaud and T. Nogier, *'Action des rayons X très pénétrants, filtrés, sur le derme et l'épiderme de la peau'*, Association française pour l'avancement des sciences, 41° session, Nîmes, 1912, résumé p. 213.
61 R. Huguenin, op. cit., p. 164.
62 'Réunion du Conseil de l'Institut Pasteur du 15–12–1909', quoted by J. Regaud, *Claudius Regaud*, Paris, Maloine, 1982, p. 63.
63 'Lettre de L. Liard, vice-recteur, Président du Conseil de l'Université de Paris, au Dr Roux', quoted by J. Regaud, op. cit., p. 63.

3 Academicism and marginality

1 For an history of these short-lived 'Ligue contre le cancer', see R. Ledoux-Lebard, *La Lutte contre le cancer*, op. cit, pp. 29–42.
2 R. Ledoux-Lebard, op. cit., p. 31.
3 Ibid., p. 32.
4 Ibid., p. 32.
5 Ibid., p. 41.
6 Ibid., p. 42.
7 'Intervention du Président Bouchard', Séance du 15 juin 1908, *Bulletin de l'AFEC*, 1908, I, 15.
8 For the list of the members of the Association française pour l'étude du cancer, see *Bulletin de l'AFEC*, 1908, I, 11–12.
9 H. Jamous, *La réforme des études médicales et des structures hospitalières*, Paris, CNRS, Centre d'études sociologiques, 1967.
10 Ibid.
11 The Ecole de santé de Paris (14 frimaire an II), was created with only two 'clinical' chairs, one for medicine, the other for surgery and obstetrics. In 1823, the chairs of general medicine and general surgery, respectively, were raised to four and three (four in 1829); a special chair for obstetrics was created in 1889. Between 1877 and 1890, six chairs of specialised clinics were opened (mental illnesses, children's diseases, opthalmology, skin diseases and syphilis, neurology, urology). See A. Prévost, *La Faculté de médecine de Paris, 1794–1900*, Paris, Maloine, 1900.
12 Most of the newly admited professors cannot obtain directly a clinical chair. They are nominated first to so-called theoretical chairs, like the chairs of anatomy, internal or external pathology, therapeutic, comparative medicine, operation and apparatus, experimental pathology, etc. These chairs of lower prestige are known as 'waiting chairs'. See on this point H. Jamous, op. cit.
13 See B. Lécuyer, *'L'hygiène avant Pasteur'*, op. cit.
14 L. Murard and P. Zylberman, 'La raison de l'expert ou l'hygiène comme science sociale appliquée', *Archives européennes de sociologie*, 1985, XXVI, 1, pp. 58–89.
15 See E. Ackerknecht, *La médecine hospitalière...*, op. cit. All the important French contributors to experimental medicine and biomedical sciences of the nineteenth century worked outside the medical faculties whether they were physicians (like Legallois, Magendie, Poiseuille, Dutrochet, Brown-Séquard, Claude Bernard) or not (Flourens, Regnault, Berthelot, Pasteur). J.B. Dumas, the 'father' of experimental embryology was one of the very few exceptions to that 'rule'.

16 H.W. Paul, *From Knowledge to Power : The Rise of the Science Empire in France, 1860–1939*, New York, Cambridge University Press, 1985.

17 J. Léonard, '*Comment peut-on être pasteurien'*, in C. Salomon-Bayet, *Pasteur et la révolution pasteurienne*, op. cit.

18 For a more complete analysis of the opposition beetwen technical versus social abilities within the medical field, see P. Bourdieu, *Homo academicus*, Paris, Ed. de Minuit, 1984.

19 See H. Jamous, op. cit.

20 Nearly half (27/60) of the professors listed by Claire Salomon-Bayet and collaborators (*Pasteur et la révolution pasteurienne*, op. cit.), as Pasteur's allies will be members of the AFEC in 1908.

21 A. Antonin, 'Charles Bouchard (1837–1915)', *Bulletin de l'académie de médecine*, 1950, pp. 732–9.

22 C. Mocquot, 'Pierre Delbet (1861–1957)', *Bulletin de l'académie de médecine*, 1957, pp. 630–8.

23 Ibid.

24 Zimmern, 'A propos de la fulguration', *Bulletin de l'AFEC*, 1909, II, p. 91.

25 J.L. Faure, 'Sur la fulguration', *Bulletin de l'AFEC*, 1909, II, p. 73.

26 Tuffier, 'Recherches expérimentales et cliniques sur la fulguration', *Bulletin de l'AFEC*, 1909, II, pp. 94–5.

27 P. Delbet, 'Sur la fulguration', *Bulletin de l'AFEC*, 1910, IV, p. 130.

28 O. Pasteau, Degrais and J. Belot, 'Modifications cliniques et histologiques d'une tumeur de la prostate', *Bulletin de l'AFEC*, 1913, VI, pp. 113–21.

29 A. Borrel, 'Le problème étiologique du cancer', *Bulletin de l'AFEC*, 1908, I, p. 2.

30 P. Ménétrier, 'Les états morbides précancéreux et la formation du cancer à leurs dépens', *Bulletin de l'AFEC*, 1908, I, p. 29.

31 P. Marie and J. Clunet, 'Végétations atypiques de l'épiderme cutané après injections intradermiques d'huile d'olive saturée de Sarlach', *Bulletin de l'AFEC*, 1909, II, pp. 146–8.

32 P. Ménétrier, G. Legros and A. Mallet, 'Hyperplasie et métaplasie épithéliales expérimentalement produites chez le rat par l'action réitérée de rayons X', *Bulletin de l'AFEC*, 1909, II, pp. 150–60.

33 P. Marie, J. Clunet and G. Raulot-Lapointe, 'Contribution à l'étude des tumeurs malignes sur les ulcères de Roentgen', *Bulletin de l'AFEC*, 1910, III, pp. 404–10.

34 G. Petit, 'Cystercerque et cancer de l'épiploon chez le lapin', *Bulletin de l'AFEC*, II, 1909, 25–27; J. Bridé and E. Conseil, 'Sarcome à cystercerques chez le rat', *Bulletin de l'AFEC*, 1909, II, 171–173 and 1910, III, pp. 318–20.

35 M. Mayet, 'Faits expérimentaux propres à éclairer la pathogénie du cancer', *Bulletin de l'AFEC*, 1909, II, pp. 120–40.

36 Contamin, 'Rayons X et cancer expérimental de la souris', *Bulletin de l'AFEC*, 1910, III, pp. 160–4.

37 J. Clunet, 'Le cancer au Maroc', *Bulletin de l'AFEC*, 1912, V, p. 167.
Trolard, 'Le cancer à Saffi (Maroc)', *Bulletin de l'AFEC*, 1912, V, p. 168.
Juillerat, 'Les maisons à cancer de Paris', *Bulletin de l'AFEC*, 1909, II, pp. 61–2.

38 See R. Ledoux-Lebard, *La lutte contre le cancer*, op. cit.

39 Ibid.

40 J. Austoker, op. cit.

41 J. Bertillon, 'De la fréquence des principales causes de décès à Paris pendant la seconde moitié du XIXᵉ siècle et notamment la période 1886–1905', in *Annuaire statistique de la ville de Paris*, Paris, Masson, 1906, pp. 113–346.

42 Ibid.

43 E. Forgue, 'Gesta Cancerologiae per Francos', op. cit., pp. 164–5.

44 Ibid., p. 172.

45 R. Huguenin, 'L'apport de la France . . .', op. cit., p. 149.

46 Ibid., p. 148.
47 E. Forgue, op. cit., p. 181.
48 Desfosses and Vitoux, *L'enseignement médical à Paris, renseignements pratiques à l'usage des médecins, 1913–1914*, op. cit., 1914.
49 R. Ledoux-Lebard, 'Causerie sur la radiothérapie profonde', in *Assemblée générale du 4 avril 1922*, op. cit., p. 31.
50 J. Bergonié, 'Le radium au point de vue médical . . .', op. cit., p. 123.
51 J. Belot, *Traité de radiothérapie*, op. cit., p. 525.
52 Ibid., pp. 513–14.
53 J. Rullière, op. cit. p., 217
54 R. Ledoux-Lebard, op. cit., p. 32.
55 *Rapport soumis par la sous-commission chargée de l'étude de la radiothérapie du cancer.* Chapter IV. Le département radiologique de la clinique gynécologique de l'université de Munich, Société des nations, Commission du cancer, Genève, 1929, pp. 42–51.
56 Desfosses and Vitoux, *L'enseignement médical à Paris, renseignements pratiques à l'usage des médecins, 1912–1913*, Paris, Masson, 1913. For information on gynaecology, see pp. 77–82.
57 G. Meyniel, 'Tribondeau, collaborateur de Bergonié', op. cit., p. 404.
58 For a detailed biography of Claudius Regaud, see the book written by his son: Jean Regaud, *Claudius Regaud*, Paris, Maloine, 1982.
59 Regaud published, between 1897 and 1900, in the 'comptes rendus et mémoires de la Société de biologie', no less than twelve articles related to the histology of testicles.
60 J. Regaud, *Claudius Regaud*, op. cit., p. 44.
61 C. Regaud, 'Lettre à Emile Roux du 3 juillet 1909', quoted by J. Regaud, ibid., p. 60.
62 A. Lacassagne, 'L'oeuvre de Regaud cancérologiste', *LCC*, 1941, pp. 69–70, 102.
63 Between 1906 and 1909, Regaud published twenty-four papers dealing with normal and pathological histophysiology and only seven papers on X-rays. Between 1910 and 1913, the ratio was inverted with fourteen papers on X-rays and three on histophysiology questions.
64 A. Lacassagne, op. cit., pp. 103–4.
65 Ibid., p. 103.
66 Ibid., p. 104.
67 C. Regaud, 'Lettre à Emile Roux . . .', op. cit., p. 61.
68 J. Regaud, op. cit., pp. 70–2.
69 J. Regaud, *Claudius Regaud*, op. cit., p. 91.

4 War and the birth of the Anti-Cancer League

1 See F. Braudel, *L'identité de la France*, Paris, Arthaud, 1986, p. 124.
2 See L. Le Lorier, 'L'oeuvre de la Ligue française', in *Le cancer*, Paris, Masson, 1944, p. 8; and R. Ledoux-Lebard, 'La lutte contre le cancer', op. cit.
3 See P. Bernard, *La fin d'un monde, 1914–1929*, Paris, Le Seuil, 1975, op. cit., p. 108.
4 D. Dessertine and O. Faure, *Combattre la tuberculose*, Presses Universitaires de Lyon, 1988, p. 29.
5 L. Murard and P. Zylbermann, 'L'idée de "service social" dans la pensée hygiéniste (1928–1936)', *Vie sociale*, 1978, 8–9, p. 467.
6 D. Dessertine and O. Faure, op. cit.
7 L. Murard and P. Zylbermann, 'L'autre guerre, la santé publique sous l'oeil de l'Amérique', *Revue historique*, 1986, 560, pp. 367–98.

8   C. Quetel, *Le mal de Naples*, Paris, Seghers, 1986.
9   A. Mignon, *Le service de santé pendant la guerre de 1914–1918*, Paris, Masson, vol. IV, pp. 723–5.
10 F. Thébaud, *La femme au temps de la guerre de 14*, Paris, Stock/ Laurence Pernoud, 1986, pp. 136–40.
11 C. Quetel, op. cit.
12 A. Mignon, op. cit.
13 E. Forgue, 'Le cancer et la guerre', *Bulletin de l'AFEC*, 1918, VII, p. 590.
14 Ibid., p. 588.
15 Ibid., p. 588.
16 P. Ménétrier, 'Relations des traumatismes, et plus particulièrement des traumatismes de guerre, avec le développement des néoplasmes' *Bulletin de l'AFEC*, VII 1918, pp. 556–62; P. Masson, des 'Rapports sur les relations des néoplasmes cutanés avec les traumatismes', *Bulletin de l'AFEC*, VII 1918, pp. 562–4; C. Walter, 'Rapports sur les cancers de la cavité pharyngienne développés sur les cicatrices de blessures de guerre', Bulletin de l'AFEC, VII 1918, p. 565; G. Lion, 'Relations du traumatisme avec les cancers de l'estomac et de l'intestin', *Bulletin de l'AFEC*, VII 1918, (pp. 565–8); M. Chevassu, des 'Relations des traumatismes du testicule avec les néoplasmes de cet organe', *Bulletin de l'AFEC*, VII 1918, pp. 568–71; J.L. Faure, 'Traumatisme et cancer du sein', *Bulletin de l'AFEC*, VII 1918, pp. 571–2; O. Pasteau, des 'Relations des néoplasmes du rein avec les traumatismes de guerre', *Bulletin de l'AFEC*, VII 1918, pp. 572–3; P. Delbet and Brault, des 'Relations des traumatismes avec les sarcomes', *Bulletin de l'AFEC*, VII 1918, pp. 573–581.
17 L. Murard and P. Zylbermann, 'Généalogie de la loi préventive: la lutte contre les maladies contagieuses en France, 1893–1925', *JEVI*, 1989, pp. 263–92.
18 A. Mignon, op. cit.
19 About Justin Godart, see: *'Pour le travail et pour la paix'. Hommage de ses amis à Justin Godart à l'occasion de son élection à l'Académie de médecine*, Paris, Quillet, 1939; 'Justin Godart (1871–1956)', Elegy given by M. Xavier Leclainche to l'Académie de médecine, at the meeting of 12 December 1972.
20 *'Pour le travail et pour la paix'*, op. cit.
21 A. Mignon, op. cit.
22 A. Lacassagne, op. cit., p. 5.
23 A. Mignon, op. cit., pp. 245–59.
24 F. Thébaud, op. cit., p. 84.
25 Y. Knibielher, *Cornettes et blouses blanches*, Paris, Hachette, 1984, p. 90.
26 A. Mignon, op. cit.
27 A. Lacassagne, op. cit., p. 6.
28 J. Bergonié, 'La faculté future', *Journal de médecine de Bordeaux*, 1908, 49, pp. 773–8.
29 F. Thébaud, op. cit., p. 92.
30 A. Mignon, op. cit.
31 Ibid.
32 P. Douérin, *Essai biographique sur M. le professeur Bergonié*, op. cit., pp. 82–4.
33 G. Jacquetty and J. Bergonié, 'Le travail agricole médicalement prescrit et surveillé comme traitement des séquelles de blessures de guerre', *Archives d'électricité médicale et de physiothérapie*, July 1917, pp. 418, 305.
34 A. Mignon, op. cit.
35 C. Mocquot, 'Jean-Louis Faure', op. cit., p. 69.
36 M.H. Rouvillois, 'Discours prononcé aux obsèques du Dr Tuffier *Bulletin de l'académie de médecine*, 1929, 102, pp. 246–7.
37 B. Cuneo, 'Notice nécrologique sur M. Edouard Quenu', op. cit., pp. 141–2.
38 A. Mignon, op. cit.

39 H. Hartmann, 'Emile Forgue (1860–1942)', *Bulletin de l'académie de médecine*, meeting of 9 March 1936, pp. 138–41.

40 A.M. Moulin, 'Les doctoresses russes du XIXe siècle . . .', op. cit.

41 'Nécrologie du Dr Sonia Fabre', *LCC*, 1948, pp. 86, 27.

42 About A. Lumière see L. Bérard, 'Mon ami Auguste Lumière', *LCC*, 1954, 107, pp. 1–6; P. Lépine, 'Auguste Lumière (1862–1954)', *Bulletin de l'académie de médecine*, séance du 22 juin 1954.

43 'Nécrologie du Dr Sonia Fabre', op. cit., pp. 2–7.

44 A. Mignon, op. cit.

45 R. Le Bret, *Assemblée générale du 4 avril 1922*, op. cit., p. 8.

46 *Annuaire de l'office central des œuvres de bienfaisance*, 1902–3.

47 'Concours de la Dentelle de France', *La France charitable*, 1906, 25, pp. 5–6.

48 Quoted by L. Murard and P. Zylbermann in 'L'idée de 'service social' dans la pensée hygiéniste . . .', op. cit., p. 467.

49 F. Thébaud, op. cit., p. 107.

50 Y. Knibielher, op. cit.

51 F. Thébaud, op. cit., p. 109.

52 L. Murard and P. Zylbermann, 'L'idée de "service social" dans la pensée hygiéniste . . .', op. cit.

53 'Statuts de la Ligue franco-anglo-américaine contre le cancer', *LCC*, 1925, 10, 98.

54 Ibid., p. 108.

55 Ibid., p. 107.

56 A. Schwartz, 'Intervention à propos de la lutte sociale contre le cancer', *Bulletin de l'AFEC*, 1919, VIII, pp. 46–7.

57 P. Delbet, 'Réponse à Schwartz', ibid., p. 47.

58 'Liste des fondateurs de la Ligue', in *Assemblée générale du 4 avril 1922*, op. cit., p. 54.

59 'Assemblée générale extraordinaire', *Bulletin de l'AFEC*, 1921, X, pp. 219–22.

60 'Allocution de P. Delbet à l'Assemblée générale de 1922', *Bulletin de l'AFEC*, 1922, XI, pp. 118–19. Also, 'Rapport de R. Le Bret', in *Assemblée générale du 4 avril 1922*, op. cit., pp. 15–16.

61 Duchesse d'Uzès, *Souvenirs de la duchesse d'Uzès, née Mortemart*, Paris, Plon, 1939, p. 126.

62 Ibid., p. 172.

63 Z. Sternhell, *La droite révolutionnaire*, Paris, Le Seuil, 1978.

64 Comte Cossé de Brissac, 'Préface' à *Souvenirs de la duchesse d'Uzès*, op. cit. The duchesse d'Uzès was born Mortemart, one of the oldest families of feudal France.

65 E. Bonnefous, *Avant l'oubli. La vie de 1900 à 1940*, Paris, Laffont/Nathan, 1984, p. 26.

66 Ibid., p. 26.

67 J.N. Jeanneney, *François de Wendel en République, l'argent et le pouvoir*, Paris, Le Seuil, 1976.

68 See *Assemblée générale du 4 avril 1922*, op. cit., pp. 54–8; *LCC*, 1925, 8, 406–9; and *LCC*, 1927, 16, pp. 333–7.

5 The beginnings of a policy for the fight against cancer

1 'Rapport de Robert Le Bret', *Assemblée générale du 4 avril 1922*, op. cit., p. 7.

2 Ibid., p. 7.

3 Ibid., p. 11.

4 A. Lacassagne, 'L'oeuvre de Regaud cancérologiste', op. cit.

5 Ibid., p. 106.

6 A. Lacassagne quoted by J. Regaud in *Claudius Regaud*, op. cit., p. 93.

7 J. Regaud, ibid., p. 94.

8 C. Regaud, 'Discours au banquet des agrégés du 8 juin 1912', in J. Regaud, op. cit., p. 67.

9 C. Bernard, *Introduction à l 'étude de la médecine expérimentale*, op. cit., p. 301.

10 Ibid., p. 300.

11 J. Regaud, op. cit., pp. 93–5.

12 See list of the founding members, *Assemblée générale du 4 avril 1922*, op. cit., pp. 54–5.

13 A. Lacassagne quoted by J. Regaud, op. cit., p. 95.

14 R. Reid, *Marie Curie, derrière la légende*, Paris, Le Seuil, coll. Points, 1979.

15 C. Regaud, 'Discours prononcé le 23 décembre 1924', quoted by J. Regaud, op. cit., p. 127.

16 Ibid., p. 126.

17 Ibid.

18 Ibid.

19 J. Lhermitte, 'Gustave Roussy', meeting of 21 June 1948, *Bulletin de l'académie de médecine*, 450–9.

20 Ibid., p. 452.

21 J. Delarue, 'Allocution prononcée pour le dixième anniversaire de la mort de Gustave Roussy', *LCC*, 1958, 129, 9–13.

22 Ibid., p. 10.

23 J. Lhermitte, op. cit., p. 156.

24 Ibid., p. 153.

25 J. Lhermitte, op. cit., p. 455.

26 *Assemblée générale du 4 avril 1922*, op. cit., p. 111.

27 G. Roussy, R. Leroux and E. Peyre, 'Le cancer expérimental du goudron chez la souris. Premiers résultats', *Bulletin de l'AFEC*, 1922, XI

28 G. Roussy, S. Laborde, R. Leroux and E. Peyre, 'Réactions locales et générales de l'organisme au cours du traitement des cancers du col utérin par les rayons X et γ ', *Bulletin de l'AFEC*, 1922, XI. G. Roussy, S. Laborde and R. Leroux, 'A propos de la durée d'irradiation dans la curiethérapie des cancers malpighiens', *Bulletin de l'AFEC*, 1923, XII

29 See J. Lhermitte, op. cit., p. 454.

30 *Assemblée générale du 4 avril 1922*, op. cit., p. 11.

31 Ibid., p. 11.

32 'Allocution de Justin Godart', Assemblée générale du 8 mai 1923, *LCC*, 1923, 1, p. 12.

33 'Rapport de Robert Le Bret', Assemblée générale du 8 mai 1923, op. cit., p. 15.

34 'Commission du Cancer', *Journal officiel du 9 juin 1922*, reproduced in *LCC*, 1923, 2, p. 101.

35 This Commission was divided into 5 sections: (1) expérimentation, pathogénie et pathologie comparées; président: Pr Letulle; (2) etiologie et démographie; président: Dr Pottevin; (3) pathologie et clinique humaine; président: Prof. Delbet; (4) thérapeutique; président: Dr Tuffier; (5) assistance, prophylaxie, propagande; président: Prof. Hartmann; in 'Commission du cancer', ibid., p. 104.

36 For a list of the members of the Commission, see 'Commission du cancer', ibid., pp. 101–4.

37 P. Douérin, *Essai biographique sur M. le Pr Bergonié*, op. cit.

38 R. Le Bret, *Assemblée générale du 4 avril 1922*, op. cit., p. 10.

39 J. Bergonié, 'Comment doivent être organisés les centres régionaux de lutte contre le cancer', rapport devant la Commission du cancer, *Paris médical*, 1923, 48, pp. 146–9.

40 Ibid.

41 Ibid.
42 R. Le Bret, *Assemblée générale du 4 avril 1922*, op. cit., p. 9.
43 'L'enseignement de la radiologie', in *L'Enseignement médical à Paris, renseignements pratiques à l'usage des médecins, 1913–1914*, op. cit., p. 172.
44 'L'industrie du radium', reproduction of M.L. Houllevigne's paper, published in *Le Temps* 26 June 1927, op. cit., pp. 13–18.
45 See 'Commission du cancer', op. cit., p. 107.
46 J. Bergonié, 'Comment doivent être organisés . . .', op. cit.,
47 A.P. Lachapelle, 'La radiothérapie en 1905', op. cit.
48 J. Bergonié, 'Comment doivent être organisés . . .', op. cit.,
49 Ibid.
50 F. Muel, 'L'école obligatoire et l'invention de l'enfance anormale', *Actes de la recherche en sciences sociales*, 1975, p. 1.
51 P. Bernard, *La fin d'un monde, 1914–1929*, op. cit.
52 J. Bergonié, 'Comment doivent être organisés . . .', op. cit.
53 Ibid.
54 Ibid.
55 'Principes d'après lesquels . . .', op. cit., pp. 104–5.
56 Ibid.
57 Ibid.
58 Ibid.
59 L. Bérard, 'Fondation et fonctionnement des centres anticancéreux', in *Le Cancer*, op. cit., p. 29.
60 L. Le Lorier, 'L'oeuvre de la Ligue française', in *Le Cancer*, op. cit., p. 11.
61 See 'Commission du cancer', op. cit., p. 106.
62 C. Regaud quoted by A. Lacassagne, 'L'oeuvre de Regaud cancérologiste', op. cit., pp. 106–7.

6 The policy for the fight against cancer: first contradictions first reorganisations

1 R. Le Bret, 'Assemblée générale du 8 mai 1923', *LCC*, 1923, 1, p. 16.
2 P. Strauss, ibid., p. 9.
3 R. Le Bret, *Assemblée générale du 4 avril 1922*, op. cit., pp. 8–9.
4 J. Worth, 'Compte rendu financier', *Assemblée générale du 4 avril 1922*, op. cit., pp. 19, 26.
5 R. Le Bret, *Assemblée générale du 4 avril 1922*, op. cit., p. 14.
6 Mme Hartmann, 'Rapport de la section d'assistance', *Assemblée générale du 4 avril 1922*, op. cit., pp. 24–5.
7 Ibid., p. 25.
8 'Comités, Associations affiliées – Lyon', *LCC*, 1923, 1, pp. 51–2.
9 R. Le Bret, *Assemblée générale du 4 avril 1922*, op. cit., p. 15.
10 'Lyon', op. cit., p. 52.
11 'Rennes – Comité régional de l'Ouest', *LCC*, 1923, 1, pp. 52–4.
12 'Toulouse – Ligue régionale contre le cancer', *LCC*, 1923, 2, pp. 147–8.
13 'La Ligue bourguignonne', *LCC*, 1923, 1, pp. 49–50.
14 'L'Association contre le cancer de Bordeaux et du Sud-Ouest', *LCC*, 1923, 2, pp. 148–9.
15 Reported by R. Le Bret, 'Assemblée générale du 8 mai 1923', op. cit., p. 21.
16 'Circulaire aux préfets du 15–11–1922', reproduced in *LCC*, 1923, 2, pp. 108–9.
17 'Intervention de Duboys-Fresney', reproduced in *LCC*, 1923, 2, p. 110.
18 C. Regaud, 'Les idées directrices de la lutte contre le cancer', *LCC*, 1923, 2, pp. 99–100.

19 'Centres de traitement du cancer. Faut-il en augmenter le nombre ?', *LCC*, 1924, 4, p. 355.

20 Ibid., p. 356.

21 Ibid.

22 'Alpes-Maritimes-Nice', *LCC*, 1923, 1, 48–9; and *LCC*, 1924, 3, pp. 254–6.

23 'La Ligue bourguignonne', *LCC*, 1924, 6, pp. 91–3.

24 'Nîmes', *LCC*, 1924, 3, 249–52; *LCC*, 1924, 4, 373–4; and *LCC*, 1925, 5, pp. 59–62.

25 'Orléans', *LCC*, 1923, 2, pp. 152–3.

26 'Montargis', *LCC*, 1924, 3, p. 258.

27 'Toulouse (Albi)', *LCC*, 1923, 2, pp. 147–8; Montauban, *LCC*, 1924, 3, p. 259.

28 'Rodez', *LCC*, 1924, 3, p. 257; and *LCC*, 1924, 4, p. 375.

29 'Limoges', *LCC*, 1924, 6, p. 94.

30 'Besançon', *LCC*, 1925, 10, pp. 164–6.

31 'Rouen', *LCC*, 1925, 6, p. 100.

32 'Le Havre', *LCC*, 1928, 21, p. 31.

33 C. Regaud, 'Doit-on augmenter le nombre des centres de thérapeutique anti-cancéreuse ?', Rapport fait à la Commission du cancer au Ministère du travail et de l'hygiène, le 4 avril 1925, reproduced in *LCC*, 1925, 10, pp. 137–44.

34 'Extraits des débats parlementaires sur le budget du cancer du 27 novembre 1928', intervention of Emile Vincent, reproduced in *LCC*, 1928, 22, pp. 94–8.

35 C. Regaud, 'Doit-on augmenter . . . ?', op. cit., p. 144.

36 Pr Marquis, 'Inauguration des nouveaux bâtiments de Rennes', *LCC*, 1937, 55, pp. 6–13.

37 'La Ligue bourguignonne', *LCC*, 1930, 27, pp. 566–7.

38 'Conseil général de la Seine: Question posée n° 222', reproduced in *LCC*, 1931, 31, p. 825.

39 M. Moine, 'Aperçu de l'action exercée en 1928 contre le cancer', *LCC*, 1930, 28, pp. 672–3.

40 'Données sur l'activité des services anticancéreux de Besançon, Dijon, Nîmes et Tarbes', *LCC*, 1930, 27, pp. 568–71 and 581–2.

41 France, during the inter-war period had very poor statistics of mortality. In 1925, the official data of mortality by cancer was 30,195 cases. This data was obviously underestimated because of the high percentage of deaths from unknown causes (36 per cent). Hence the estimation of 40,000 deaths per year put forward by the League. The number of 100,000 cancer patients in the population is, of course, of very little statistical value. Nevertheless, one must consider that the 4,800 patients treated in the anti-cancer centres represent only a small proportion of the whole population of cancer patients.

42 C. Regaud, 'Doit-on augmenter . . . ?', op. cit., pp. 137–8.

43 Ibid., pp. 139–40.

44 Ibid., pp. 143–4.

45 J.L. Faure, 'La cure chiurgicale du cancer', *LCC*, 1923, 1, p. 35.

46 Ibid., pp. 35–6.

47 C. Regaud, J. Roux-Berger, A. Lacassagne, M. Cesbron, M. Coutard and G. Richard, 'Sur la technique de la curiethérapie dans le cancer du col de l'utérus', *Bulletin de l'AFEC*, 1920, IX, pp. 224–57.

48 Ibid., p. 226.

49 Ibid., pp. 255–7.

50 P. Delbet, 'A propos de la curiethérapie', *Bulletin de l'AFEC*, 1920, IX, p. 422.

51 P. Delbet, 'A propos de la curiethérapie', op. cit., p. 422.

52 J.L. Faure, op. cit., pp. 40–1.

53 J.L. Faure, op. cit., p. 41.

54 C. Regaud, 'Les idées directrices de la lutte contre le cancer', op. cit., pp. 95–6.

55 J.L. Faure, op. cit., p. 42.
56 C. Regaud, 'Les idées directrices de la lutte contre le cancer', op. cit., p. 98.
57 Ibid., p. 98.
58 Degrais,' A propos des communications sur la curiethérapie faites par M. Regaud à l'Association française pour l'étude du cancer', *Bulletin de l'AFEC*, 1920, IX, p. 416.
59 Ibid., pp. 417 and 419.
60 A. Mignon, 'Le service de santé aux armées . . .', op. cit.
61 About the rise of the cost of the technical material in the *Assistance Publique* of Paris, see 'Hôpitaux de l'A.P. – Les dépenses de radiologie', extrait du compte rendu moral et administratif de l'exercice 1924, reproduced in *LCC*, 1926, pp. 13, 73–4.
62 *Rapport soumis par la sous-commission chargée de l'étude de la radiothérapie du cancer –* Chapter IV, La Fondation Curie, Société des nations, op. cit., pp. 53–5.
63 Ibid.
64 C. Regaud, 'Doit-on augmenter . . . ?', op. cit., pp. 141–2.
65 On 30 January 1925, a day before Regaud had to submit his report to the parliament, a leader of the surgical lobby (and a surgeon himself), Senator Daraignez, was advocate of a project of law related to the jurudical status of the anti-cancer centres, for the 'High Assembly'. He suggested that the 'Sénat' should adopt a recommendation stipulating that the physician in charge of the consultation of the patients should always be the surgeon of the centre. The idea was, of course, to assure surgeons a key position in the centre. The 'Sénat' accepted the proposal but it was rejected later by Justin Godart who argued that it was impossible to give such a monopoly to the surgeons. On that controversy, see 'La personnalité civile aux centres anticancéreux', *LCC*, 1925, 7, p. 211.
66 The province are represented in the Commission by medical professors of Lille (2), Toulouse (2), Lyon (3), Bordeaux (1), Strasbourg (3), Nancy and Alger, and by several people's representatives from the 'départements'. See 'Commission du cancer', op. cit.

7 The rise of 'big medicine'

1 'Commission d'examen des demandes de subvention des centres régionaux de lutte contre le cancer', *Journal officiel du 23 mai 1931*, 5690.
2 'CAC Bordeaux', *LCC*, 1924, 4, pp. 360–5.
3 'CAC Bordeaux', *LCC*, 1924, 7, pp. 217–18.
4 'CAC Lyon', *LCC*, 1923, 1, pp. 51–2; 'CAC Lyon', *LCC*, 1924, 4, p. 369; 'CAC Toulouse', *LCC*, 1924, 4, pp. 376–7; 'CAC Toulouse', *LCC*, 1924, 5, pp. 29–30; 'CAC Toulouse', *LCC*, 1924, 7, pp. 220–1.
5 'CAC Nancy', *LCC*, 1925, 8, pp. 323–7; *LCC*, 1926, 11, pp. 251–3.
6 R. Lainé, *Le centre régional de lutte contre le cancer de Nantes 1924–1925*, Thèse de médecine, Paris, 1929, p. 92.
7 A. Gunsett, 'La lutte sociale contre le cancer', *La vie sociale*, 1924; 'CAC Strasbourg', *LCC*, 1931, 31, 860–4.
8 'Calvados', *LCC*, 1924, 5, p. 24.
9 'CAC Caen', *LCC*, 1930, 30, pp. 817–18.
10 'Loire-Inférieure', *LCC*, 1929, 24, pp. 290–3. 'Seine-Inférieure', *LCC*, 1931, 34, pp. 60–2.
11 'CAC Reims', *LCC*, 1926, 11, p. 253. 'CAC Reims', *LCC*, 1930, 27, pp. 575–8.
12 'CAC Angers', *LCC*, 1925, 10, pp. 162–4.
13 'Ardennes', *LCC*, 1930, 30, pp. 815–16.
14 'Blois', *LCC*, 1927, 15, pp. 222–3; 'Loir-et-Cher', *LCC*, 1929, 24, pp. 287–90.

15 'Nice', *LCC*, 1925, 9, pp. 58–9. 'CAC Rennes', *LCC*, 1924, 6, pp. 95–8; 'CAC Montpellier', *LCC*, 1925, 9, pp. 56–7.

16 'Règlement de la Fondation Curie', *LCC*, 1926, 13, p. 39.

17 'Centre anticancéreux de la région parisienne', *LCC*, 1925, 9, pp. 42–51.

18 Ibid., p. 47.

19 Ibid., p. 51.

20 *Rapport soumis par la sous-commission chargée de l'étude de la radiothérapie des cancers*, SDN, op. cit.

21 G. Guillain, 'Pierre Marie 1853–1940', *Bulletin de l'académie de médecine*, 1940, pp. 524–35.

22 'Proposition de création d'un Institut pour l'étude et le traitement du cancer', *LCC*, 1925, 9, pp. 51–3.

23 'Séparation du centre anticancéreux de la banlieue parisienne d'avec l'hospice Paul Brousse à Villejuif', *LCC*, 1926, 13, pp. 50–1.

24 'L'Institut du cancer', *LCC*, 1926, 13, pp. 39, 41.

25 'L'Institut du cancer', *LCC*, 1926, 15, pp. 216–20.

26 'Conseil général de la Seine, Séance du 27–12–1930', *LCC*, 1931, 31, pp. 877–90.

27 'Inauguration de L'Institut du cancer', *LCC*, 1930, 28, p. 620.

28 Ibid., p. 621.

29 H. Dubief, *Le déclin de la IIIᵉ République*, Paris, Le Seuil, 1976, pp. 17–18.

30 'Loi sur le perfectionnement de l'outillage national', *Journal officiel* du 29–12–1931, pp. 13251–7.

31 'Chambre des députés. Extraits des débats parlementaires', *LCC*, 1931, 31, pp. 889–94.

32 'Chambre des députés, Deuxième séance du 3 décembre 1931', *LCC*, 1932, 35, p. 33.

33 'Loi sur le perfectionnement . . .', op. cit., p. 13256.

34 'Conseil général de la Seine, Séance du 27–12–1930', op. cit.

35 'CAC Caen', *LCC*, 1932, 38, p. 245.

36 C. Oberling, 'Inauguration de l'Institut du cancer à Villejuif', *Paris médical*, 1934, p. 94, annexe 82–84.

37 'Un tube de rayons X géant', *LCC*, 1931, 32, pp. 1013–14.

38 'L'Institut du cancer', *LCC*, 1937, 57, p. 186.

39 'Conseil général de la Seine', *LCC*, 1933, 41, pp. 451–6.

40 'Un don de M. Elie Lazard', *LCC*, 1932, 35, p. 33.

41 'Conseil municipal, Séance du 9 avril 1938', *LCC*, 1938, 60, pp. 114–19.

42 'Inauguration du centre anticancéreux de Lyon', *LCC*, 1935, p. 48.

43 'CAC Lille', *LCC*, 1931, 34, p. 98.

44 'Un don anonyme', *LCC*, 1934, 46, p. 241.

45 'CAC Strasbourg', *LCC*, 1936, 54, pp. 263–74.

46 Ibid., p. 271.

47 The value of the french franc decreased from 65.5 mg of gold in 1925 to 27.5 mg in 1938. See H. Dubief, op. cit. p. 212.

48 Prof. Hoche, 'Le CAC de Lorraine', *LCC*, 1936, 54, pp. 338–9.

49 For a preliminary outline of international comparison of cancer policies during the inter-wars period, see P. Pinell 'Cancer in the first half of the XXth century', in P.J. Bowler and J. Pickstone (eds), *The Cambridge History of Science*, vol. 6: *Life and Earth Sciences Since 1800*, Cambridge University Press, 2000; For an analysis of cancer policy in the UK, see D. Cantor, 'The MRC's support for experimental radiology during the inter-war years', in S. Austoker and L. Bryder (eds), *Historical Perspectives of the Role of the MRC*, Oxford University Press, 1989, pp. 181–204.

50 P. Guillaume, Du désespoir au salut . . ., op. cit., pp. 219–39.

51 'CAC Toulouse', *LCC*, 1930, 27, p. 572.

52 M. Steffen, *Régulation politique et stratégies professionnelles; médecine libérale et émergence des centre de santé*, Thèse d'Etat de Sciences politiques, Grenoble, March 1983.

53 E. Lenglet, 'Thérapeutique, mais science d'abord', *Le Médecin syndicaliste*, 1925, pp. 178–82.

54 'Syndicats médicaux – Caisses d'assurances et organisation de soins', *Le Médecin syndicaliste*, 1926, p. 161.

55 'CAC Toulouse', op. cit., pp. 572–3.

56 'La Fondation Foch', *LCC*, 1930, 30, p. 810.

57 R. Le Bret, 'Rapport devant l'Assemblée générale du 28 avril 1931', *LCC*, 1931, 32, p. 994.

58 Ibid., p. 995.

59 R. Le Bret, 'Rapport devant l'Assemblée générale du 16 mai 1930', *LCC*, 1930, 28, p. 638.

60 'Les personnes fortunées soignées dans les hôpitaux de l'Assistance publique', *LCC*, 1934, 14, pp. 122–4.

61 Ibid.

62 Ibid., p. 123.

63 'Admission des malades dans les hôpitaux et dispensaires. Projet de loi déposé par M. Raoul Brandon du 28 juillet 1936', reproduit in *LCC*, 1937, 56, pp. 128–30.

64 R. Le Bret, 'Rapport devant l'Assemblée générale du 26 mai 1936', *LCC*, 1936, 53, p. 191.

65 Ibid., p. 192.

66 Ibid., p. 192.

67 These fantasies concerning the nationalisation of medicine were so present, at that time, that Hazemann, chief secretary to the minister of health, Henry Sellier, invited by the League at its annual meeting, in May 1937, felt it necessary to insist, in his speech, on the attachment of the popular front's government to the exercise of private medicine, claiming: 'if you knew how busy the minister was dealing with the work going on in his ministry, it will be obvious to you that he has no time to keep himself busy with things that work pretty well on their own'. To conclude: ' We don't want to nationalise, nor to organise on the lines of the civil service the anticancerous fight. We trust in the private practitioners and we trust in the Ligue contre le cancer. You started twenty years ago, you are moving in the right direction, and I thank you in the name of the minister [applause]'. 'Assemblée générale du mai 1937', *LCC*, 1937, 56, p. 117.

68 Ibid., p. 113.

69 Concerning the hostility of the french medical trade unions to social insurances, see H. Hatzfeld, *Du paupérisme à la Sécurité Sociale, 1850–1950*, Paris, Armand Colin, 1971.

70 Since the beginning, the League kept up close relations with some insurance companies, first, through the participation of R. Le Bret to the administrative council of the Phénix-Vie (which is, with two other companies, a member of the League). Then, in 1938, M. Armand Pottier, honorary director of the company 'Union', became the treasurer of the League.

71 'Autour du problème du cancer', *LCC*, 1938, p. 242.

73 R. Le Bret, 'Assemblée générale du 4 mai 1937', op. cit., p. 103.

8 Between science and charity: the question of incurables

1 Mme Hartmann, 'Un voyage en Amérique latine', *LCC*, 1928, 22, p. 80.

2 See M.V. Cornil, 'Sur les greffes et inoculations de cancer', *Bulletin de l'académie de médecine*, 1891, p. 906.

3 M.V. Cornil, ibid., p. 907.

4 Ibid., p. 907.

5 Ibid., p. 908.

6 Ibid., p. 906.

7 The correspondant of the *British Medical Journal* present in Berlin for the Congress of the German medical association made this comment: 'The question whether a surgeon is justified in inoculating a patient with minute particles of cancer is being as much discussed in medical circles in Berlin as it is in Paris', *British Medical Journal*, 1891, July 25, p. 214.

8 Report of Mme Hartmann, *Assemblée générale du 4 avril 1922*, op. cit.

9 Mme Hartmann, 'Le Comité d'assistance de la Ligue franco-anglo-américaine contre le cancer', *LCC*, 1924, 3, p. 201.

10 Report of Mme Hartmann, *Assemblée générale du 4 avril 1922*, op. cit., p. 23.

11 Report of Mme Guernez, 'Assemblée générale du 17 juin', *LCC*, 1941, 69–70, p. 129.

12 F. Thébaud, op. cit.

13 Report of R. Le Bret, *Assemblée générale du 4 avril 1922*, op. cit., p. 7.

14 'Extrait de la correspondance', *LCC*, 1924, 4, p. 345.

15 'Extrait de la correspondance', *LCC*, 1924, 3, p. 205.

16 Report of Mme Hartmann, *Assemblée générale du 4 avril 1922*, op. cit., p. 24.

17 Mme Hartmann, 'Un voyage en Amérique latine', op. cit., p. 84.

18 Mme Hartmann, 'Le Comité d'Assistance . . .', op. cit., p. 197.

19 Report of Mme Hartmann, *Assemblée générale du 4 avril 1922*, op. cit., p. 27.

20 Report of R. Le Bret, *Assemblée générale du 4 avril 1922*, op. cit., p. 12.

21 Ibid., 13.

22 Report of R. Le Bret, 'Assemblée générale du 16 mai 1939', op. cit., p. 115.

23 'Extrait de la correspondance', *LCC*, 1924, 4, p. 345.

24 R. Le Bret, 'Hommage au Dr Récamier', *LCC*, 1931, 34, p. 70.

25 Report of R. Le Bret, *Assemblée générale du 4 avril 1922*, op. cit., p. 13.

26 'Administration générale de l'Assistance publique, Extrait du compte moral et administratif de l'exercice 1923', *LCC*, 1925, 9, p. 30.

27 R. Le Bret, 'L'aide médico-sociale aux incurables', Rapport présenté au Congrès international de lutte scientifique et sociale contre le cancer', Bruxelles, September 1936, reproduced in *LCC*, 1937, 55, pp. 20–30.

28 R. Le Bret, 'Hommage au Dr Récamier', op. cit.

29 'Chronique', *LCC*, 1924, 3, p. 228.

30 'Chronique', *LCC*, 1924, 5, p. 20.

31 Report of Mme Le Bret, 'Séance du Comité des Dames', *LCC*, 1926, 12, p. 360.

32 Report of R. Le Bret, 'Assemblée générale du 8 mai 1923', op. cit., p. 19.

33 Report of Mme Le Bret, 'Séance du Comité des Dames', *LCC*, 1925, 7, p. 151.

34 Report of R. Le Bret, Assemblée générale du 4 avril 1922, op. cit., p. 12.

35 R. Le Bret, 'L'aide médico-sociale aux incurables', op. cit.

36 Prof. Marie, 'Note sur l'organisation et le fonctionnement du centre régional de Toulouse pour la lutte contre le cancer', *LCC*, 1925, 7, pp. 168–73.

37 It is more particularly the case of the centre of Strasbourg, with 622 treated patients for a total of 2,071 consulting patients, and of the centre of Nancy with 333 treated patients for 1,055 consulting patients.

38 'Lettre adressée par le Dr Baud, directeur du CAC de Reims, à tous les médecins des départements de l'Aisne, des Ardennes et de la Marne', reproduced in *LCC*, 1925, 10, pp. 169–70.

39 M. Renaud, 'Que peut la médecine pour les cancéreux dits incurables ?', *LCC*, 1930, 30, p. 783.

40 Ibid., p. 784.

41 T. Marie, 'Sur la nécessité de la création d'établissements hospitaliers pour les cancéreux dits incurables', *LCC*, 1932, 36, p. 86.
42 R. Le Bret, 'L'aide médico-sociale aux incurables', op. cit., p. 26.
43 Report of R. Le Bret, 'Assemblée générale du 4 mai 1937', op. cit., pp. 105–6.
44 *Rapport soumis par la sous-commission chargée de l'étude de la radiothérapie des cancers*, SDN, op. cit., p. 59.
45 Ibid., see more particularly the chapter 2 'Règles adoptées par la sous-commission dans le but d'établir des statistiques complètes et comparables'.
46 C. Regaud, 'Comment on peut concevoir actuellement l'organisation de la lutte contre le cancer' (2nd edn), *LCC*, 1929, 24, pp. 225–42.

9 Publicity, education, supervision

1 C. Regaud, 'Les idées directrices de la lutte contre le cancer', op. cit., p. 93.
2 C. Regaud, 'Le rôle du médecin sans spécialité dans le diagnostic du cancer', *LCC*, 1925, 10, p. 112.
3 H. Hartmann, 'Le péril cancéreux', *Paris médical*, 1923, 48, p. 149.
4 C. Regaud, 'Comment on peut concevoir actuellement l'organisation de la lutte contre le cancer', *LCC*, 1927, 24, p. 229.
5 H. Hartmann, op. cit.
6 'Publication de la Ligue franco-anglo-américaine', *LCC*, 1926, 11, p. 284.
7 Report of R. Le Bret, 'Assemblée générale du 7 avril 1927', *LCC*, 1927, 16, p. 220.
8 Report of R. Le Bret, 'Assemblée générale du 28 avril 1925', *LCC*, 1925, 8, p. 274.
9 Mme Hartmann, 'Un voyage en Amérique latine', op. cit., p. 81.
10 Report of R. Le Bret, 'Assemblée générale du 4 mai 1937', op. cit., p. 96.
11 See C. Herzlich and J. Pierret, *Malades d'hier, malades d'aujourd'hui,* Paris, Payot, 1984, pp. 88–97, and P. Pinell, 'How do cancer patients express their point of view ?', op. cit.
12 Report of R. Le Bret, 'Assemblée générale du 28 avril 1925', op. cit., p. 274.
13 See N. Elias, *The Civilizing Process*, op. cit.
14 M. Moine, 'Les principales causes de décès en France', *LCC*, 1939, 65–6, pp. 215–20.
15 'Institut National d'Hygiène. Importance du cancer en France', *LCC*, 1946, 75, pp. 5–8.
16 See in particular the report of Prof. Gunsett, 'CAC de Strasbourg', *LCC*, 1931, p. 31, 863; the report of Prof. Papin, 'CAC d'Angers', *LCC*, 1935, 50, p. 295; the report of Prof. Hoche, 'CAC de Nancy', *LCC*, 1938, 61, p. 200.
17 R. Le Bret, 'L'aide médico-sociale aux incurables', op. cit.
18 See the report of Prof. Moulonguet and Prof. Taillefer published in *LCC*, 1947, 82, pp. 180–5.
19 Report of R. Le Bret, 'Assemblée générale du 8 avril 1924', op. cit., p. 324.
20 'Chronique', *LCC*, 1924, 5, p. 18.
21 Op. cit., pp. 19–20.
22 Report of R. Le Bret, 'Assemblée générale du 8 mai 1923', op. cit., p. 17.
23 Vote taken by the national Council of French Women, quoted by Mme Hartmann, in 'Assemblée générale du 8 avril 1924', op. cit., pp. 335–6.
24 Report of Mme Le Bret, 'Séance du Comité des Dames', *LCC*, 1926, 12, 361.
25 'Chronique', *LCC*, 1923, 7, p. 64; 'Chronique', *LCC*, 1924, 5, p. 20.
26 'Chronique', *LCC*, 1929, 24, p. 277.
27 'Chronique', *LCC*, 1923, 1, p. 64.
28 'Chronique', *LCC*, 1925, 9, p. 24.

29 'Chronique', *LCC*, 1929, 24, p. 276.
30 'Cours sur le cancer', *LCC*, 1928, 21, p. 59.
31 Report of R. Le Bret, Assemblée générale du 4 avril 1922, op. cit.
32 Report of R. Le Bret, 'Assemblée générale du 27 avril 1926', *LCC*, 1926, 12, p. 346.
33 Report of R. Le Bret, 'Assemblée générale du 5 avril 1927', op. cit., p. 293.
34 'Compte rendu de la Semaine du cancer', *LCC*, 1930, 32.
35 'Causerie radiophonique de M. Lucien Viborel', *LCC*, 1930, 29, p. 701.
36 'Causerie radiophonique de M. Justin Godart', *LCC*, 1930, 29, p. 705.
37 Ibid., p. 704.
38 'Causerie radiophonique de M. Robert Le Bret', *LCC*, 1930, 29, p. 716.
39 L. Viborel, op. cit., p. 701.
40 P. Jacques, 'Causerie à propos du cancer de la gorge, cancéreux et cancrophobes', *LCC*, 1932, 36, p. 203.
41 Ibid.
42 'La Semaine du cancer du 23 au 30 juin 1931', *LCC*, 1931, 33, pp. 6–13.
43 'La Semaine du cancer du 21 au 27 juin 1937', *LCC*, 1937, 57, pp. 217–19.
44 P. Jacques, op. cit., p. 201.
45 J.L. Faure, 'La lutte contre le cancer utérin', talk given on Radio Paris, reproduced in *LCC*, 1931, 33, p. 21.
46 E. Forgue, 'Le cancer du sein peut être guéri s'il est traité à son début', talk given on Radio Paris, reproduced in *LCC*, 1931, 33, p. 16.
47 B. Ketcham-Wheaton, *L'office et la bouche*, Paris, Calmann-Lévy, 1984.
48 E. Forgue, op. cit., p. 16.
49 'It is obviously painful for a patient to present herself, more or less soiled with blood, but her interest commands her to do so'; Prof. Rechou, 'Pour endiguer le fléau', *LCC*, 1934, 45, p. 219.
50 Report of R. Le Bret, 'Assemblée générale du 17 mai 1938', op. cit., p. 95.
51 Report of R. Le Bret, 'Assemblée générale du 26 avril 1932', *LCC*, 1932, 36, p. 94.
52 C. Regaud, 'Le rôle du médecin sans spécialité dans le diagnostic du cancer', op. cit., p. 113.
53 'Contre les charlatans', *LCC*, 1924, 6, pp. 78–9.
54 R. Le Bret, 'Méfiez-vous des guérisseurs, des remèdes illusoires, des annonces fallacieuses'. I, *LCC*, 1930, 30, p. 802.
55 'Contre les charlatans', op. cit., pp. 78–9.
56 R. Le Bret, 'Méfiez-vous des guérisseurs . . .', op. cit., p. 802.
57 'Unfortunately, the director of a newspaper cannot control the advertisements that have paid for a place. He doesn't have the time to do it and, moreover, he is not qualified to do it', ibid., p. 804.
58 Ibid., p. 804.
59 Report of R. Le Bret, 'Assemblée générale du 9 mai 1933', *LCC*, 1933, 40, p. 364.
60 'L'Ordre des médecins', *LCC*, 1939, 65–66, p. 227.
61 R. Le Bret , 'Méfiez-vous des guérisseurs . . .'. II, *LCC*, 1931, 31, pp. 865–7.
62 'Autour du problème du cancer', *LCC*, 1934, 44, p. 119.
63 Report of R. Le Bret, 'Assemblée générale du 9 mai 1933', op. cit., p. 364.
64 'L'Ordre des médecins', op. cit., p. 228.
65 Report of R. Le Bret, 'Assemblée générale du 9 mai 1933', op. cit., p. 365.
66 See for example L. Bérard, 'A propos des traitements du cancer. Techniques modernes et guérisseurs', conference at the T.S.F., 2 February 1932, reproduced in *LCC*, 1932, 35, pp. 6–17.
67 Circular quoted in *LCC*, 1933, 40, p. 365.
68 Report of R. Le Bret, 'Assemblée générale du 4 mai 1937', op. cit., p. 106.

69 Concerning the long story of the idea of controlling medical practice in France, see J. Léonard, *La médecine entre les pouvoirs et les savoirs,* Paris, Aubier Montaigne, 1981, particularly pp. 13–17.

70 *Proposition de loi relative à la création d'un Ordre des médecins,* Documentation parlementaire, 1928, annexe 819 (deuxième séance du 28 novembre 1928).

71 We can find amongst them the 'Académie de médecine', the trade union of the hospitals' physicians, the medical trade union of the 'département de la Seine'.

72 Quoted in 'Autour du problème du cancer', op. cit., p. 124.

73 Ibid., p. 124.

74 France was then the third European country, after Portugal and Belgium to adopt the structure of an order for the regulation of the practices of the medical profession.

75 C. Regaud, 'Quelques préceptes généraux déduits de l'état actuel de la thérapeutique', *Paris médical,* 1923, 48, pp. 149–52.

76 C. Regaud, 'Memorandum pour la sous-commission de radiothérapie à la Commission du cancer', in SDN, op. cit., p. 79.

77 Ibid., p. 80.

78 'If I was in charge of organising the fight against cancer in a new country, I would institute first a centre both for scientific research and for therapeutical practices . . . I would like the heads of the wards and their assistants to be full time, that is to say, paid enough to devote themselves completely to the common task.' C. Regaud, 'Comment peut-on concevoir actuellement l'organisation de la lutte contre le cancer ?', op. cit., pp. 236–7.

79 C. Regaud, 'Memorandum pour la sous-commission. . .', op. cit., p. 81.

80 Ibid., p. 81.

81 Still included in the structure for training radiologists, the part devoted to the teaching of radiotherapy increased significantly in Paris, between 1914 (a seventh of the programme) and 1924 (a third of the programme). Most of the teaching was done by members of the radium institute (C. Regaud gave ten lessons and Marie Curie, two). 'Enseignement de la radiologie, programme pour l'année 1924–1925', reproduit in *LCC,* 1924, 6, pp. 136–8.

82 The evolution of the question of cancer in France shows us that the process of medicalisation is not simply related to an increase of medical power. On the one hand, the progress in cancer treatment induced a growing medicalisation of cancer patients. On the other hand, the hospital specialists in oncology, in the name of their scientific and technical efficiencies, tried to impose their legitimacy on general practitioners and to submit them to their authority. They claimed a rational division of medical labour, involving a strict limitation of the GPs practices to diagnostic, referral and follow-up activities. As we have seen, during the inter-wars period, it was hard for cancer specialists to persuade GPs to renounce their prerogatives in treatment matters, a renouncement they saw as a loss of social power. Several decades later, different investigations have shown dramatic changes. GPs seem now to have completely accepted the limitation of their technical abilities in diseases like cancer. Such a change must be related to the more general changes that occurred in medical studies with the development of specialities and their symbolic domination over general medicine. The growing hierarchisation of the medical profession has created the social conditions for the GPs (who are mostly doctors who have failed to win a position as a specialist) to accept, during the time of their training, the limitations of their skills. See P. Aïach, *Cancer et médecine, rapport de recherche INSERM,* 1984; M. Arliaud, *Le corps étranger,* LEST, 1984; F. Muel, 'Le fantôme du médecin de famille', *Actes de la recherche en sciences sociales,* 54, 1984, pp. 70–1.

10 A modern illness

1 See F. Mesle and J. Vallin, 'Reconstitution des tables annuelles de la mortalité pour la France au XIXe siècle', *Population*, 1989, 6, pp. 1121–57.

2 About social concerns in demography matters, in France before the First World War, see M. Rebérioux, *La République radicale, 1898–1914*, Paris, Le Seuil, 1975, pp. 204–8. The question of depopulation and ageing in France became even more important during the inter-war years, fed by alarmist papers concerning demographics. Indeed, it was true that between 1900 and 1939, the French population only grew by 3 per cent, whereas the population of the other European countries and of the USA was growing strongly (UK 23%, Italy 33%, Germany 36%, United States 72%). See *Histoire économique et sociale de la France*, vol. 2., *1914–années 1950*, Paris, PUF, 1980, pp. 607–23.

3 Prof. Hartmann, 'Le péril cancéreux', op. cit.

4 Ibid.

5 Ibid.

6 It is only at the beginning of the 1960s that data on mortality through cancer disappeared from the posters of the League.

7 'How far are we, with cancer, of the romantism . . . where people were softly dying, reciting verses . . . Everything is tragic with cancer; the problems it sets are those of despair. Does a man, in the presence of a calvary he dare not face, have the right to commit suicide? Does a son have the right to kill his mother in order to shorten her suffering? Can a wife kill her husband who asks for death for pity's sake?, 'Assemblée générale du 6 mai 1930', op. cit.

8 *Assemblée générale du 4 avril 1922*, op. cit., p. 14.

9 'The cancer enigma is linked to the problem of ageing, of the evolution of the cellular life. . . . Why does the harmony that presides over our life, disappear? We cannot explain what makes the child lithe, the conflict between the litheness and the growing strength of the adult, then the decline of the litheness and of the strength, finally the slower life of a man of age'. Assemblée générale du 28 avril 1931', op. cit., p. 990.

10 See P. Guillaume, op. cit.

11 'Assemblée générale du 4 mai 1937', op. cit., p. 101.

12 For a general analysis of the French situation, see A. Chauvenet, *Médecine au choix, médecine de classe*, Paris, PUF, 1978.

13 N. Elias,*The Civilizing Process*, op. cit.

14 N. Elias, *The Society of Individuals*, Oxford, Blackwell, 1991.

15 See L. Boltanski, *Prime éducation et morale de classe*, op. cit.; O. Baudelot and E. Plaisance, 'L'évolution des objectifs de l'école maternelle', *Cahiers du CRESAS*, 1973, 9; J. Goudsblom, 'Les grandes épidémies et la civilisation des moeurs', *Actes de la recherche en sciences sociales*, 1987, 68, pp. 3–14.

16 J. Goudsblom, op. cit.

17 E. Goffman, *La mise en scène de la vie quotidienne*, Paris, Ed. de Minuit, 1973, vol. 2, chap. 2.

18 See I. Grellet and C. Kruse, *Histoires de la tuberculose*, Paris, Ramsay, 1983, pp. 201–11.

19 Ibid., p. 204.

20 For a development of this analysis, see P. Pinell, 'Modern medicine and the civilizing process', *Sociology of Health & Illness*, 1996, 18, 1, pp. 1–16.

21 N.D. Jewson, 'The disappearance of the sick-man from medical cosmology, 1770–1870', *Sociology*, 1976, 10(2), pp. 225–44.

22 Quoted by C. Sinding, *Le clinicien et le chercheur*, Paris, PUF, 1991.

23 See P. Pinell, 'La relation médecin-malade cancéreux: l'enjeu des manipulations symboliques', *Prévenir*, 1985, 11, pp. 9–16.

24 J. Schlanger, *Les métaphores de l'organisme*, Paris, Vrin, 1971.

25 Born during the Great War, the League is heir to the 'spirit of the sacred unity'. The references to the fight against cancer as a total war are permanent during the whole inter-war period, as shown in the three following quotations: (1) 'Money is missing. We need it. We need it again and again. We need it always in wartime. We need it for the supply, for the cantonment, for the weapons: the surgeon's knife and that prodigious radium, a gram of which costs a fortune'. Speech of H. Bordeaux, 'Assemblée générale du 6 mai 1930', op. cit., pp. 655–6. (2) 'The lessons of the war were exerting a salutary influence on the creation of the League. Facts proved that success can only be obtained by the coordinated use of all the battle weapons and that the warriors' actions should be supported by the forces of the whole country.' R. Le Bret, 'Assemblée générale du 4 mai 1939', op. cit., p. 98. (3) 'To give a good idea of the situation of the present day, I can't do better than evoke this period so painful, so distressing, so dull, where, after the immense hope given by a victory, we were powerless to pass through or to turn over the front line of the enemy'. R. Le Bret, 'Assemblée générale du 28 avril 1931', op. cit. About war metaphors in medicine, see also A.M. Brandt, *No Magic Bullet*, Oxford University Press, 1987; P.J. Weindling, 'Theories of the Cell State in Imperial Germany', in C. Webster (ed.), *Biology, Medicine and Society 1840–1940*, Cambridge, 1981.

26 J. Schlanger, op. cit., p. 185.

27 S. Sontag, *Illness as Metaphor*, New York, Farrar, Stauss and Giroux, 1978.

28 C. Quetel, *Le mal de Naples*, op. cit.

29 See L. Murard and P. Zylberman, 'La cité eugénique', *Recherches*, 1978, pp. 313–14; and I. Grellet and C. Kruse, op. cit., pp. 215–22.

30 I. Grellet and C. Kruse, op. cit., p. 227.

31 P. Pinell, 'How do cancer patients express their point of view ?', op. cit.

32 I. Löwy, 'The immunological construction of the self', in A. Tauber (ed.), *Organism and the Origins of Self*, Dordrecht, Kluwer Academic Publishers, 1991, pp. 43–75.

33 R. Le Bret, 'Assemblée générale du 20 mars 1934', op. cit., p. 102.

34 Ibid., p. 103.

35 Ibid., p. 105.

Bibliography

Primary Sources

Bulletin de l'association française pour l'étude du cancer (Bulletin de l'AFEC), volumes 1–12.

Lutte contre le cancer (la) (LCC), Bulletin of the Ligue franco-anglo-américaine contre le cancer (until 1927), then of the Ligue nationale française contre le cancer, nos 1–71.

Annuaire de l'office central des œuvres de bienfaisance, 1902–1903.

Assemblée générale du 4 avril 1922, Paris, Ligue franco-anglo-américaine contre le cancer, 1922.

Belot, J., *Traité de radiothérapie*, Paris, G. Steinheil, 1905.

Bérard, L., 'A propos des traitements du cancer. Techniques modernes et guérisseurs', *LCC*, 1932, 35, 6–17.

Bergonié, J., 'Où en sont aujourd'hui les applications à la médecine et à la chirurgie de la découverte de Roentgen ? Nouveaux faits', *Journal de médecine de Bordeaux*, 1897, 1, 14– 22.

Bergonié, J., 'Le radium au point de vue médical', *Archives d'électricité médicale*, 1904, 2, 123–32 and 1904, 3, 175–83.

Bergonié, J., 'Effets des rayons X dans le cancer du sein', *Journal de médecine de Bordeaux*, 1904, 13, 228–30.

Bergonié, J., 'La faculté future', *Journal de médecine de Bordeaux*, 1908, 49, 773–8.

Bergonié, J. (with G. Jacquetty), 'Le travail agricole médicalement prescrit et surveillé comme traitement des séquelles de blessures de guerre', *Archives d'électricité médicale et de physiothérapie*, July 1917, 418, 297–317.

Bergonié, J., 'Comment doivent être organisés les centres régionaux de lutte contre le cancer', Rapport devant la Commission du cancer, *Paris médical*, 1923, 48, 146–9.

Bernard, C., *Introduction à l'étude de la médecine expérimentale*, Paris, Flammarion, 1984.

Bertillon, J., 'De la fréquence des principales causes de décès à Paris pendant la seconde moitié du XIXe siècle, et notamment la période 1886–1905', in *Annuaire statistique de la ville de Paris*, Paris, Masson, 1906, pp. 113–346.

Borrel, A., 'Le problème étiologique du cancer', *Bulletin de l'AFEC*, 1908, I, 15–25.

Bouchacourt, L., *De l'exploration des organes internes à l'aide de la lumière éclairante et non éclairante. Endoscopie par les rayons de Roentgen*, Thèse, Paris, 1898.

Bridé, J. and Conseil E., 'Sarcome à cystercerques chez le rat', *Bulletin de l'AFEC*, 1909, II, 171–3 and 1910, III, 318–20.

Cancer (Le), Paris, Masson, 1944.

Chavannaz, Prof. 'A propos du cancer de l'utérus', *LCC*, 1934, 45, 219–20.

Chevassu, M., 'Des relations des traumatismes du testicule avec les néoplasmes de cet organe', *Bulletin de l'AFEC*, 1918, VII, 568–71.

Clunet, J., 'Le cancer au Maroc', *Bulletin de l'AFEC*, 1912, V, 167.

Contamin, 'Rayons X et cancer expérimental de la souris', *Bulletin de l'AFEC*, 1910, III, 160–4.

Cornil, M.V., 'Sur les greffes et inoculations de cancer', Séance du 23 juin 1891, *Bulletin de l'Académie de médecine*,1891, 906–9.

Degrais, P., 'A propos des communications sur la curiethérapie faites par M. Regaud à l'Association française pour l'étude du cancer', *Bulletin de l'AFEC*, 1920, IX, 415–19.

Delbet, P., 'Sur la fulguration', *Bulletin de l'AFEC*, 1910, IV, 130.

Delbet, P., 'A propos de la curiethérapie', *Bulletin de l'AFEC*, 1920, IX, 419–24.

Delbet, P. and Brault, A., 'Relations des traumatismes avec les sarcomes', *Bulletin de l'AFEC*, 1918,VII, 573–81.

Desfosses, P. and Vitoux, G., *L'enseignement médical à Paris. Renseignements pratiques à l'usage des médecins, 1912–1913*, Paris, Masson, 1913.

Desfosses and Vitoux, *L'enseignement médical à Paris. Renseignements pratiques à l'usage des médecins, 1913–1914*, Paris, Masson, 1914.

Dominici, H., 'Du traitement des tumeurs malignes par le rayonnement ultra-pénétrant du radium', *Bulletin de l'AFEC*, 1908, I, 124–55.

'Eighteenth Congress of the German Medical Association', *British Medical Journal*, 1891, July 25, 214.

Faure, J.L., 'Sur la fulguration', *Bulletin de l'AFEC*, 1909, II, 73–5.

Faure, J.L., 'Traumatismes et cancer du sein', *Bulletin de l'AFEC*, 1918,VII, 571–2.

Faure, J.L., 'La cure chiurgicale du cancer', *LCC*, 1923, 1, 35–46.

Faure, J.L., 'La lutte contre le cancer utérin', *LCC*, 1931, 33., 20–3.

Forgue, E., 'Le cancer et la guerre', *Bulletin de l'AFEC*, 1918, VII, 585–93.

Forgue, E., 'Le cancer du sein peut être guéri s'il est traité à son début', *LCC*, 1931, 33, 14–17.

Forgue, E., 'Gesta cancerologiae per Francos', *LCC*, 1936, 53, 160–85.

Furetière, A., *Dictionnaire universel*, Paris, Le Robert, 1978.

Geoffroy, E.L., *Manuel de médecine pratique*, 1800.

Godart, J., 'La réhabilitation de l'incurable', *LCC*, 1946, 77, 126–36.

Gunsett, A., 'La lutte sociale contre le cancer', *La vie sociale*, 1924.

Gunsett, A., 'Le CAC Strasbourg', *LCC*, 1931, 31, 861–4.

Hartmann, H., 'Le péril cancéreux', *Paris médical*, 1923, 48, 141–5.

Mme Hartmann, 'Un voyage en Amérique latine', *LCC*, 1928, 22, 70–86.

Mme Hartmann, 'Le Comité d'assistance de la ligue franco-anglo-américaine contre le cancer', *LCC*, 1924, 3, 197–206.

Hoche, Prof., 'Le CAC de Lorraine', *LCC*, 1936, 54, 338–9.

Houllevigne, M.L., 'L'industrie du radium', *LCC*, 1927, 17, 13–18.

Huguenin, R., *'L'apport de la France dans l'étude du cancer'*, in *Ce que la France a apporté à la médecine depuis le début du XXe siècle*, Paris, Flammarion, 1946, pp. 139–73.

Jacques, Prof., P., 'Causerie à propos du cancer de la gorge, cancéreux et cancrophobes', *LCC*, 1932, 36, 200–4.

Juillerat, Dr, 'Les maisons à cancer de Paris', *Bulletin de l'AFEC*, 1909, II, 61–2.

Lachapelle, A.P., 'La radiothérapie en 1905', *Journal de radiologie et d'électrologie*, 1958, 39, 5–6, 383–96.

Laîné, R., *Le centre régional de lutte contre le cancer de Nantes 1924–1925*, Thèse de médecine, Paris, 1929.

Le Bret, R., 'Hommage au Dr Récamier', *LCC*, 1931, 34, 69–71.

Le Bret, R., 'L'aide médico-sociale aux incurables', *LCC*, 1937, 55, 20–30.

Le Bret, R., 'Méfiez-vous des guérisseurs, des remèdes illusoires, des annonces fallacieuses'. I. *LCC*, 1930, 30, 789–805; and II. *LCC*, 1931, 31, 865–7.

Le Bret, R., 'Les propagandes parasites', *LCC*, 1932, 35, 18–23.

Ledoux-Lebard, R., *La lutte contre le cancer*, Thèse de Médecine, Paris, Masson, 1906.

Ledoux-Lebard, R., 'Causerie sur la radiothérapie profonde', in *Assemblée générale du 4 avril 1922*, Paris, Ligue franco-anglo-américaine contre le Cancer, 1922, 29–49.

Lenglet, E., 'Thérapeutique, mais science d'abord', *Le Médecin syndicaliste*, 1925, 178–82.

Lion, G., 'Des relations du traumatisme avec les cancers de l'estomac et de l'intestin', *Bulletin de l'AFEC*, 1918, VII, 565–8.

Loste, F., 'Hôpital', in *Dictionnaire des sciences médicales*, 1817–1821, p. 490.

Marie, P. and Clunet, J., 'Végétations atypiques de l'épiderme cutané après injections intradermiques d'huile d'olive saturée de Sarlach', *Bulletin de l'AFEC*, 1909, II, 146–8.

Marie, P., Clunet, J. and Raulot-Lapointe, G., 'Contribution à l'étude des tumeurs malignes sur les ulcères de Roentgen', *Bulletin de l'AFEC*, 1910, III, 404–10.

Marie, T., 'Note sur l'organisation et le fonctionnement du centre régional de Toulouse pour la lutte contre le cancer', *LCC*, 1925, 7, 168–73.

Marie, T., 'Sur la nécessité de la création d'établissements hospitaliers pour les cancéreux dits incurables', *LCC*, 1932, 36, 83–6.

Masson, P., 'Des rapports sur les relations des néoplasmes cutanés avec les traumatismes', *Bulletin de l'AFEC*, 1918, VII, 562–4.

Mayet, M., 'Faits expérimentaux propres à éclairer la pathogénie du cancer', *Bulletin de l'AFEC*, 1909, II, 120–40.

Ménétrier, P., 'Les états morbides précancéreux et la formation du cancer à leurs dépens', *Bulletin de l'AFEC*, 1908, I, 25–57.

Ménétrier, P., 'Des relations des traumatismes, et plus particulièrement des traumatismes de guerre, avec le développement des néoplasmes', *Bulletin de l'AFEC*, 1918, VII, 556–62.

Ménétrier, P., Legros, G. and Mallet, A., 'Hyperplasie et métaplasie épithéliales expérimentalement produites chez le rat par l'action réitérée de rayons X', *Bulletin de l'AFEC*, 1909, II, 150–60.

Mignon, A., *Le service de santé pendant la guerre de 1914–1918*, Paris, Masson, vol. IV.

Oberling, C., 'Inauguration de l'Institut du cancer à Villejuif', *Paris médical*, 1934, 94, appendices 82–4.

Pasteau, O., Degrais and Belot, J., 'Modifications cliniques et histologiques d'une tumeur de la prostate', *Bulletin de l'AFEC*, 1913, VI, 113–21.

Pasteau, O., 'Des relations des néoplasmes du rein avec les traumatismes de guerre', *Bulletin de l'AFEC*, 1918, VII, 572–3.

Petit, G., 'Cystercerque et cancer de l'épiploon chez le lapin', *Bulletin de l'AFEC*, 1909, II, 25–7.

Prévost, A., *La Faculté de médecine de Paris, 1794–1900*, Paris, Maloine, 1900.

Rapport soumis par la sous-commission chargée de l'étude de la radiothérapie des cancers, SDN, Commission du cancer, Genève, 1929.

Rechou, Prof., 'Pour endiguer le fléau', *LCC*, 1934, 45, 217–18.

Regaud, C., 'Les idées directrices de la lutte contre le cancer', *LCC*, 1923, 2, 87–100.

Regaud, C., 'Le rôle du médecin sans spécialité dans le diagnostic du cancer', *LCC*, 1925, 10, 111–21.

Regaud, C., 'Comment on peut concevoir actuellement l'organisation de la lutte contre le cancer', *LCC*, 1929, 24, 225–42.

Regaud, C., 'Doit-on augmenter le nombre des centres de thérapeutique anti-cancéreuse?', *LCC*, 1925, 10, 137–44.

Regaud, C., 'Quelques préceptes généraux déduits de l'état actuel de la thérapeutique', Paris médical, 1923, 48, 149–52.

Regaud, C. and Nogier, T., 'Action des rayons X très pénétrants, filtrés, sur le derme et l'épiderme de la peau', *Association française pour l'avancement des sciences*, 41° session, Nîmes, 1912.

Regaud, C., Roux-Berger J. *et al.*, 'Sur la technique de la curiethérapie dans le cancer du col de l'utérus', *Bulletin de l'AFEC*, 1920, IX, 224–57.

Renaud, M., 'Que peut la médecine pour les cancéreux dits incurables ?', *LCC*, 1930, 30, 782–8.

Rocquain, F., 'L'Œuvre des dames du Calvaire', *LCC*, 1924, 3, 207–13.

Roussy, G., Leroux R. and Peyre, E., 'Le cancer expérimental du goudron chez la souris. Premiers résultats', *Bulletin de l'AFEC*, 1922, XI, 8–15.

Roussy, G., Laborde, S., Leroux, R. and Peyre, E., 'Réactions locales et générales de l'organisme au cours du traitement des cancers du col utérin par les rayons X et γ', *Bulletin de l'AFEC*, 1922, XI, 431–44.

Roussy, G., Laborde, S. and Leroux, R., 'A propos de la durée d'irradiation dans la curiethérapie des cancers malpighiens', *Bulletin de l'AFEC*, 1923, XII, 467–75.

Sabrazes, Prof. J., 'Peut-on éviter le cancer et prévenir son incurabilité ?', *LCC*, 1934, 45.

Schwartz, A., 'Intervention à propos de la lutte sociale contre le cancer', *Bulletin de l'AFEC*, 1919, VIII, 46–7.

'Syndicats médicaux, caisses d'assurances et organisation de soins', *Le Médecin syndicaliste*, 1926, 159–62.

Trolard, 'Le cancer à Saffi (Maroc)', *Bulletin de l'AFEC*, 1912, V, 168.

Tuffier, T., 'Recherches expérimentales et cliniques sur la fulguration', *Bulletin de l'AFEC*, 1909, II, 94–5.

Viborel, L., Causerie radiophonique: 'Il faut démasquer le cancer', *LCC*, 1930, 29, 700–8.

Walther, C., 'Des rapports sur les cancers de la cavité pharyngienne développés sur les cicatrices de blessures de guerre', *Bulletin de l'AFEC*, 1918, VII, 565.

Zimmern, A., 'A propos de la fulguration', *Bulletin de l'AFEC*, 1909, II, 87–91.

Biographies

Antonin, A., 'Charles Bouchard (1837–1915)', *Bulletin de l'Académie de médecine*, 1950, 732–9.

Baudouin, A.M., 'Hommage à Antoine Béclère', *Bulletin de l'Académie de médecine*, 1939, 121, 351–6.

Bengolea, A.J., 'Madame Garnier', *LCC*, 1936, 54, 249–59.

Chanoine Chaffanjon, *Les veuves et la charité. Vie de Madame Garnier*, Paris, Vitte, 1922 (5th edition).

Cuneo, B., 'Notice nécrologique sur M. Edouard Quenu', *Bulletin de l'Académie de médecine*, 1933, 131–44.

Delarue, Prof. J., 'Allocution prononcée pour le dixième anniversaire de la mort de Gustave Roussy', *LCC*, 1958, 129, 9–13.

Douérin, P., *Essai biographique sur Monsieur le Professeur Bergonié*, Thèse en médecine, Bordeaux, 1978.

Guillain, G., 'Pierre Marie 1853–1940', *Bulletin de l'Académie de médecine*, 1940, 524–35.

Hartmann, H., 'Bernard Cuneo', *Bulletin de l'Académie de médecine*, 1945, 53–5.

Hartmann, H., 'Emile Forgue (1860–1942)', Séance du 9 mars 1943, *Bulletin de l'Académie de médecine*, 1943, 138–41.

Hommage à Justin Godart à l'occasion de son élection à l'Académie de médecine, Paris, Quillet, 1939.

Jeanneney, J.N., *François de Wendel en République, l'argent et le pouvoir*, Paris, Le Seuil, 1976.

Lacassagne, A., 'L'œuvre de Regaud cancérologiste', *LCC*, 1941, 69-70, 95–112.

Leclainche, X., 'Justin Godart', Séance du 12 décembre 1972, *l'Académie de médecine*, 1972.

Legueu, F., 'Félix Guyon', *Bulletin de L'Académie de médecine*, 1931, 39, 561–88.

Lépine, P., 'August Lumière', Séance du 22 juin 1954, *Bulletin de l'Académie de médecine*.

Lhermitte, J., 'Gustave Roussy', Séance du 21 juin 1948, *Bulletin de l'Académie de médecine*, 1948, 450–9.

Mathieu, P., 'Eloge d'Edouard Quenu', *Bulletin de l'Académie de médecine*, 1953, 651–6.

Meyniel, G., 'Tribondeau collaborateur de Bergonié', *Journal de radiologie et d'électrologie*, 1958, 403–5.

Mocquot, C., 'Pierre Delbet', *Bulletin de l'Académie de médecine*, 1957, 630–8.

Mocquot, C., 'Jean-Louis Faure', *Bulletin de l'Académie de médecine*, 1945, 67–71.

Monod, O., 'Notice nécrologique sur le Professeur Hartmann', *Bulletin de l'Académie de médecine*, 1952, 11, 14–17.

'Nécrologie du Dr Sonia Fabre', *LCC*, 1948, 86, 27.

Reclus, P., 'Eloge de Paul Berger', *Bulletin de l'Académie de médecine*, 1913, 568–84.

Regaud, J., *Claudius Regaud*, Paris, Maloine, 1982.

Reid, R., *Marie Curie derrière la légende*, Paris, Le Seuil, 1979.

Rouvillois, M.H., 'Discours prononcé aux obsèques du Dr Tuffier', *Bulletin de l'Académie de médecine*, 1929, 102, 246–7.

Uzès, Duchesse d', *Souvenirs de la duchesse d'Uzès, née Mortemart*, Paris, Plon, 1939.

Secondary sources

Ackerknecht, E., *A Short History of Medicine*, Baltimore, Johns Hopkins University Press, 1982.

Ackerknecht, E., 'Hygiene in France (1815–1848)', *Bulletin of History of Medicine*, 1948, 22, 562–93.

Ackerknecht, E., *La médecine hospitalière à Paris (1794–1848)*, Paris, Payot, 1986.

Ackerknecht, E., 'Le cancer dans l'oeuvre de l'Ecole de Paris 1800–1850', *Cliomedica*, 1986, 20, 10, 125–33.

Aïach, P., *Cancer et médecine*, rapport de recherche INSERM, 1984.

Ariès, P., *L'enfant et la vie familiale sous l'Ancien Régime*, Paris, Le Seuil, 1973.

Arliaud, M., *Le corps étranger*, rapport de recherce LEST, 1984.

Arnold, O., *Le corps et l' âme: la vie des religieuses du XIXe siècle*, Paris, Le Seuil, 1984.

Austoker, J., *An History of Imperial Cancer Research Fund, 1902–1980*, Oxford University Press, 1988.

Baudelot, O. and Plaisance, E., 'L'évolution des objectifs de l'école maternelle', *Cahiers du CRESAS*, 1973, 9.

Bell, R.M., *Holy Anorexia*, Chicago, University of Chicago Press, 1985.

Bernard, P., *La fin d'un monde, 1914–1929*, Paris, Le Seuil, 1975.

Boltanski, L., *Prime éducation et morale de classe*, Paris, Mouton, 1971.

Bonnefous, E., *Avant l'oubli. La vie de 1900 à 1940*, Paris, Laffont/Nathan, 1984.

Borsa, S. and Michel, C.R., *La vie quotidienne des hôpitaux en France au XIXᵉ siècle*, Paris, Hachette, 1985.

Bourdieu, P., *Le sens pratique*, Paris, Ed. de Minuit, 1980.

Bourdieu, P., *Homo academicus*, Paris, Ed. de Minuit, 1984.

Brandt, A.M., *No Magic Bullet*, Oxford University Press, 1987.

Braudel, F., *L'identité de la France*, Paris, Arthaud, 1986.

Breslow, L., *A History of Cancer Control in the United States, 1946–1971*, Bethesda, Department of Health, Education and Welfare, 1977.

Cantor, D., 'The MRC's support for experimental radiology during the inter-war years', in Austoker, S. and Bryder, L. (eds), *Historical Perspectives of the Role of the MRC*, Oxford University Press, 1989.

Castel, R., *L'ordre psychiatrique*, Paris, Ed. de Minuit, 1976.

Christies Hospital and Holt Radium Institute, Manchester', *Cancer Bulletin*, 1961, 13, 11.

Cocheton, J.J., Guerre J. and Pequignot, H., *Histoire illustrée de l'hépato-gastro-entérologie*, Paris, Roger da Costa, 1987.

Delaporte, F., *Le savoir sur la maladie*, Paris, PUF, 1991.

Dessertine, D. and Faure, O., *Combattre la tuberculose*, Presses Universitaires de Lyon, 1988.

Dubief, H., *Le déclin de la IIIᵉ République*, Paris, Le Seuil, 1976.

Duvignaud, J. and Corbeau, J.P., *Les tabous des Français*, Paris, Hachette, 1981.

Elias, N., *The Civilizing Process*, Oxford, Blackwell, 1994.

Elias, N., *The Society of Individuals*, Oxford, Blackwell, 1991.

Encyclopédie du catholicisme, hier, aujourd'hui et demain, Paris, Letouzey et Ane, vol. II, 1954.

Foucault, M., *Naissance de la clinique*, Paris, PUF, 1963.

Goffman, E., *La mise en scène de la vie quotidienne*, vol. II, Paris, Ed. de Minuit, 1973.

Goudsblom, J., 'Les grandes épidémies et la civilisation des moeurs', *Actes de la recherche en sciences sociales*, 1987, 68, 3–14.

Grellet, I. and Kruse, C., *Histoires de la tuberculose*, Paris, Ramsay, 1983.

Grmek, M., *Les maladies à l'aube de la civilisation occidentale*, Payot, Paris, 1983.

Guiart, J., 'Le cancer dans l'histoire de la médecine', *LCC*, 74, 1945, 23–9.

Guillaume, P., *Du désespoir au salut. Les tuberculeux aux XIXᵉ et XXᵉ siècles*, Paris, Aubier, 1986.

Hatzfeld, H., *Du paupérisme à la Sécurité sociale, 1850–1950*, Paris, Armand Colin, 1971.

Herzlich, C. and Pierret, J., *Malades d'hier, malades d'aujourd'hui*, Paris, Payot, 1984.

Histoire économique et sociale de la France, vol. 2., 1914–années 1950, Paris, PUF, 1980.

Jamous, H., *La réforme des études médicales et des structures hospitalières*, Paris, CNRS, Centre d'études sociologiques, 1967.

Jewson, N.D., 'The disappearance of the sick-man from medical cosmology, 1770–1870', *Sociology*, 1976, 10(2), 225–44.

Ketchman-Wheaton, B., *L'office et la bouche*, Paris, Calmann-Lévy, 1984.

Knibielher, Y., *Cornettes et blouses blanches*, Paris, Hachette, 1984.

Le Brun, J., 'Cancer Serpit. Recherches sur la représentation du cancer dans les biographies féminines au XVIIIe siècle', *Sciences sociales et santé*, 1984, 2, 2, 9–31.

Le Brun, J., 'Représentations du cancer à l'époque moderne (XVIIe–XVIIIe siècles)', *Prévenir*, 1988, 16, 9–14.

Lécuyer, B., 'L'hygiène avant Pasteur', in C. Salomon-Bayet, *Pasteur et la révolution pasteurienne*, Paris, Payot, 1986, pp. 65–139.

Léonard, J., *La médecine entre les pouvoirs et les savoirs*, Paris, Aubier Montaigne, 1981.

Léonard, J., 'Comment peut-on être pasteurien', in C. Salomon-Bayet, *Pasteur et la révolution pasteurienne*, Paris, Payot, 1986.

Löwy, I., 'The immunological construction of the self', in A. Tauber (ed.), *Organism and the Origins of Self*, Dordrecht, Kluwer Academic Publishers, 1991, pp. 43–75.

Mesle, F. and Vallin, J., 'Reconstitution des tables annuelles de la mortalité pour la France au XIXe siècle', *Population*, 1989, 6, 1121–57.

'Middlesex Hospital', *Cancer Bulletin*, 1959, 11, 53.

Moulin, A.M., 'Les doctoresses russes du XIXe siècle', *Revue de l'AGEMP*, 1986, 21–6.

Muel, F., 'L'école obligatoire et l'invention de l'enfance anormale', *Actes de la recherche en sciences sociales*, 1975, 1.

Muel, F., 'Le fantôme du médecin de famille', *Actes de la recherche en sciences sociales*, 1984, 54, 70–1.

Murard, L. and Zylbermann, P., 'L'idée de "service social" dans la pensée hygiéniste (1928–1936)', *Vie sociale*, 1978, 8–9, 467.

Murard, L. and Zylberman, P., 'La raison de l'expert ou l'hygiène comme science sociale appliquée', *Archives européennes de sociologie*, 1985, XXVI, 1, 58–89.

Murard, L. and Zylbermann, P., 'L'autre guerre, la santé publique sous l'oeil de l'Amérique', *Revue historique*, 1986, 560, 367–98.

Murard, L. and Zylbermann, P., 'Généalogie de la loi préventive: la lutte contre les maladies contagieuses en France, 1893–1925', *JEVI*, 1989, 263–92.

Murard, L. and Zylbermann, P., 'La cité eugénique', in *L'Haleine des faubourgs*, Recherches, 1978, 313–14.

Murphy, I. and Gerald, P., 'Roswell Park Memorial Institute', *Oncology*, 1980, 37, 426–8.

'Netherlands Cancer Institute', *Cancer Bulletin*, 1959, 11, 85.

Pasveer, B., 'Knowledge of shadows, the introduction of X-ray images in medicine', *Sociology of Health and Illness*, 1989, 11, 4, 360–81.

Patterson, J.T., *The Dread Disease*, Harvard University Press, 1987.

Paul, H.W., *From Knowledge to Power: The Rise of the Science Empire in France, 1860–1939*, New York, Cambridge University Press, 1985.

Peter, J.P., 'Les mots et les objets de la maladie', *Revue d'histoire*, 1974, 246, 499, 13–38.

Pinell, P. and Zafiropoulos, M., *Un siècle d'échecs scolaires*, Paris, Les Editions ouvrières, 1983.

Pinell, P., 'Cancer: images, mythe et morale', in *Concertation nationale cancer*, Synthèses thématiques, 1983.

Pinell, P., 'La relation médecin-malade cancéreux: l'enjeu des manipulations symboliques', *Prévenir*, 1985, 11, 9–16.

Pinell, P., 'How do cancer patients express their point of view ?', *Sociology of health and Illness*, 1987, 9, 1, 25–44.

Pol Gosset, Dr, 'L'hôpital pour cancérés', *LCC*, 1926, 12, 311–20.

'Pour une histoire du service social', *Vie sociale*, 1987, 8/9.

Quetel, C., *Le mal de Naples*, Paris, Seghers, 1986.

'Radiumhemmet', *Cancer Bulletin*, 1959, 11, 72.

Rather, L.J., *The Genesis of Cancer*, Baltimore, Johns Hopkins University Press, 1978.

Rebérioux, M., *La République radicale, 1898–1914*, Paris, Le Seuil, 1975.

Rettig, R.A , *Cancer Crusade, The Story of the National Cancer Act of 1971*, Princeton, 1977.

'Royal Marsden Hospital', *Cancer Bulletin*, 1962, 14, 53.

Rullière, R., *Abrégé d'histoire de la médecine*, Paris, Masson, 1981.

Salomon-Bayet, C., *Pasteur et la révolution pasteurienne*, Paris, Payot, 1986.

Schlanger, J., *Les métaphores de l'organisme*, Paris, Vrin, 1971.

Sinding, C., *Le clinicien et le chercheur*, Paris, PUF, 1991.

Sontag, S., *La maladie comme métaphore*, Paris, Le Seuil, 1979.

Steffen, M., *Régulation politique et stratégies professionnelles; médecine libérale et émergence des centre de santé*, Thèse d'Etat de sciences politiques, Grenoble, March 1983.

Sternhell, Z., *La droite révolutionnaire*, Paris, Le Seuil, 1978.

Thébaud, F., *La femme au temps de la guerre de 14*, Paris, Stock/ Laurence Pernoud, 1986.

Thomas, L.V., 'Mort redécouverte, mort escamotée', in *La mort aujourd'hui*, Marseille, Rivages, 1982.

Vuilbeau, A., *Orthopédie et pédagogie*, Thèse de 3ème cycle, Paris VII, 1980.

Waro, N., 'A Pilgrim's Progress', *Cancer Research*, 1974, 34, 1767–74.

Weindling, P.J., 'Theories of the cell state in Imperial Germany', in C. Webster (ed.), *Biology, Medicine and Society 1840–1940*, Cambridge, Cambridge University Press, 1981.

Index